POPULATION CHANGE IN THE RURAL WEST 1975-1990

16

Edited by

John M. Wardwell
James H. Copp

University Press of America, Inc.
Lanham • New York • London

Copyright © 1997 by
University Press of America, ® Inc.
4720 Boston Way
Lanham, Maryland 20706

3 Henrietta Street
London, WC2E 8LU England

Library of Congress Cataloging-in-Publication Data

Population change in the rural West, 1975-1990 / edited
by John M. Wardwell and James H. Copp.
p.   cm.
1. Rural population--West (U.S.)--History. 2. West (U.S.)--
Population--History. I. Wardwell, John M. II. Copp, James H.
HB2403.U6P67   1996   304.6'0978'09045--dc20   96-34952 CIP

ISBN 0-7618-0512-5 (cloth: alk. ppr.)
ISBN 0-7618-0513-3 (pbk: alk. ppr.)

♾™ The paper used in this publication meets the minimum
requirements of American National Standard for information
Sciences—Permanence of Paper for Printed Library Materials,
ANSI Z39.48—1984

Dedication

This book is appreciatively and affectionately dedicated to

Jean and Veronica

Acknowledgments

A work of this nature cannot be completed without the assistance of many individuals, most of whose names do not appear within the pages of this book. We particularly appreciate the critical review of the entire manuscript provided by Dudley L. Poston, Jr., Professor and Chair of the Department of Sociology at Texas A & M University. James J. Zuiches, Dean of the College of Agriculture and Home Economics of Washington State University, supported the project throughout its existence and provided essential assistance at key points in the preparation of this book. Vicki A. McCracken, Associate Director of the Agricultural Research Center of Washington State University, has provided administrative support and encouragement in the current phase and form of the project.

Viktor Gecas, Chair of the Department of Rural Sociology of Washington State University, provided support for preparation of the final camera-ready draft of the manuscript. This work was accomplished by John Porter of the Department of Rural Sociology. J.P. contributed his experience in type-setting as well as his excellence in word processing to produce the manuscript you are now holding

The Department of Sociology at Washington State University provided financial support for the publication of the manuscript. Jennifer Lincoln Hanson assisted in preparation and review of the bibliography in Chapter One.

Finally, as editors we wish to express our appreciation of the participation of all of the chapter authors whose work is presented within. Without the excellence of their research and writing, and their timely collaboration throughout the project, there would be no book on Population Change in the Rural West.

Population Change in the Rural West
1975 - 1990

edited by John M. Wardwell and James H. Copp

TABLE OF CONTENTS

CONTENTS

Chapter 7   **Social Change in Resource Development**   163
Communities
James H. Copp and Edward Knop

LIST OF FIGURES

LIST OF TABLES

Chapter Five

Chapter Six

Chapter Eight

Preface

The History and Context of Regional Research

James J. Zuiches and Dennis Oldenstadt[1]
Washington State University

Innovation, invention and discovery occur in many contexts as a result of the pursuit of new knowledge by motivated individuals. Some organizational contexts, however, are themselves innovations, and these encourage and stimulate the process of discovery. This book is a product of such an institutional innovation, regional research in the state agricultural experiment stations, and of talented and committed researchers from multiple disciplines. In this preface, we will briefly describe the nature of regional research and the development of the W-118 regional research project. The topic is population change and, more specifically, the migration of people and the primary and secondary impacts of these migrations on families, communities and states in the western region from 1975 to 1990. The strategy used to support this multi-state regional research effort, which involved agricultural economists, home economists, rural sociologists and demographers, is a regional research project.

One often forgets that how work is organized can itself be a major innovation. Henry Ford achieved such an organizational change in creating the assembly line. In a less mechanistic manner, the research process was transformed in 1946 when Congress authorized and the U.S. Department of Agriculture (USDA) and State Agricultural Experiment Station (SAES) directors implemented a system of funding regional research. The purpose of this new funding mechanism was to stimulate and facilitate interstate cooperation on high priority regional or national issues. Such research projects would require a coordinated team effort among federal and university scientists of many states, thus eliminating duplication and improving research quality. The vision called for teams of scientists to be supported and funded by SAES and USDA to address regional or national problems, not merely state-specific or disciplinary questions.

The results of the research are published in journal articles, entire books, chapters in books, research bulletins, extension bulletins, and in other outlets useful to research and policy professionals and other users of the research. This book is one form in which two decades of productivity is being disseminated. The general topic of the research has always been migration and population change in the nonmetropolitan West. But the progress of research and shifts in behavior and in regional and national emphases required periodic updating of the objectives and procedures.

The 1950s and 1960s were a period of massive outmigration from rural to urban areas. The movement of rural peoples was caused by significant differentials in educational and income opportunities and by the continued modernization of agriculture. Severe losses of human capital resulted. The ability of local communities to provide basic services to a dispersed, declining and aging population diminished.

The USDA model for responding to the concerns generated by these social and demographic developments was to convene conferences, study groups and task forces to develop a plan for needed research to address these problems. USDA is a decentralized organization with scientists in every state. The next step meant assembling experts within regions to develop the agenda for research. In the West, priority topics included examinations of the patterns, causes and consequences of migration to and within the region. This focus become the core of the research around which W-118 was organized.

In 1970, an Ad Hoc Technical Committee of researchers from eleven Western states and USDA met to detail research plans and develop a formal proposal for a coordinated study of migration. The objectives were:

(1) To determine the empirically significant features which influence migration decisions and which can be used to predict the magnitude, routes and timing of migration;

(2) To determine the benefits and costs of migration on an

individual or family basis;

(3) To determine social (community, regional, national) costs and benefits of migration; and,

(4) To specify policy implications resulting from these analyses.

The proposal for this research was approved through the SAES/USDA hierarchy and Project W-118 began in 1971. Participating researchers and advisors met at least yearly, sometimes more often, and communicated frequently by telephone and mail, in order to coordinate the research underway through their respective state Experiment Stations. After five years, at the conclusion of the first phase of the project, a summary report was prepared that synthesized the findings and implications of the many project publications.[2]

A revised project proposal was developed for the next five years. The objectives remained similar to those of the first project period, with one major revision. The original project had had its roots in the concern with rural outmigration and its implications for the sustenance of rural population and places. New analyses of current data emerging in the early to mid-1970s, particularly those of USDA demographer Calvin L. Beale, showed that the long-established rural-to-urban net migration flow had been "turning around" in the United States. More people were moving from metropolitan to nonmetropolitan areas than were leaving rural places for cities. The consequences of the new pattern were not well understood. Even if it were a real change in trends rather than an artifact of data recording procedures, political boundaries, or the like, there was no certainty that the "turnaround" would last. These issues became important concerns of the second phase of W-118 research.

Upon the conclusion of the second phase of W-118, much of the first decade of research from the project was provided and interpreted as a book on the nonmetropolitan migration turnaround[3] and the project again underwent revision. The turnaround of net rural-urban migration was holding and much was being learned about it, but several other migration-related developments emerged in the West during the second phase of the research. These new developments would also demand research attention.

The oil embargo in 1974 had caused national energy prices to skyrocket. Alternative energy sources were being developed quickly and profitably, and many of these were located in the rural West. The earlier "boom town" phenomenon returned as a part of the region's migration picture. A counterpoint to this use of rural environments appeared in the changing structure of migrant motivations. Much of the turnaround flow

xxiii

contributing to growth of the rural West appeared to be due to the increasing interest and ability of people to move for amenities reasons. The attraction of natural and social environments in the West began to rank along with, or even to supersede, economic considerations in making migration decisions. Inevitably, increasing emphasis on environmental concerns within the region would conflict with the economic interests of many in the energy, forest products and agricultural industries and occupations.

The migration picture within the region was further complicated by changes in federal laws regulating foreign migratory labor. Concerns over the presence and labor force participation of undocumented aliens were growing. Much of the illegal flow into the United States impacted the West more than other regions, and much of it involved workers in agriculture. The third phase of the W-118 project included these new developments, and this book includes chapters reflecting these new emphases.

But by the mid-1980s, migration issues in the West appeared to be changing again. An already-complicated situation had become more so. National and regional project data suggested that the nonmetropolitan net migration turnaround was faltering. The energy boom had largely run its course with a return to lower oil prices. Amenities-directed migration was holding for some nonmetropolitan locations but yielding to new economic realities in many others. Economic hardship was increasing in much of the rural West as agricultural and extractive industries markets softened. Retirement relocation was proving to be a mixed blessing in many parts of the rural West. Crises in urban centers were draining resources and attention away from continuing rural concerns. The global economy was also emerging as a challenging uncertainty with profound but poorly understood implications for rural and nonmetropolitan areas.

The fourth phase of W-118 was initiated in this new context. The final set of revised objectives included:

(1) To describe and explain population changes involving rural and nonmetropolitan areas through the mechanisms of changes in migration, mortality and fertility;

(2) To refine further the decision models of migrants and potential migrants to, from, and within the West; and,

(3) To analyze the interdependencies of agriculture and natural resource production, food and fiber employment, and population change.

Three themes predominate in this review of the more than twenty-year history of regional research project W-118:

(1) Continuity of interest in the primary topic. Through more than 35 scientists participating over the course of the twenty-one years and a nearly complete turnover from the initial technical committee to the final participants, the common ingredient has been an intense interest in understanding migration and its effects on rural people and places.

(2) The diversity of the participants. The regional research mechanism easily incorporated scientists from all states in the West and, over time, from other states experiencing similar and related demographic phenomena. Michigan, for example, participated in project W-118 to contribute to analyses of the rural turnaround, as did Texas in studies of natural resource boom and bust cycles. W-118 twice formally hosted national and interregional conferences including scientists from similar projects in other regions of the country.

(3) The variety of methodologies used to study shared objectives. Descriptive studies, in-depth field research, individual surveys, census and other documentary data analyses, data files of labor statistics, socioeconomic and religious subgroup datasets, boom towns, economic and ecological models, computer software developments for processing large data files, and public policy analyses have all at one time or another been introduced to the project. Research results have been disseminated through reports, maps, charts, more traditional scientific publications, presentations at professional meetings and other talks. Whatever means might effectively communicate the research results have been employed throughout the duration of the project.

This product of the research is being made available at a time when the role of migration in rural and nonmetropolitan growth and change appears once again to have changed. Newly-released analyses of Federal-State Cooperative county population estimates and Current Population Survey data indicate renewed net inmigration to nonmetropolitan areas. Comparison of annual county net migration rates suggest that nonmetropolitan outmigration may have bottomed out in 1985. Net migration rates have steadily increased since that time, and once again exceed metropolitan for the first two years of the 1990s. The research reported in this book is thus appearing at a time of renewed interest in nonmetropolitan and rural migration, and in the West as a region of dynamic population change.

Rather than summarize results or accomplishments in this Preface, we would encourage the reader to choose a chapter of interest and read it. We extend our congratulations to the technical committee for the excellent product they have achieved. As the administrative advisors to the project over the last twenty-one years (Oldenstadt from 1971 to 1986, Zuiches from 1986 through its conclusion in 1992), we are proud of the many insights, understandings, and contributions of these social and economic scientists. It is their product, and it was made possible by the regional research mechanism.

Notes

1. We acknowledge and appreciate the effort of Edward Knop in reconstructing much of the project history reviewed in this preface.

2. Published as Knop, Edward, Joel Hamilton, Donald West and C. Jack Gilchrist. 1978. The Social and Economic Significance of Human Migration in the Western Region. Pullman: Washington State University College of Agriculture Research Center Bulletin No. 859.

3. Published as Brown, David L. and John M. Wardwell (editors). 1980. New Directions in Urban-Rural Migration. New York: Academic Press.

Chapter 1

Migration Research in the West, 1982-1992[1]

John M. Wardwell
Washington State University

Introduction

Since the early 1970s, land grant universities in the western United States have supported a regional project to conduct research on migration to, from, and within the region. In association with the Cooperative State Research Service of the U.S. Department of Agriculture, these universities have maintained the largest continuing collaborative research enterprise devoted to population description and analysis in the Western States. The focus of this project, designated as W-118, remained on the causes and consequences of migration throughout its more than twenty-year existence from its initiation in 1971 through its termination in 1992.

The work was organized in a series of four, five-year projects. The summary results of the first phase of the project were published as an Agricultural Research Center Bulletin from Washington State University in 1978.[2] The second phase results were published as a book on the nonmetropolitan migration turnaround (Brown and Wardwell 1980). This chapter is an annotated review of the research literature generated during the final (1982-87 and 1987-92) project phases. The chapter also serves as an introductory overview of this book by putting the chapters in the context of the research conducted through W-118 over the past decade.

The book itself summarizes, describes and explains major socio-demographic trends of the Western States in the latter 1970s and through the 1980s. Through this work it is hoped that a foundation has been established to better understand and adapt to the trends of the 1990s, with the recent evidence of renewed nonmetropolitan growth in the region and throughout the nation.

Scientists participating in W-118 generated almost 200 research papers on population issues of concern to the West.   Researchers working in other regions may be unaware of these research products. The descriptions provided herein are necessarily brief, and several papers are often cited for the same research finding. Many of the papers identified in the bibliography and described in this chapter might be difficult for the interested user to obtain other than by writing directly to the author. A primary purpose of this chapter is simply to make others aware of the existence of these research products so that they may obtain and study them in detail. The names and addresses of the authors of the papers are provided in the Appendix for this purpose.

Research conducted in the collaborative USDA and land grant framework is formally organized by objective. This chapter follows that format, providing the objective itself and a brief characterization of the nature of the work. Specific applications of each objective are then identified and described, and the research papers themselves introduced and cited. Several of the studies reported and described below are related to more than one objective of the project. Wherever possible, the study is reported under the objective to which it is most closely related. Where the overlap between objectives demands further treatment of the study, it is considered again under later objectives.

The research of W-118 calls attention to the dynamic nature of demographic processes and to the difficulties associated with forecasting population shifts (Swanson 1988; Wardwell and Cook 1982). Since the initiation of the project, the nation has experienced the nonmetropolitan migration turnaround and also its diminution and reversal in the 1980s. While dramatic shifts such as these generate a significant and worthwhile body of research, the relative absence of research during periods of lower public interest leaves serious gaps in the accumulating body of knowledge regarding social and economic changes, population shifts, and quality of rural living (Wardwell 1986a).

The continuity of research under W-118 through times when demographic patterns seemed more stable as well as through the times of dramatic shifts in population change was one of the greatest strengths of this project. It is instructive in this context to recall that research on rural population change had largely been neglected throughout the nation prior to the nonmetropolitan turnaround, apart from the efforts of regional project NC-97, conducted in the North Central states in collaboration with continuing research sponsored or conducted by USDA. When the time came to understand how the turnaround could have happened in so unanticipated a fashion, it was necessary to reconstruct what had taken place in the 1950s and 1960s, because the necessary research had been largely neglected in those decades when patterns of urban expansion seemed clear, inexorable, and continuing (Wardwell 1982b).

This book appears at a time when it once again seems likely that rural and nonmetropolitan areas are growing compared to metropolitan centers, while remaining relatively disadvantaged in terms of income and employment growth and the development and maintenance of the material components of the quality of living (Wardwell 1986c). It is our hope that by providing these research results, the circumstances under which the conditions of working and living in rural and nonmetropolitan regions may once again dominate migration flows will be more fully understood.

Objective 1
To describe and analyze changes in population distribution patterns, monitor the stability of growth in nonmetropolitan areas of the West, and examine policy options and implications related to these patterns.

Population change in the West has been unusual when compared with the nation and with other regions (Swanson 1984, 1988). The region contains large and unique subregions such as the Mormon Culture Area with its distinctive population dynamics (Toney, Stinner and Byun, Chapter 3), and scores of sparsely settled mountainous counties in which migration has been particularly responsive to amenities attractions (Knop and Jobes, Chapter 5) and resource development (Copp and Knop, Chapter 7).

Other parts of the region are impacted more by immigration than is typically the case in the rest of the nation (Martin, Chapter 4). The Pacific Northwest has shown the influence of traditional resource dependence shifting toward recreation-retirement industries (Cook, Chapter 2). All of these factors are related to the distinctive and rapid growth rates of nonmetropolitan western counties in the 1980s, when compared to the dramatic slowdown of nonmetropolitan growth nationally.

The primary focus of this first objective has been explanatory and descriptive, to monitor and report trends in nonmetropolitan migration and population growth with a focus of continued research on the explanations of these trends. During the final (1987-1992) phase of W-118, a separate focus on the interactions of population change and food and fibre industries was separated from this first objective. Research literature pertaining to this more specific objective that was generated during the prior (1982-87) phase is treated with the later research in the final section of this chapter.

Variations Within the Region

Three of the chapters of the book are explicitly designed to describe and explain variations in patterns of migration and population change within the West. In Chapter 2, Cook examines population change from 1960 to 1990 in the Pacific Northwest. Toney, Stinner and Byun describe the Mormon Culture Region in Chapter 3. Martin examines in Chapter 4 the impacts of immigration on population growth in California.

The foundations for this subregional research were established in a number of studies conducted throughout the last decade. Swanson (1984) examined nonmetro counties for the proportion of 1980 residents that had been residing in another nonmetro area in 1975: of the four regions, the West had the highest proportion of counties in which 15 percent or more of the 1980 residents had moved to the counties from another nonmetropolitan area since 1975. All western states were then compared in terms of the geographic origins of these migrants, with particular focus on whether migration streams had changed in the 1975-80 period when compared with these streams in earlier decades. Significant variations by state were discovered. States such as Wyoming and Idaho received migrants by quite different paths from different geographic origins than they had previously, and differed from nonmetropolitan counties in other western states.

In New Mexico, Eastman (1983a, 1984b) noted that the turnaround pattern was not characteristic. Population increases were most rapid in the urban and urban fringe counties, while the smallest rural counties in northeastern New Mexico steadily lost population. In work similar to Swanson's, Williams (1987) showed that while most movement occurs between New Mexico and nearby southern and western states, north eastern and north central states provided the largest net migration into New Mexico.

Changes in the distribution of Utah's population also revealed more rapid growth of metropolitan than of nonmetropolitan population between 1950 and 1980 (Stinner and Kan 1983; Stinner and Toney 1981; Stinner and Al-Massarweh 1988). The most noteworthy shift within this period however occurred in nonmetropolitan areas. Between 1950 and 1970, the 24 nonmetropolitan counties of Utah grew by only 4,000 persons, but in the next decade, these counties added nearly 91,000 people to their populations. In the earlier decades the only nonmetropolitan counties to grow were those which were adjacent to metropolitan centers. In the 1970s, the bulk of nonmetropolitan county growth was captured by the nonadjacent counties.

Nonmetropolitan areas in Utah were experiencing net migration losses after 1980 (Stinner and Al-Massarweh 1989). Adjacent and nonadjacent counties had net migration gains from 1980 to 1983 but both groups of counties experienced losses from 1983 to 1986. The rate of loss for nonadjacent counties was triple that of adjacent counties. Natural increase compensated for net migration losses in adjacent but not in nonadjacent counties between 1983 and 1986. These patterns diverge somewhat from those reported by Swanson (1988) for the region, wherein adjacent counties were still experiencing net migration gains between 1983 and 1988.

In Washington, Cook (1991a) demonstrated that projected change in county populations placed the bulk of anticipated growth in the large metro counties of King (Seattle), Snohomish (Everett), and Pierce (Tacoma). Many nonmetro counties were projected to grow at a more rapid rate between 1988 and 2000 than they did in the 1980s.

Cook also addressed population shifts among various segments of the nonmetro population in Washington (1990a). Nonmetro migration trends for the population aged 65 and over and for the general population from 1970 to 1980 were compared with 1980-85 trends, focusing on similarities and differences between the two groups in times of economic prosperity and recession, variations in retirement migration by county economic base, and factors related to retirement migration (1990b). The population aged 65 and over grew faster in Washington with no indication of the slowing in growth evident at the national level. Retirement migration into Washington continued in the 1980s and may even have increased over the level observed in the prior decade (Cook 1990c). However, substantial county variability was noted in population aging, with some aging due to retirement inmigration and some to young adult outmigration.

Stinner and Byun (1990) analyzed National Longitudinal Survey Data on retirement migration decision making. Their particular focus was on men aged 59 to 69 for whom retirement and a move occurred simultaneously. The association of migration and poverty among Hispanic youths was also explored (Wilson-Figueroa 1990; Wilson-Figueroa, Berry, and Toney 1991). Including socioeconomic, demographic and contextual variables, the research demonstrated partial support for the hypothesis that poor Hispanics are less likely to migrate than are Hispanics who are not poor.

Washington's minorities increased much more rapidly than the state's majority population or than minority populations nationally (Cook 1991b). Asian and Pacific Islanders were the most rapidly growing minority. Like the African-American population, they remained concentrated in the largest urban counties. American Indian, Eskimo and Aleut populations were more dispersed, Growth of the Hispanic population was substantial throughout the state, particularly in central rural counties.

Structural Change and Population Shifts

An historical analysis of trends in population change revealed interesting but potentially misleading parallels between the demographic situation of the 1970s and that of the 1930s (Wardwell 1985; 1987). In the earlier as well as the more recent decade, the population of the United States engaged in movement patterns such that the pace of urbanization slowed and even reversed, with more people moving from urban to rural areas than were making the more traditional rural-to-urban move. Fertility levels reached all-time lows, below replacement, in these two decades.

Wardwell's comparison of the recent turnaround period with the 1930s revealed that the demographic similarities of these two periods were the result of very different social and economic forces. In the 1930s, fertility was low because couples delayed both marriage and child-bearing as they sought to interpret the meaning for them of the difficult economic circumstances of those years. Their choices were constrained by economic considerations that limited their options and forced them to delay household formation and family growth.

In the 1980s, the same behavior resulted from an expanded array of choices facing individuals, in the West and throughout the United States. Marriage was delayed as alternative roles grew, as more women completed their education and entered the labor force in larger and larger numbers. Increased female enrollment ratios and labor force participation rates also delayed the onset of childbearing and reduced the number of children desired and expected.

Similarly, the phenomenon of increased nonmetropolitan and rural growth through migration throughout the nation in the 1970s, persisting in the West through the early 1980s, was the result of expanded opportunities for choice. In the 1930s, individuals and families left depressed urban centers to seek subsistence in the countryside, either on their own or to rejoin extended families resident on farms. Economic circumstances forced them to move from city to country: free and unconstrained choice played little if any role in the phenomenon. However in the 1970s and 1980s, a superficially similar movement pattern was the result of economic and social change in rural and nonmetropolitan areas such that individuals and families experienced a greater freedom of choice as to where they could live and work, a freedom to move from city to country without giving up opportunities for employment, incomes, and participation in the modern lifestyles of an industrialized society.

    The economic and social changes in rural America that have brought about this greater freedom of choice were documented in the form of structural correlates of nonadjacent nonmetropolitan county growth in a national study using the National County Data Base at Montana State University (Wheat, Wardwell, and Faulkner 1984). This study indicated that climate was strongly associated with nonadjacent nonmetropolitan county growth. Manufacturing base, racial composition, retirement-recreation, and mining were also associated with migration. Similar factors were collected by Wardwell (1983b) in a projection of nonmetropolitan growth into and through the 1980s. This work was then extended to include the trends of the 1980s; despite the slowdown in nonmetropolitan growth, the past decade more closely resembled the growth of the 1970s than it did the decline of the 1950s or 1960s (Wardwell 1988).

    The strong association of climate with nonmetropolitan growth patterns led to an examination of the sociodemographic impacts of global climate change and variability (Wardwell 1990; 1991). From the perspective of human ecology, the demographic impacts of climate change are mediated through rural social institutions, primarily employment opportunities, production, and energy costs. Apart from minor and perhaps even unmeasurable impacts on mortality and fertility in the region, the major demographic impacts come about through migration. Migration responds to differentials in opportunities. It is impossible to speculate on the impacts of global climate change in any given region without reference to an adjacent region, since interregional migration is dependent upon those differentials.

Nonmetropolitan Migration and Structural Theory Building
    Theories and explanations of the nonmetropolitan migration turnaround were critically compared and applied to the migration trends of the 1980s in order to assess the extent to which the 1980s data were

consistent with each of these alternative explanations (Wardwell and Gilchrist 1987; 1988). No single explanation was consistent with all of the later trends. However, the theories could be compared as to which were consistent with more or less of the facts of the past decade.

The ecological explanation of structural convergence in metropolitan and nonmetropolitan areas seemed to more effectively account for the trends observed in the 1980s than did either noneconomic motivational explanations or traditional economic explanations (Wardwell 1988). Residential preference explanations based on changes in values were least supported. Wardwell further argued that explanations based on residential preferences must be integrated with contextual ecological-economic considerations in order to identify the conditions under which residential preferences may affect nonmetropolitan migration in the 1990s and beyond (1989b).

Trends in national occupational change during the 1980s were analyzed comparing two theoretical perspectives, that of metropolitan dominance vs. decentralization (Cook and Beck 1991). The finding that the presence of executive and professional positions increasingly dominated occupational structures of larger metropolitan areas but showed no change in nonmetropolitan areas lends support to the metropolitan dominance perspective.

Population Turnover

An unanticipated finding of research under this objective has been documented by Jobes and Knop (Jobes 1984c, 1986b; Jobes et al. 1984b; Knop and Bacigalupi 1983; 1984; 1985) who found that population growth in high amenity areas of the West is remarkably unstable. Bacigalupi (1983) showed how rapid in and outmigration were related to the values that drew migrants to rural Colorado communities. Longitudinal analysis of migrants in areas of continuing high growth rates showed that nearly as many residents were moving out as were moving in (Jobes 1985a, 1986b; Jobes et al. 1984b). Their analyses are elaborated in Chapter 5 of this book.

One key issue in regional economics has traditionally been whether "people follow jobs" or "jobs follow people." There is some evidence in the literature that the two are jointly determined but that the latter effect is the stronger. Stevens and Owen (1982) however found that the "people follow jobs" effect was much stronger for a set of Pacific Northwest counties. To the extent that people are willing to sacrifice income for environmental goods, on the other hand, it may be that households are more footloose and migration harder to predict than has been the case historically.

That households may be more footloose is also the interpretation of the longitudinal data gathered in Colorado and Montana (Knop and Jobes, Chapter 5). The resulting transience of populations in high amenity areas is an important factor to consider in developing policy. Few persons remain in an area long enough to become informed about issues. With rapid in and out migration, it is more difficult for migrants to become effective participants. Political decision making is likely to gradually consolidate in the hands of a small group of longer term residents who may not be representative of the community (Bohren et al. 1985).

Transience also masks a major source of economic input. Newcomers bring assets with them. Communities in high amenity areas depend on this source of fresh money, while generally favoring a stable population. This dependence may be seen as similar to that based on tourism. This should be acknowledged as part of the planning process and should be included in policy deliberations.

Policy makers might modify their approaches regarding migration and development. Newcomers and oldtimers have expectations at odds with each other. Newcomers would benefit from being informed by community leaders that they are unlikely to become stable permanent residents by virtue of inadequate opportunities or unrealistic expectations. In fact, even an increased level of opportunities would seem to be unlikely to increase the proportion of newcomers who stay for more than a few years. Oldtimers would benefit from being informed regarding the economic contributions made by newcomers, however temporary their residence. Longer-term residents are an industry in themselves and perhaps would benefit if the community were more able to see them as such.

These findings, drawn from longitudinal surveys conducted in the region in the course of the project, point to the necessity for time series data. Other secondary data were assessed in Utah with this end in mind (Toney and Swearengen 1984). One national survey of young adults, the age group for whom migration rates are highest, contained a subsample of 2,000 individuals in states in the West. These individuals had been interviewed annually since 1979. This enabled more complete analysis of the future consequences of migration, since the separation of determinants and consequences is often quite difficult with data in which measures are reported for one point in time only.

Descriptive Statistics for Applied Agencies

As part of these efforts, W-118 participants in four states collaborated in the use of the National County Data Base at Montana State University [itself a product of prior W-118 efforts] to develop and publish wall charts on population trends in western counties by state. These states include Montana, Utah, Colorado and New Mexico (Jobes 1984b; Toney 1984; Knop 1984b; and, Eastman 1984b and 1984c, respectively; see also Eastman and Williams, 1982-85).

The charts included information on population changes for counties, each individual western state, the West, and the United States. In addition to information on population trends, including migration, social and economic characteristics of the geographical units were included in the charts. The charts were widely distributed, and the feedback received indicated that they became a valued source of information to policy makers and others in public agencies throughout the region. The publication and distribution of these charts fulfilled in part the intent to give attention to the policy implications of the findings of W-118 research. Samples of the charts are available from the individuals cited above (see Appendix for addresses).

Objective 2

To identify and assess the decision models used by migrants and potential migrants to, from and within the West, and to integrate these models with those based in structural changes in an effort to better inform policy analysts of future migration trends.

Under this objective, work was focused on refining and assessing models of migration decision-making, and on integrating these models with those based on structural change and aggregate data (Swanson 1986b). Rowe (1984) describes the complexity of the decision making process for individuals and households, emphasizing that with greater freedom of choice brought on by structural changes, micro models must incorporate and integrate more motivational bases for the choices made by migrants.

The role of choice in the models explaining migration changed in at least two ways in the 1970s, changes that were explored in the research conducted in the 1980s (Jobes, Stinner, and Wardwell 1992). The array of choices expanded, as has been indicated above (Wardwell 1983c), and the bases on which the choices were made changed to include a larger number of noneconomic considerations, and to permit individuals and families to place a greater weight on these noneconomic factors than had previously been possible (Wardwell 1982b; Stinner and Khosrashahin 1985).

Community Integration and Migration Decision-Making
The bases of choices regarding migration intentions and behavior form the key elements in the models developed by Stinner and Toney and their colleagues. The distinctive sociological fabric of the rural communities in the Mormon Culture Region provides a natural setting for integrating structural and social psychological approaches to migration.

The communities in which Stinner and Toney conducted their research are remote from major metropolitan centers (Kan et al. 1984). They have traditionally manifested a highly integrated social structure attributed to the numerical dominance of Mormons, the organizational effectiveness of the Mormon Church, its well-established belief system, and a lifestyle oriented largely about church activities. Geographic isolation has reinforced cohesiveness and homogeneity (Van Loon and Stinner 1991).

Socioeconomic developments in the region in the 1970s brought sizeable inmigration to the communities, including energy exploration, industrial decentralization, tourism, and an expansion of transportation and communication systems linking these once-remote communities into state, regional and national economic, social and cultural networks. In this ferment of change these communities provide a context within which to examine the micro-level processes involved in migration decision-making of nonmetropolitan residents and recent migrants, among both Mormon adherents to the dominant belief system and nonMormons (Toney and Stinner 1990).

The model is organized in three stages: community attachment, migration intentions, and actual migration. Community attachment is defined as a joint function of social position, behavioral attachment as measured by community involvement, and perceptual attachment as measured by satisfaction in three domains: social relations, urbanity and cohesion.

The concept of the community of limited liability guides their research. This holds that individuals' orientations and attachments are limited and variable. Migration, viewed as physical withdrawal from the community, is dependent upon subjective satisfaction. Need fulfillment is achieved through the decision to migrate. Variations in community satisfaction are influenced by background attributes and social or community bonds which tie individuals and households to communities, partly through community satisfaction. Stronger bonds yield higher levels of satisfaction which in turn offset desires to move. Stronger bonds may also mean options for reducing dissatisfaction without having to depart. Other types of bonds may act to constrain outmigration, even when dissatisfaction persists. Similarly, background attributes may constrain or facilitate migration independent of community satisfaction or social bonds.

In a very basic sense, the ability of nonmetropolitan communities to hold their residents in place is a pivotal issue for the collective well-being of these communities. From the perspective of the resident, the decision to remain or depart is a litmus test of their commitment to the community.

Community satisfaction is a multidimensional concept with three domains: social relations, amenities and community problem-solving capacity. Each domain meets a specific need for affiliation, quality of living or power. Background attributes condition social roles and thus facilitate or constrain migration.

Contrary to the reasoning of the linear development model, community size does not have an independent inverse effect on any of the community attachment indicators. But, contrary to the systemic model, duration of residence did not consistently have a positive effect on attachment. Important interaction effects were evident, but these interactions were also not consistent. In some cases, significant effects were present in villages but not cities, while the opposite interaction was evident in other cases (Byun et al. 1990). The analysis demonstrated and reaffirmed the necessity of viewing community attachment as a multidimensional process. In no case did the researchers observe a duplication of variable configuration and patterning across the four indicators of community attachment.

Assessment of the persistent distinctiveness of the Mormon Cultural Region required attention to the interactive role of religion in migration to, from, and within this area (Golesorkhi and Toney 1981; Kan and Kim 1981; Toney et al. 1983). Multiple measures of community satisfaction, life cycle stage, duration of residence, home ownership and socioeconomic status were also included (Tinnakul and Stinner 1985). This research revealed that religion exerted a significant influence upon migration intentions after controlling for these other variables. However, community satisfaction was also significantly related after controls were introduced.

Other research (Stinner and Byun 1991; Stinner et al. 1991; Stinner et al. 1992; Van Loon and Stinner 1991) evaluated the influence of community size preference and six domains of community satisfaction on migration intentions. Community size preference dominated the time frame of migration intentions. In the largest places in both metropolitan and nonmetropolitan areas, preference for residence in a smaller-sized location was linked to a greater likelihood of migration plans. In the smallest communities, both those with and without a preference for a larger community exhibited more migration intentions compared to those in the largest communities who did not prefer a different community size.

An analytical model of out-of-state migration intentions in the short and long term was begun with background characteristics, socioeconomic attachment, and psychic attachment (Toney et al. 1981). Younger residents employed full-time in metropolitan locations indicated that they were more likely to leave the state (Seyfrit 1986). NonMormons, regardless of degree of religious involvement, were also more likely to leave. Higher educated residents, those who were unmarried, or who had no children or were single parents, indicated a greater likelihood of leaving. If their residence in the state had been of shorter duration, they had no kin within the state, were less active in their communities of residence or indicated dissatisfaction, they were also more likely to leave.

Among nonmetropolitan residents, the least educated, those with kin only outside the state, the most active in their communities but the most dissatisfied, those aged 55 and over, those who were never married, formed an empty nest household, or were single parents, indicated that they were more likely to leave in the short rather than the long term.

In a 1988 statewide survey of migration intentions in Utah, duration of residence, religious affiliation and involvement, educational attainment, family life cycle stage and employment status were significantly related to migration intentions while annual family income and gender were not (Stinner et al. 1992). Analyzing social ties, the researchers noted that the number of kin or friends in the community was inversely related to migration intentions while home ownership and social participation were not significantly related. It was interesting, however, to note that those respondents with the highest and lowest participation levels were the most likely to express intentions to migrate.

The high expressed likelihood of the most active persons illustrated the perspective of limited liability; people could be very active yet still ready to move. This has important implications for community development. The higher the level of dissatisfaction with the community the more likely the expression of migration intentions.

Within specific satisfaction domains, they observed that items pertaining to government responsiveness were not significantly related to migration intentions. Within an urbanity domain respondents who were dissatisfied with adult education opportunities and public parks/playgrounds exhibited a greater anticipation of migrating than those satisfied with these two items. Within a local economy domain people who were dissatisfied with job advancement and the local tax rate were significantly more likely to express migration intentions.

In the public services domain, persons who were dissatisfied with public schools and health services were more likely to intend to migrate than persons who were satisfied. Finally, in the natural environment domain, dissatisfaction with air and water quality and scenic beauty was related to a greater likelihood of migration intention.

These bivariate results demonstrated a variety of community conditions, both noneconomic and economic, linked to expressed migration intentions. This research also incorporated concepts from ecological perspectives in describing the structural context within which migration decisions were being made, further contributing to the integration of motivational and structural models (Kan et al. 1981; Stinner and Kan 1984).

Regional Variations in Migration Motivations

Many commentators on the status of the social sciences have observed that genuine replication is rare, compared with other sciences. Data collected in 1982 in a rapidly growing nonmetropolitan area of Idaho and Washington oriented on the metropolitan center of Spokane were designed in part to replicate research that had been conducted in the 1970s in other regions of the nation, including a study in rapidly growing counties of the North Central region (Rowe and Wardwell 1987). The results of this replication are presented in Chapter 6.

The study sought to identify regional variations in the mix of migrant motivations for movement to nonmetropolitan areas. The Western study showed a much greater emphasis on environmental considerations, and a lower emphasis on family and other ties to the destination community or region (Wardwell and Rowe 1983). This difference was explained in terms of differences in settlement history of the North Central and Pacific Northwest regions. Residents of large urban areas in the North Central region are more likely to have moved there from the rural parts of the same region, and thus to retain family and other ties to those rural areas. In the Northwest, residents of large urban areas are much more likely to have moved from large urban areas in other regions of the nation, and are less likely to have family ties to the rural areas of the Northwest. Consequently, when these urbanites do move to those rural areas, they are more likely to cite environmental considerations than family ties as their reason for making such a move (Rowe and Wardwell 1988).

Research conducted in high natural amenity areas of Colorado and Montana underscores the Idaho-Washington findings. This study is presented in Chapter 5. Migrants to these areas of the Rocky Mountains were also more likely to cite quality of life reasons for their move, such as living in a small community near natural recreation areas, than is typical even for the Western region (Jobes 1985a; 1986a; 1986b; 1990a; 1990b).

Williams and Jobes (1990) reported a strong association between reasons for leaving place of origin and reasons for choosing the Gallatin Valley of Montana as their destination. This association varied with socioeconomic status. The higher the status of the migrant, the greater the likelihood of stressing both economic and quality of living factors in the decision-making process. For migrants of lower socioeconomic status, quality of living reasons dominated.

In 1985, a survey was conducted of a small metropolitan area in the Northern Rockies (Great Falls, Montana), to compare reasons given for migration to a regional trade center with reasons for migration to nonmetropolitan areas. Employment and other economic reasons were reported far more frequently in this study than had been the case for migrants to nonmetropolitan areas in the West. Migrants were also far more likely to indicate that they considered the move temporary, and might move on again if conditions warranted (Wardwell 1986b; 1986d).

In this research, as well as in that reported by Jobes, men were more likely than women to report employment and income factors as central to their decision to move. Women were more likely to cite social factors characteristic of the community to which they had moved (Williams et al. 1986). These findings lend support to the argument advanced by Jensen and Blevins (1982), who criticize models of migration for their uniform failure to incorporate women workers into their labor force predictions.

Salience of Infrastructure

In addition to environmental factors, migrants to nonmetropolitan counties of the Spokane region cited structural factors other than economic changes as important to their move. The 1982 study was the first to include these factors, in an attempt to integrate structural and motivational explanations of the migration turnaround. This was done by expressing the most frequently presented structural explanations of the nonmetropolitan turnaround in terms of the residential preferences of migrants (Wardwell 1984). That is, migrants were asked to assess the importance of structural changes in the region of their destination, in exactly the same format that had been used to assess the importance of family ties, environmental factors and economic considerations.

The results indicated that migrants placed at least as much importance on changes in infrastructure such as transportation improvements (Shearman 1983) and easier access to cities, as they did on economic considerations in their move (Wardwell 1984). Changes in road and highway maintenance, improved urban access, shopping convenience, community services and reduced social isolation were rated by migrants as being at least as important to their decision as standard economic factors such as employment opportunities, income, and cost of living. School consolidation, access to air transportation, loan availability and cable television in small towns were rated least important. The importance to the migrant of economic motivators and the salience of this type of structural change were positively associated (Wardwell 1992).

The effect of this research has been to change the context of the debate over migrant motivation from an excessively simple dichotomy employing economic-noneconomic factors to the more complete cross-classification of structural/individual and economic/ noneconomic factors (Jobes, Stinner, and Wardwell 1992).

Effects of the Economic Recession

The role of economic factors was also explored. This became more important through the 1980s, as rates of growth in nonmetropolitan areas slowed in the West and even more dramatically in the rest of the nation. Since the Idaho-Washington study was conducted in 1982 at the depth of the economic recession, it included opportunities for the respondents to indicate how the recession was influencing their ability to remain in their chosen location, and whether the changed economic circumstances had caused them to reconsider the bases on which they had made the decision to move to the area (Wardwell and Rowe 1984). This research is presented in Chapter 9 of this volume.

The results suggest the possibility that the slowdown in nonmetropolitan growth came about more through reduced metropolitan outmigration than through increased nonmetropolitan outmigration. The likelihood of lower retention was not indicated by the responses of the new nonmetropolitan residents of the Spokane nonmetropolitan region.

There was however a relationship between reason for moving and the respondent's indication of the likelihood of a future move based upon the economic climate of the region (as there is between the reason for moving and the individual economic outcomes associated with the move, as is shown in the research conducted by Kershaw 1985). Respondents who had moved primarily for economic reasons were much more likely to say that the economic circumstances of the recession could cause them to move on again than were respondents who had moved for any other reasons.

Jobes and his colleagues point out, however, that a move to a high amenity area primarily for noneconomic reasons does not necessarily imply a strong commitment to remain in the area. About forty percent of their initial subsample had moved away within five years. The absence of anticipated employment and income opportunities was the most important reason for moving away in this study as it was in the Washington-Idaho study (Jobes 1992a). Many newcomers based their moves on expectations which were unrealistic, given the characteristics of the community to which they were moving. They then reevaluated the relative importance of the variables they had considered (or failed to consider) at the time of their arrival (Jobes 1986a).

The long and deep recession in the Pacific Northwest continued to condition the research (Cook 1987; Stevens and Owen 1982). Statewide survey data were collected in 1988 in Idaho to update and extend the original research (Rowe 1988). At that later date, about one-half of the respondents believed that economic reasons might force a move from their present community within five years, while one-fourth indicated that nothing could cause them to move and the remainder cited noneconomic reasons for an anticipated move.

No significant differences were found between metropolitan and nonmetropolitan residents in perceived probability of a move, but nearly one-half (47%) of the nonmetropolitan residents indicated a preference for another Idaho city of under 10,000. By a two-to-one margin, metropolitan residents were more likely to move to another metropolitan area outside the state, while less than half the nonmetropolitan residents would so move.

The migrant population in Oregon was surveyed to shed light on the question of how people perceived and evaluated public services. Because of their geographic mobility, migrants are in a position to evaluate these services in at least two different situations. If their perceptions are accurate, this approach may allow more accurate predictions of migration trends, since secondary data on quality indicators are often available by place.

Stevens (1984b; 1984c) showed that inmigrants' perceptions of air quality and safety from crime were generally consistent with the regional differences in crime rates and levels of suspended particulates, ozone and carbon monoxide. There were both high and low demanders for these public services, however, in spite of a high degree of shared perception. Those inmigrants most vulnerable to crime, particularly the elderly, those with young children, females, and those with more wealth, felt they had gained the largest increases in satisfaction from the generally lower crime rates in Oregon (Stevens 1985). Younger household heads, those with young children, and those with higher incomes felt they had gained the most from the generally improved air quality (1986a).

The understanding gained from this research on inmigrants led to a study of public service satisfaction among a cross-section of Oregon households, with an emphasis upon adaptations by those who were the most dissatisfied (Ahearn 1984; Stevens 1985; 1986a). Rural residents were the most dissatisfied with local police protection even though crime rates were lowest in rural areas. Along with previous crime victims and those who live alone, rural residents were the most likely to purchase market goods for household protection (such as lights and alarms). The degree of unmet need in public safety appeared to be greater in cities, where residents voiced a higher willingness to pay for safety, than in rural areas.

The accuracy of perceptions was even greater for air quality than safety. Dissatisfaction with air quality was greatest among young people, those with more education, and those with respiratory illness. These people were also the most active in making market and political adaptations to secure better air quality. To the extent that migration is oriented to securing improved air quality and public safety, these results suggest that the participants were reasonably well informed in their decision making.

Quality of Living and Income Tradeoffs

Through most of the studies, whenever income comparisons were asked of recent nonmetropolitan migrants, respondents were as likely as in any other study to indicate that they had sacrificed income in order to make their move to a nonmetropolitan destination in the Inland Northwest, the Pacific Northwest, or the Rocky Mountains of Montana,

Colorado and Utah. National research with documentary data conducted by Gilchrist and Wardwell (1982) cast some doubt upon this frequently-reported finding.

When migrants from large metropolitan areas to nonmetropolitan counties were compared with all other types of movers, there was no finding of change in the propensity of movers to nonmetropolitan destinations to accept an income loss associated with their move. Using data on patterns of income change associated with movement between metropolitan and nonmetropolitan areas, Gilchrist and Wardwell (1992) found movers to nonmetropolitan destinations to be no more likely to have experienced income losses associated with their move than were movers to other destinations. Most of the income loss at the time of a move could be attributed to the effects of inflation. This was true for all types of movers.

These findings call into question the widely-accepted explanation of nonmetropolitan migration in terms of the increased willingness of migrants to accept lower incomes in exchange for higher quality of living (Jobes et al. 1992). Resolution of this apparent discrepancy of findings based upon primary survey data and documentary data awaits further research. In a related study, Stinner et al. (1985) found that metropolitan to nonmetropolitan migrants during the period of the turnaround had suffered a loss in occupational status.

Objective 3a [3]
To analyze the socioeconomic consequences of migration flows on migrants and sending/receiving communities with the intent of providing local, state and national policy makers with current information.

Research conducted under this objective was focused on the consequences of trends in migration and of the act of moving itself for individuals, households, and families. Particular consequences of nonmetropolitan migration have been emphasized in several studies. This section includes research on community impacts, simulation modeling of impacts, retirement migration and community development, migration impacts on local education, changes in population composition and policy implications.

Community Impacts
Energy industries are subject to well-known boom and bust cycles, and it is widely believed that the rapidity of change in these cycles

negatively impacts energy-dependent communities (Copp 1984a; Jobes 1984a; Jobes and Branch 1983; Jobes et al. 1984a; Knop 1987a). Community studies in Colorado, Montana and Texas have explored these change relationships. Colorado and Montana communities are addressed in Chapter 5 while Chapter 7 examines socioeconomic impacts in Colorado and Texas.

Social change has been monitored in five Texas communities throughout the project (Copp 1990; Backman and Copp 1988). Two were impacted by an oil boom, one was the proposed site for a lignite-fired electrical generating plant, and the remaining town a stagnant community adjacent to a rapidly growing metropolitan center. Litigation delayed construction of the proposed power plant, and in 1986 the price of crude oil fell sharply, leading to further cutbacks in an already retrenched oil and gas industry.

Research on social change proceeded along two lines: studies of changing economic organization brought about by the earlier oil boom; and, studies of the primary, secondary and tertiary effects of retrenchment in the oil and gas industry. The oil boom that came to Central Texas in the late 1970s and early 1980s lifted agricultural communities to a higher level of economic activity (Copp 1984b). There was more wealth, measured by bank deposits, and a higher level of business activity, measured by sales tax receipts. The stock of housing increased greatly. Despite the recession in the oil industry, the population of the small towns remained steady, but open country areas were more likely to show slight depopulation (Copp 1984a).

Ironically, the higher level of activity attracted chain stores, motels, and highway shopping centers. Although the variety and quality of goods and services available to shoppers improved, the economic well-being of local merchants declined because of the greater sophistication of the chain store competition. Sales fell off for many merchants. Some survived by diversifying activities or personalizing services. A surprising amount of innovation in merchandising was detected in the attempts to survive (Copp 1985c). Excess apartment construction worked to the detriment of local owners.

The decline in the oil and gas industry had been going on for four years, taking a sharp drop in 1986. The primary effect was manifested in drilling activity which came to an abrupt stop. Secondary effects were evident in the oil service industry, first in those related to bringing wells into production and later in those related to production maintenance. In the first three years of the decline, the companies failing were those with poor job performance or costly debt service (Copp 1984d). The disappearance of service companies was related to the scarcity of work. The major companies all survived, but a heavy toll was taken of independents. Oil field services closely allied with the majors survived, but were increasingly forced into bidding contract competition and strict performance standards.

The tertiary effects of the industrial decline were evident in the failures of motels, restaurants, motion picture theaters, convenience stores, taverns, and other service businesses. At the same time, new businesses were initiated to secure income for local residents. The new businesses included nursery schools, salvage, video rentals, modernized business places, or diversifications into new lines of service, such as the bail bondsman who added a dry cleaning service. Other effects involved a fall in assessed valuation for tax purposes of oil field property and oil producing land. These changes did not lead to revenue shortfalls in education or local government because of upward adjustments in rates (Copp 1990).

The history of the proposed lignite fired electrical plant took unusual turns involving high finance and complex maneuvering in the state bureaucracy and River Authority (Copp 1985a). It appeared that no power plant would be built. The other major employer, an aluminum smelter, cut back employment, and the overall level of commercial activity in the community appeared to be stable, not declining. Field work continued in monitoring the three communities through oil boom and bust cycles (Copp 1990).

The industry declined further in the 1990s. Drilling activity resumed after successes in the Austin Chalk formation with horizontal drilling. The price of oil rose in 1990 and drilling activity picked up, but was limited by a shortage of trained workers. Workover rigs and new drilling sites were in abundance, and more wells had been brought back into production. Drilling declined with the end of the Gulf War but remained above previous levels.

The economic community generally responded in a quite conservative manner to the renewal of economic activity. Little social effect of the boomlet was observed. Sales tax revenues increased, surplus rental housing in the rural communities was absorbed, but there were few new business start-ups or community improvements. Copp concluded that the oil bust tended to accentuate secular trends for trade center centralization and regionalization, with particularly adverse effects on small towns under 2,500 (1984d; 1990).

The fourth community, adjacent to a growing metropolitan center, remained stagnant (Copp 1984d). Major employers were retained and a few small community improvement projects were successfully completed. A number of small crises in local government occurred but were all resolved successfully. The situation remained one of stagnation rather than decline, but with improved self-direction.

In summary, this research revealed a good deal of change in the four communities over a short period of time. Yet it also revealed a good deal of resilience and innovation as local citizens adjusted to changing economic conditions (Copp 1984c; 1985b). The greatest outmigration flows were found among open country residents living in mobile housing. Even here, population movement was mixed: some oil industry workers left, but this movement was counteracted by the movement in of commuters and retirees. Community leaders and their linkages to other institutions in and outside the community played a major role in adapting to change (Copp 1985c). The key role that must be played by financial leaders in local government and in economic development activities continued to be underscored in these four communities (Copp 1984c).

Simulation of Community Impacts

Work accomplished under this heading has been directed along several routes including the development and testing of county typologies, simulation modelling, and community impact assessments. Rowe (1988) developed for Idaho counties an adapted version of the USDA typology.[4] The goal was to provide a framework for the analysis of changes and adaptations by people and communities impacted by structural changes occurring in natural resource industries.

From a different orientation Knop (1989) developed a basic dynamic computer simulation model which demonstrated the direct and indirect interactional effects of migration processes on host community well-being. Developed for use on three nonmetropolitan Colorado communities that have been studied longitudinally for two decades (Knop and Bacigalupi 1984), the preliminary model was tested with data for the Navajo Nation, at the Tribe's request (Eckert et al. 1989). This gave insights to its transferability to other sociodemographic units. This activity contributed to an understanding not only of population dynamics for a special situation but, in the process, served to refine methodologies relevant to local areas and the interrelations with external settings.

The model simulates demographic processes with input rates by age and selected social and economic characteristics. The units include the

United States, Colorado, and seven sub-state regions. The migration component assumes net flows in the direction of perceived greater opportunity, which is defined differently for different age, social and economic categories. Differential rates by categories were obtained from 1970-1980 data and modified according to changes in the state and nation since 1980, and from information obtained in Colorado community case studies.

Migration of the Aged and Retirement as Community Development

Research in Washington and Utah supported the viability of viewing retirement migration as part of an economic development strategy in resource-based nonmetropolitan counties (Cook 1990a). Development efforts to attract retirees to rural areas could effectively offset declines in traditional resource-based industries (Cook 1990b; Stinner and Nam 1984). The feasibility of this strategy is enhanced if county-level migration patterns of persons 65 or older shift over time and differ from those of the general population, particularly during economic recessions. Amenities, service availability, and cost of living influenced nonmetropolitan retirement migration between 1980 and 1985 (Stinner and Khosrashahin 1985).

Impacts of Migration on Education

Research in Oregon and Washington concentrated on outcomes for the support and integration of local schools. Education was an early emphasis in the first phase of project W-118 (Knop and Knop 1982; 1985). The determinants of support for school budget elections in Oregon public school districts was a primary focus in the work of Stevens and Mason (1988). Prior research had identified 100 problem districts with nonexistent or inadequate tax bases, requiring a popular vote for local levies to sustain the costs of education. Budget elections from 1981-1986 were analyzed; 15-18 variables were statistically significant in explaining annual operating expenses per student. These included price, incomes, tastes, demographics, technology, voting processes and the use of state aid. These variables operated differently for elementary schools, union high schools, and conventional K-12 districts (Stevens and Mason 1988).

Economies of size, for example, did not appear in elementary or union high districts, but became apparent in conventional K-12 school districts. Voter age structures definitely influenced budget election outcomes. Older voters, and particularly older voters who had recently moved to a district, reduced school spending. A K-12 district one standard deviation above the mean in percent of population aged 60 or older had school expenditures 5.7 percent lower than a district that was average in terms of population age composition. Elderly inmigration reduced spending 1.7 percent; the combined effect of these two variables reduced spending 7.4 percent.

Research studies in Oregon and Washington examined migration-related impacts on local schools as part of an endeavor to understand how population changes affect various community subsystems. The Oregon research was conducted to cast light on local school finance issues (Stevens and Mason 1988). These issues have been of much concern to state policy-makers, who see school funding instability as a major deterrent to inmigration and economic growth. The major focus has been to explain why school budget elections pass or fail and why some school districts spend substantially more than others. Data have been assembled for those 100 districts that accounted for nearly all of the region's school budget elections between 1981/82 and 1985/86. These districts have small or zero tax bases and must seek annual approval by the voters of large excess levies. They are also the districts where numerous school closures have occurred because tax levies have failed as many as six times.

A preliminary analysis of operating expenditures in these districts over the five years has been accomplished by regression analyses of pooled time-series and cross-sectional data. About seventy-five percent of the variation in operating expenditures per student can be explained by a set of about twenty independent variables, representing tax level, demographics, attitudes and preferences of voters, revenue sources, costs of producing education, and voter process (Stevens and Mason 1988). Results suggested that average expenditures per student were:

- positively related to family income, but with a relatively low income elasticity.
- negatively related to the tax level, but also in a relatively inelastic way.
- related to the age distribution of voters in a fairly complex way.
- negatively related to enrollment, indicating economies of size.
- positively related to state aid, but with substantial "leakage" to property tax relief.
- positively related to voter turnout.

Wardwell and Cornelius (1988) analyzed relationships between migration and K-12 enrollment patterns in Great Falls, Montana, a small, isolated metropolitan area in the Northern Rockies that has been severely impacted by declining economic employment in manufacturing and processing industries in the past two decades. The community attained a stable economic base but remained subject to fluctuations as a consequence of national trends in agriculture, tourism-recreation and federal employment. Economic stability could not provide the employment growth needed to retain young adults in the community; this was made evident by the declining crude birth rates in the city and county, and indeed throughout Montana. Without other changes in the economic base, the declining numbers of births would be certain to lead to declining kindergarten enrollments in the near future.

Research on migration and education also concentrated on methodologies of projecting enrollments in local school districts. Wardwell and Judson (1990) examined the school enrollment projections formerly in use by the Washington State Office of the Superintendent of Public Instruction and compared these results to those obtained from 23 alternative projection methods. On the basis of this research, they recommended changes to the most accurate method available, a simple unweighted cohort progression.

The methods previously in use had projected 50 percent of state school districts within ± 5 percent and 63-65 percent within ± 8 percent. The methods recommended increased the proportions within these accuracy limits to 70-73 percent and 83 percent respectively. These methods improved projection accuracy in all categories of district size and direction/rate of change. In five-year accuracy tests, the recommended methods (which were subsequently adopted) placed 53-65 percent of larger districts within ± 8 percent. The preferred methods also yielded the lowest errors for the smallest school districts.

Wardwell and Stewart (1991) completed data collection on migration and school enrollments in the Northern Rockies region and preliminary analyses of relationships. The analysis measured population turnover in the local community by comparing enrollment change with total migration at the county level. Gross and net migration rates as estimated from enrollment data compared more favorably with census inmigration and turnover rates for the 1975-80 period than with net or gross outmigration rates.

Changes in Population Composition
The population composition of both areas of origin and destination may frequently change quite substantially through migration. Swanson

(1986a) examined the extent to which the exchange of migrants between nonmetropolitan areas had disruptive [i.e., changing] effects or equalizing effects. Inmigrants to nonmetropolitan counties were classified into those originating in metropolitan and other nonmetropolitan counties. They were then compared in terms of their characteristics to the prior residents of destination nonmetropolitan counties. Whether migrants brought additional economic and human resources to an area or a greater need for public services was a central focus of the analysis. Nonmetropolitan areas were chosen which received migrants from other nonmetropolitan areas at a rate higher than the U.S. average. Ten of the resulting seventeen states were located in the West, with the remainder in the neighboring Central region.

Migrants from nonmetropolitan areas brought some employment and income-related benefits. Among those in the labor force, metropolitan origin migrants were more likely to be unemployed, but slightly less likely to rely on public assistance, than were longer-term residents. Inmigrant groups from both origins had a slightly greater percentage of school children than did longer-term residents, and a lower proportion of retirees. Higher levels of education were brought to nonmetropolitan destinations by migrants from both types of origins.

In these Western and Central study areas, there were small net gains of school children and people with higher education through migrant exchange with other nonmetropolitan areas. In the exchange with metropolitan areas, there were small net gains of retirees, moderate net gains of school children, and large net gains of highly educated people.

While less than one percent of the nation's population is Mormon, 70 percent of the residents of the Mormon Cultural Region are Mormon. This area includes all of Utah and portions of Idaho, Colorado, Arizona, Nevada and Wyoming. It has been described by population geographers as being one of the most distinctive features in the social mapping of the United States. This region is identified, described and discussed in Chapter 3.

The impact of recent migration on this pattern of population distribution has been a major focus of W-118 (Toney et al. 1983; Kan and Kim 1981; Toney et al. 1985). This research has shown that migration has played a key role in maintaining the area's unique population composition (Stinner and Kan 1983; Stinner and Toney 1981). A majority of the inmigrants to this cultural area were Mormon, while a majority of those leaving were not. Migration was thus not altering the area's predominantly Mormon religious composition. Survey data collected from Montana supported the Utah-based study by revealing a low preference on the part of nonMormons for destinations within the Mormon Culture Region (Jobes et al. 1984b).

Because of the considerable concern expressed in migration literature over potential conflicts between migrants and natives of different social backgrounds, the policy relevance of these studies is important. The high proportion of nonMormons intending to leave the area suggests the need for local areas to make special efforts to facilitate the integration of these individuals into the community. This is especially important in the context of efforts by political leaders to attract a diversity of industries as part of their economic development policies, a point emphasized by Blevins and Bradley in Chapter 8 of this volume.

Another nationally-based study lead by W-118 researchers in Utah examined the extent to which racial differences exist in the selection of nonmetropolitan destinations. The results from the young male cohort of the National Longitudinal Surveys showed African Americans to be much less likely than whites to select nonmetropolitan destinations. The persistence of this trend would increase racial distinctiveness along the metropolitan-nonmetropolitan dimension (Keywon et al. 1986; Larson and Toney 1984; Pitcher et al. 1985).

Related research also analyzed the consequences of migration for the family size expectations of individuals (Golesorkhi and Toney 1981; Toney et al. 1985). This study compared the family size expectations of migrants with those of natives in high fertility areas of the West. Inmigrants were found to have expectations similar to those of natives, once compositional differences were controlled.

The effects of community population change on satisfaction was studied (Byun et al. 1990). Global and domain specific satisfaction levels were evaluated for three types of communities, stable growing, reversal slow declining, and reversal rapid declining. No differences in community satisfaction across community type were found. Duration of residence had the greatest influence on community satisfaction. Religious affiliation was also found to be an important indicator of community satisfaction, except in the rapidly declining communities.

An unusual study in Washington examined the effects of migration on the population composition of areas and those effects in turn upon large-scale organization and federal revenues. The findings of this study indicate that population redistribution affects revenues. This in turn affects the need for regional location of federal agencies and staffing strengths. The effects come about through the associated shifts in labor force participation, income change, and subregional shifts in compliance with federal mandates, rather than directly (Wardwell 1986a; see also Rowe 1985). The compositional and behavioral changes associated with population movements appear to have had a greater effect on the total demand for services than did the volume of movement itself, or the related changes in population size. Complexity of returns and patterns of compliance affected staffing needs.

Policy Implications

Changes in population growth, composition, and social infrastructure of rural areas imply changes in the policies appropriate to the quality of living of rural and nonmetropolitan peoples (Copp and Moe 1984; Rowe 1989). The role of rural infrastructure in attracting growth was explored in the study of the Inland Northwest region of Washington and Idaho. On the bases of these results, a reconsideration of rural policies toward infrastructure is in order. Wardwell (1986c) argued that greater attention must be given to the rural per capita costs of maintaining infrastructure in place if the social and economic vitality of rural regions are to be maintained.

The political subsystem may be directly impacted by the public policy orientations of migrants vis-a-vis natives (Stinner et al. 1986; 1987). The issue is examined closely by Stinner and Paita in Chapter 10 of this book. This chapter is focused on the contribution of migrant-native variations in public policy orientations to metropolitan-nonmetropolitan differences. The investigation evaluates the "urban way of life," "convergence," and "institutionalist" models. Their findings suggest that no one model could account for the patterns observed in the data; however, the "institutionalist" model generally predominated.

Analyses of 1984 statewide survey data in Utah revealed striking similarities among natives, returning, and nonreturning migrants in attitudes regarding several public policy issues. This was contrary to expectations. On some issues metropolitan-nonmetropolitan differences were observed, while on others there was no difference. Similarly, inmigrants contributed to contraction in metropolitan differences on some issues while reinforcing preexisting differences between metropolitan and nonmetropolitan natives on other issues [see Chapter 10].

Objective 3b [5]

To analyze the interdependences of agriculture and natural resource production, food and fiber employment, and population

change.

Under this objective, research studies covered a range of food and fiber industries, including the wood products industry in the Pacific Northwest, impacts of population growth and development on agriculture in the Rocky Mountains, immigration effects on agricultural labor in California, interactions between recreation industries and wilderness management, and analyses of county growth patterns by economic resource base.

Wood Products Industries and Community Impacts

Research in Oregon has focused on monitoring population and economic trends in natural resource-dependent communities, especially those related to the wood products industry. This research had documented the existence of a dual labor market with limited possibilities for local jobs or residential migration. More recently, a series of economic crises buffeted the timber region. Inflation led to reductions in housing starts about 1978 and wood products employment plummeted. Land withdrawals for wilderness and overcutting on private lands also turned long-term job prospects downward.

The ability of workers to respond to these crises was studied in mill closures (Stevens 1983), forest resources for rural development (Stevens 1984a), and forest products and rural labor incomes (Stevens 1986b). Wood products output climbed back to prerecession levels but employment only rose from a low of 55,000 in 1982 to about 65,000 workers in the early 1990s. Over 80,000 people had worked in the industry prior to the recession. Many jobs were lost as firms mechanized in order to remain competitive. It seemed unlikely that workers or small communities would have the political power to use a base in forest-related activities to enhance jobs in the future. As issues of accelerated timber harvest, log exports and wilderness areas are resolved in the political arena, workers will need to look to other regions and other industries for employment.

An analysis of changes in timber-dependent areas of Washington found pervasive outmigration during the 1980s. The outmigration was related to slow growth or absolute losses in the labor force and to slow growth in per capita incomes (Cook 1992). In addition, these areas experienced much more rapid growth in single-parent families and more rapid aging. Some of the resource dependent communities adjacent to metropolitan areas were making the transition to a suburban community economic base, but the more remote areas experienced substantial difficulties.

Growth and Development Impacts on Agriculture

Agricultural impacts of growth and development were emphasized in research focused on communities in Colorado, Montana and Texas. New residents in agricultural areas were unlikely to compete directly with local farmers and ranchers (Copp 1985b). Few entered agriculture as an occupation. Those who did were likely to do so on a part-time and frequently alternative basis (Jobes 1984c).

Population growth in rapidly expanding rural communities had direct impacts on agriculture (Copp 1985b). This growth converted land to nonagricultural uses as needs for commercial and residential space increased. Communities lacked coordinating systems for accommodating the growth. Conflicts over appropriate land uses and service distribution were encountered during periods of rapid change. These conflicts were magnified by outdated or nonexistent policies (Jobes 1985b). Increased land values then created an attractive economic alternative for farmers and ranchers who sold or commercially developed their land. Nonagricultural development in turn created a variety of problems for farmers and ranchers. Trespassing, poaching, and harassment of stock by dogs occurred with increasing population proximity, as new settlement expanded into agricultural or grazing areas (Jobes 1986c).

The communities serving agriculture were affected in both positive and negative ways, a theme developed in Chapter 5 of this volume. New migrants to rural areas increased the viability of the infrastructure, providing goods and services and frequently preventing their demise. This improved the availability of goods and services to resident farmers and ranchers (Jobes and Branch 1983). Although the personal attention given to oldtimers may have diminished, the variety of private and public sector activities may have increased (Jobes 1984c). Local ranchers and farmers frequently felt their economic and political influence had been undermined by growth, particularly when it was based on rapid inmigration of persons who differ from them (Jobes 1984a).

Traditional ranching activities interact with new growth based on energy developments (Jobes 1986d; 1989). Two small ranching communities, Decker and Birney, located in the midst of a sparsely settled region impacted by coal extraction, experienced transitions with rangelands converted to mines and mines in turn converted to reclaimed lands. While long-term residents continued to describe the area as a desirable place to live, substantial outmigration had taken place, and social relationships were perceived as having deteriorated.

Immigration and Agricultural Labor

As has been indicated, research in California and New Mexico emphasized illegal and undocumented immigration. The focus of this work was particularly upon its effects on agriculture (Martin et al. 1984; 1985; Martin 1990), and upon rural communities (Eastman 1983b). Martin stressed the difficulty of drawing accurate inferences about undocumented immigration from data on legal immigrants (Martin 1985a). A regular stream of undocumented migrants provided a small but critical segment of the agricultural labor force (Eastman 1983b; Martin and Mamer 1982; 1985). Currently, there is an oversupply of agricultural workers in the region (Martin and Taylor 1990).

This research suggests that illegal immigration increased and changed in composition between 1975 and 1985, as more urban residents came to the U.S. illegally and as experienced undocumented workers moved out of agriculture and into other, less rural industries (Martin and Mines 1984; Martin and Fogel 1982; Mines and Martin 1984). Additional longitudinal analysis is needed in order to assess the impacts this shift will have on Western states (Martin 1985b). Workers with rural backgrounds are willing to perform many U.S. farm tasks, and they may initially work for lower wages than U.S. workers.

Do undocumented workers compete with residents for jobs? Yes, but the displacement process is complex (Mines and Martin 1984). In California citrus, for example, illegal immigrants displaced legal green card workers and changed the labor market from unionized employer associations to farm labor contractors. However, the displaced unionized and legal workers never identified illegal immigration as the cause of their unemployment.

Any immigration reforms which attempt to reduce the flow will require adjustments in industries which employ undocumented labor. Employers will have to recruit residents or make other arrangements for the needed labor. Legislation to curtail undocumented migration will raise the cost of labor, especially for smaller producers who are most dependent on undocumented workers (Martin 1985b). At the bottom of the occupational ladder, undocumented workers perform work that U.S. citizens avoid. However, as these workers gain skills, they do compete with domestic labor (Eastman 1984a). Recent passage of the Immigration Control Act invites continued monitoring of impacts on border communities. In Chapter Four of this volume, Martin explores impacts of NAFTA on existing immigration.

Recreation Industries and Wilderness Management

Calvert and Jobes (1990) demonstrated that economic perspectives were inadequate as the sole or even primary basis for decisions on wilderness management. An economic framework was adopted to demonstrate that even in these terms preservation made more sense than did traditional use. Jobes examined the Greater Yellowstone Ecosystem as a biological concept corresponding closely to social systems of the region (1986a). Local towns and counties are economically dependent upon the Yellowstone Ecosystem, while state and federal systems determine its use and management. Local residents are simultaneously part of the ecosystem and distinct from it. Local residents and inmigrants have beliefs and activities that distinguish them from residents elsewhere. Five zones surrounding Yellowstone and Grand Teton National Parks usefully distinguished differences between residents varying in attitudes and behaviors regarding exploiting the natural resources of the region through technologies and social organization.

Housing needs within Yellowstone for employees complemented the research contrasting wilderness and recreation demands. With rapid turnover, the constant shift of workers made it difficult to find consensus on the type of housing best suited to the area (Jobes 1990a). Nonetheless there are increasing demands to improve the housing stock (Jobes 1990b).

Growth Patterns by County Type

A major focus under this objective was the delineation of structural factors accounting for migration trends, and identification of demographic profiles for varying nonmetropolitan county clusters. Renewed net migration losses did not appear in all types. Analyses in Utah revealed variations between the 1980-83 and 1983-86 periods. For counties concentrated in mining and nonlocal services, net out-migration was already evident in 1980-83 and worsened in the later period. Among agricultural, manufacturing and governmental counties, net out-migration only appeared in the 1983-86 period. Only those counties whose economic base was focused on tourism experienced continuing net migration gain through both periods.

In Washington more outmigration was observed between 1983 and 1987 than earlier in the 1980s in a number of agricultural and timber counties (Cook 1987). In Idaho net outmigration was also highly concentrated in mono-industry agricultural, mining or wood products counties.

Cook's (1987) multivariate analysis of net migration in Washington and Oregon counties between 1980 and 1984 suggests that two additional structural variables, degree of self-employment and the percent of the labor force that is female, may be necessary for explaining the factors that altered nonmetropolitan migration patterns in the 1980s.

Overview of Population Change in the Rural West

This chapter has summarized and integrated ten years of migration-related research on population and social change in the West. This volume derives from the twenty-year research history of Western Regional Project W-118. The next three chapters examine population trends in subregions of the West in the context of the sociocultural and economic changes that lie behind the more visible phenomenon of population change.

Cook examines economic and population change in the Pacific Northwest in Chapter Two. Toney, Stinner and Byun compare the sociodemographic and cultural distinctiveness of the Mormon Culture Region in Chapter Three. In Chapter Four, Martin analyzes the dynamics of immigration and changes in the domestic labor force in California.

The next several chapters examine causes and consequences of migration, particularly in rural communities and more remote nonadjacent counties. Knop and Jobes explain how an appearance of population stability or stagnation can mask extensive turnover of population in rural communities in Chapter Five. In Chapter Six, Wardwell and Lyle compare the reasons given for moving by recent nonmetropolitan migrants to the Northern Rockies with those given by similar migrants to rapidly growing rural areas of the North Central States.

Copp and Knop elaborate the socioeconomic impacts on social change of boom and bust cycles in resource extractive industries in small communities of Colorado, Montana and Texas in Chapter Seven. Wyoming is the smallest state in the West and in the nation in terms of its population size, and it has long been one of the most resource-dependent of state economies. In Chapter Eight, Blevins and Bradley examine the record and potential for economic diversification in Wyoming.

The theme of impacts of the economic recessions of the 1970s and 1980s runs throughout the research reported in this volume. In Chapter Nine, Wardwell and Lyle examine the interaction between rural economic recessions and migrant motivations, as part of the effort to integrate economic and motivational explanations of migration patterns involving rural and nonmetropolitan areas. Finally, in Chapter Ten, Stinner and Paita examine the impacts of migration on public policy orientations, comparing the distributions of metropolitan and nonmetropolitan differences in Utah. They examine whether these distributions have been affected by differences between long-term residents and recent migrants to metropolitan and nonmetropolitan areas of the State.

Notes

1. This is an updated and revised version of a bulletin published in 1988 as Migration Research in the West: A Review of the Literature by the Western Rural Development Center, Corvallis, OR, Bulletin No. 35. Jennifer Lincoln Hanson provided invaluable assistance in updating the literature review to include the 1987-1992 period. I wish to thank James H. Copp, Patrick C. Jobes, Philip L. Martin and Michael B. Toney for their helpful comments on the earlier draft, and James J. Zuiches for his continuing support and encouragement of this project. The work of conducting this review was supported by Project 0354, College of Agriculture and Home Economics, Agricultural Research Center, Washington State University, a contributing project to Western Regional Project W-118.

2. Published as Knop, Edward, Joel Hamilton, Donald West and C. Jack Gilchrist. 1978. The Social and Economic Significance of Human Migration in the Western Region. Pullman: Washington State University College of Agriculture Research Center Bulletin No. 859.

3. This was Objective 3 of the project through the completion of the 1982-87 phase.

4. See Bender, Lloyd D., Bernal L. Green, Thomas L. Hady, John A. Kuehn, Marlys K. Nelson, Leon B. Perkins and Peggy R. Ross. 1985. The Diverse Social and Economic Structure of Nonmetropolitan America. Washington, D.C.: U.S. Department of Agriculture Economic Research Service Rural Development Research Report No. 49.

5. In the third and final phase of the project, 1987-1992, this was Objective 3 of the revised proposal.

Research Papers of W-118: 1982-1992

Ahearn, Mary C.
   1984   An Analysis of Contingent Valuation Applied to Air Quality and Public Safety from Crime. Corvallis, OR: Oregon State University, Ph. D. Dissertation.

Bacigalupi, Tad
1983 Values in the Decision-Making Process: A Study of Migration in Three Rural Colorado Communities. Fort Collins, CO: Colorado State University Ph.D. Dissertation.

Backmann, Kenneth F. and James H. Copp
1988 Variations in per capita Expenditures for Services in Various Types of Rural Economies. Presented at the annual meeting of the Southwestern Sociological Association, Houston (March).

Ballard, Chester C. and James H. Copp
1982 Coping with Change in an Oil Boom Town. Small Town, : 4-8.

Ballard, Chester C., Myrna S. Hoskins and James H. Copp
1981 Local Leadership Control of Small Community Growth. College Station: Texas Agricultural Experiment Station Department of Rural Sociology Technical Report No. 81-3.

Bouvier, Leon F. and Philip Martin
1985 Population Change and California's Future. Washington, D.C.: Population Reference Bureau.

Bohren, Lenora, Edward Knop and Sheila Knop
1985 Defining Rights and Responsibilities: Theoretical and Applied Implications of an Energy Development Case. High Plains Applied Anthropologist 5: 7-13.

Brown, David L. and John M. Wardwell (editors)
1980 New Directions in Urban-Rural Migration. NY: Academic Press.

Byun, Yongchan, Mollie Van Loon and Seh-woong Chung
1990 Changes in Community Size, Individual Characteristics and Community Satisfaction. Presented at the Rural Sociological Society annual meetings, Norfolk (August).

Calvert, Jerry W. and Patrick C. Jobes
1990 The Economic Value of Wilderness: A Critical Assessment. Pp. 59-72 in John D. Hutchinson Jr., Francis P. Noe and Robert E. Snow (editors), Outdoor Recreation Policy. New York: Greenwood.

Carpenter, Edwin H.
1990 New Technologies in Social Science Research. In R.C. Buse and J.L. Driscoll (eds.), New Directions in Data and Information Systems in Rural Areas. Ames: Iowa State Press.

Carpenter, Edwin H. and S. T. Chester, Jr.
  1984   Are Federal Energy Tax Credits Effective, A Western States Survey.
         The Energy Journal, 5:139-149.

Carpenter, Edwin H., S. T. Chester, Jr., D.R. Iams and W.R. Fasse
  1981   Homeowner's Awareness and Utilization of Federal Energy Tax
         Credits. Housing and Society, 8:118-123.

Carpenter, Edwin H. and C. Durham
  1985   Federal Tax Credits Found Effective. The Energy Journal, 6:127-128.

Cook, Annabel K.
  1987   Nonmetropolitan Migration: The Influence of Neglected Variables.
         Rural Sociology 52: 409-18.

  1990a Human Resources: Implications for the 1990s.   The Changing
         Northwest, 2: 4-5.

  1990b Retirement Migration as a Community Development Option. Journal
         of the Community Development Society, 21: 83-101.

  1990c Retirement Migration, Economic Recession and Community
         Development. Presented at the Pacific Sociological Association annual
         meetings, Spokane, April.

  1991a Exceptional Growth and the Return of Population Concentration in
         Washington. Pullman: Washington Counts No. 1 (April).

  1991b Increasing Racial and Ethnic Diversity. Pullman: Washington Counts,
         No. 2 (June).

  1992   Economic and Social Change in Washington: Timber Dependent
         Counties.   Pullman: Washington State University Cooperative
         Extension EB 1674.

Cook, Annabel K. and Don Beck
  1991   Metropolitan Dominance Versus Decentralization in the Information
         Age. Social Science Quarterly 72: 284-298.

Copp, James H.
  1984a After the Boom. Presented at Southern Association of Agricultural
         Scientists annual meetings, Nashville, February.

  1984b Social Impacts of Oil and Gas Developments on a Small Rural

Community. College Station, TX: Center for Energy and Mineral Resources, Texas A&M University Monograph Series CEMR-MS-8.

1984c   Some Working Hypotheses about Rural Community Leadership. Sixth World Congress for Rural Sociology, Manila, December.

1984d   The Stagnating Community. Presented at Southwestern Sociological Association annual meetings, Fort Worth, TX, March.

1985a   Building a Power Plant: A Study in Linkages and Obstructions. Presented at Southern Sociological Society annual meetings, Charlotte, NC, April.

1985b   The Contributions of Family, Production and Marketing to the Survival of Small Farmers. Pp. 99-105 in Thomas T. Williams (ed.), Strategy for Small Farmers: International Implications. Tuskegee, Alabama: Human Resources Development Center.

1985c   Leadership and Linkage in Rural Community Growth: A Study in Resource Mobilization. Southern Association of Agricultural Scientists annual meetings, Biloxi, Mississippi, February.

1987   Community Effects of Retrenchment in the Oil and Gas Industry. Presented at the Southern Rural Sociological Association, Nashville.

1990   Patterns of Decline in Resource Dependent Communities. Presented at the Southern Rural Sociological Association annual meetings, Little Rock, February.

Copp, James H. and Edwin O. Moe
1984   Policy Implications of Migration Research in the Western Region. Presented at W-118 Technical Committee annual meeting, Reno, October.

Eastman, Clyde
1983a   1980 Census Figures for Cibola and Valencia Counties. Las Cruces, New Mexico State University Cooperative Extension Service No. 400.

1983b   Participation of Undocumented Workers in New Mexico Agriculture. Las Cruces: New Mexico State University Department of Agricultural Economics Staff Report No. 35.

1984a   Immigration Reform and New Mexico Agriculture. El Paso, TX: University of Texas at El Paso Center for Inter-American and Border

Studies, Border Policy Working Paper Series No. 15.

1984b The People of New Mexico, 1980. Las Cruces, NM: New Mexico Agricultural Experiment Station Bulletin No. 710.

1984c Population Profiles of New Mexico Counties, 1980; Mountain States and the United States. Bozeman, MT: Montana State University Center for Data Systems and Analysis.

Eastman, Clyde and James D. Williams
1982-85 New Mexico in Numbers. Las Cruces, NM: New Mexico State University Cooperative Extension Newsletter Series No. 1-9.

Eckert, J., E. Knop, J. Lopez and S. Helmericks
1989 Employment and Incomes in the Navajo Nation, 1987-88: Estimates and Historical Trends. Ft Collins, CO: Colorado State University Institute for Distribution and Development Studies.

Gilchrist, C. Jack and John M. Wardwell
1982 Metropolitan-Nonmetropolitan Changes in Employment Location and Income Level. Presented at the Population Association of America annual meetings, San Diego, April.

1992 Changes in Employment Location and Income. Pp. 255-98 in Patrick C. Jobes, William F. Stinner, and John M. Wardwell (eds), Society, Community and Migration. Lanham, MD: University Press.

Golesorkhi, Banu and Michael B. Toney
1981 Residence, Religion and Fertility Expectations: An Analysis of Mormon and NonMormon Fertility in Rural Utah. Presented at the Western Social Science annual meetings.

Jensen, Katherine and Audie Blevins
1982 Women in Boomtowns: Modeling Visible and Invisible Roles. Presented at the Northwest Women's Studies Conference, Missoula, Montana, October.

Jobes, Patrick C.
1984a The Impacts of Coal Development on Small, Rural Communities in Southeastern Montana. Montana Agricultural Research, 1:16-19.

1984b Montana Wall Chart. Bozeman, MT: Montana State University.

1984c Old Timers and New Mobile Life Styles. Annals of Tourism Research

11:181-198.

1985a Nominalism, Multiple Realities and Community Planning. Presented at Pacific Sociological Association annual meetings, Albuquerque, NM, April.

1985b Social Control of Dirty Work: Conflict Avoidance in Social Impact Assessment. The Rural Sociologist, 5:104-111.

1986a The Changing Importance of Wilderness in a High Natural Amenity Area. Presented at National Symposium of Social Science and Natural Resources, Corvallis, Oregon, May.

1986b Different Realities, Satisfaction and Planning in a Changing Community. Proceedings of the Conference for the Small City, Stevens Point, Wisconsin: University of Wisconsin Press.

1986c Rural Impacts in Ranch Land Communities. Pp.145-160 in Pamela Dee Elkind-Savatsky (ed.), Differential Social Impacts of Rural Resource Development. Boulder, CO: Westview Press.

1986d A Small Rural Community Responds to Coal Development. Sociology and Social Research, 70:174-177.

1989 Disintegration of Ranching Communities in Southeastern Montana. Environmental Impact Assessment Review, 9: 149-156.

1990a The Complementarity between Applied and Pure Research: An Examination of Housing Satisfaction in Yellowstone National Park. Presented at the Rural Sociological Society, Norfolk, August.

1990b Living in the Fishbowl: Residential Satisfaction in Yellowstone National Park. Presented at the Pacific Sociological Association annual meetings, Spokane, April.

1991a The Greater Yellowstone Social System. Conservation Biology, 3: 387-394.

1991b Migration into Small Communities: Problems and Solutions. Montana Policy Review, 1:1-8.

1992a Economic and Quality of Life Decisions in Migration to a High Natural Amenity Area. Pp. 335-362 in Patrick C. Jobes, William F. Stinner and John M. Wardwell (eds), Community, Society and Migration:

Noneconomic Migration in America. Lanham, MD: University Press of America.

1992b Migration and Community in Montana. Pp. 1-10 in Population Decline in Montana. Bozeman: Montana State University Burton K. Wheeler Center.

Jobes, Patrick C. and K. Branch
1983 Satisfaction with Community Change and Coal Development in Decker, Montana. Helena, MT: Montana Department of State Lands and U.S. Office of Surface Mining.

Jobes, Patrick C. and C. Jack Gilchrist
1992 Ecological Attachment and Community Support During the Farm Crisis. Free Inquiry in Creative Sociology, 20: 187-197.

Jobes, Patrick C., William F. Stinner and John M. Wardwell
1992a Paradigm Shift in Migration Explanation. Pp. 1-31 in Patrick C. Jobes, William F. Stinner and John M. Wardwell (eds), Society, Community and Migration: Noneconomic Migration in America. Lanham, MD: University Press of America.

Jobes, Patrick C., Anne S. Williams and Richard Ladzinsky
1984a Community Disintegration and Coal Development: A Longitudinal Case Study of the Promise and Perplexity of Social Impact Assessment. Presented at the Rural Sociological Society annual meetings, College Station, Texas, August.

1984b Migration Into the Gallatin Valley: Preliminary Findings. Presented at the Rural Sociological Society, College Station, Texas, August.

Kan, Stephen J. and Yun Kim
1981 Religious Affiliation and Migration Intentions in Nonmetropolitan Utah. Rural Sociology, 46: 669-687.

Kan, Stephen, Yun Kim and William F. Stinner
1984 Migrant-Nonmigrant Differentials, Housing Type, Community Satis faction and Migration: A Study of Nonmetropolitan Communities in Utah within the Context of Population Turnaround. Logan, Utah: Utah Agricultural Experiment Station Research Report No. 89.

Kan, Stephen, Michael B. Toney and William F. Stinner
1981 Community Satisfaction, Migration Intentions and Migration: The Case of Nonmetropolitan Utah within the Context of Rural Revival.

Presented at Rural Sociological Society, Guelph, Canada, August.

Keywon, Cheong, Michael B. Toney and William F. Stinner
  1986 Racial Differences Among Young Men in the Selection of Metropolitan vs. Nonmetropolitan Destinations. Rural Sociology 28: 222-228.

Kershaw, Terry
  1985 Attitudes Toward Economic Growth, Personal Economic Experience and Reasons for Moving. Pullman, WA: Washington State University, Ph.D. dissertation.

Knop, Edward
  1982 Craig, Colorado, Pre- and Post-Impact: Citizens' Assessments. Presented at the Western Social Science Association, Denver (April).

  1984a Community Conceptions and Development Approaches in Sociology. High Plains Applied Anthropologist, 5: 12-14.

  1984b Population Profiles of Colorado Counties; Mountain States and the United States, 1980. Bozeman, MT: Montana State University Center for Data Systems and Analysis.

  1987a Alternative Perspectives on Community Impacting: Toward Complementary Theory and Application. Sociological Inquiry, 57:273-291

  1987b Subjective and Objective Assessment of Environmental Quality. Free Inquiry in Creative Sociology, 5: 75-80

  1989 Policy and Procedural Challenges of Estimating the Navajo Population. Presented at the Society for Applied Sociology, Denver, October.

Knop, Edward and Tad Bacigalupi
  1983 Population "Turnover" in Selected Nonmetropolitan Colorado Communities, 1970-1980. Ft. Collins, CO: Research in Demography and Developmental Change Series No. 15.

  1984 Migration Patterns and Management Challenges in Three Nonmetropolitan Colorado Communities, 1970-1980. Ft. Collins, CO: Colorado State University Experiment Station and Department of Sociology Technical Report No. 84-17.

  1985 Local Implications of Net and Turnover Migration: Observations from Three Nonmetropolitan Communities. Pace, 2: 5-8.

Knop, Edward and Sheila Knop

1982   The New-Information Effect in Community Participation: Implications for Academic Research and Service Roles. Rural Sociologist, 2: 28-35.

1985   Educational Challenges of Migration. Pace, 2: 9-11.

Larson, Don C. and Michael B. Toney

1984   Direction of White/Nonwhite Migration and Occupational Mobility. Presented at Western Social Science Association 26th annual conference, San Diego.

Martin, Philip L.

1982   Select Commission Suggests Changes in Immigration Policy: A Review Essay. Monthly Labor Review, 105: 31-37.

1983   Labor-Intensive Agriculture. Scientific American, 249: 54-59.

1984   Changing Patterns in California's Harvest Labor Force. California Agriculture, 38: 6-8.

1985a   Comments, Pp. 127-132 in Vernon M. Briggs, Jr. and Marta Tienda, Immigration: Issues and Policies. Washington, DC: Washington National Council for Employment Policy.

1985b   Migrant Labor in Agriculture. Berkeley: University of California Press.

1988   The SAW Legalization Program. Pp. 115-133 in D. Meissner and D. Papademetriou (eds), The Legalization Countdown: A Third-Quarter Assessment. Washington, D.C.: Carnegie Endowment.

1990   The Outlook for Agricultural Labor in the 1990s. U.C. Davis Law Review, 23: 499-523.

Martin, Philip L. and Walt Fogel

1982   Immigration: California's Economic Stake. Berkeley: Institute of Governmental Studies.

Martin, Philip L. and Marion Houstoun

1982   European and American Immigration Policies. Law and Contemporary Problems, 45: 29-54.

Martin, Philip L. and Gary Johnston

1983   Employment and Wages Reported by California Farmers in 1982. Monthly Labor Review, 106: 27-31.

Martin, Philip L., Harmon Kaslow, Daniel Egan, Theodor Consignado
    and Lindsay Deauville
  1984   Changing Patterns in California's Harvest Labor.   California
         Agriculture, 38:6-8.

Martin, Philip L. and S. Luce
  1988   IRCA's Effect on Large Farms. California Agriculture, 42: 26-28.

Martin, Philip L. and John Mamer
  1982   Hired Workers on California Farms. California Agriculture, 36: 21-23

  1985   Labor Trends Affecting Agriculture.California Agriculture, 39: 12-14

Martin, Philip L., John Mamer, B. Mason and C. Cartwright
  1987   California Farm Employment and Wages in 1984.   California
         Agriculture, 41:18-20.

Martin, Philip L. and Greg Miller
  1990   Farm Employment and Wage Patterns in the Mid-1990s.   California
         Agriculture, 44:16-18.

Martin, Philip L. and Richard Mines
  1982   Alien Workers and Agriculture: The Need for Policy Linkage.   Yale
         Law and Policy Review, 1: 101-115.

  1983a Immigrant Workers and the California Citrus Industry.   Industrial
         Relations, 23: 139-149.

  1983b Immigration Reform and California Agriculture.   California
         Agriculture, 37: 14-15.

Martin, Philip, L., Richard Mines and Angie Diaz
  1985   Profile of California Farmworkers. California Agriculture 39:16-18.

Martin, Philip L., Gustavo Sain and Quirino Paris
  1983   A Regional Analysis of Illegal Aliens. Growth and Change: 27-31.

Martin, Philip L. and J. Edward Taylor
  1990a Immigration Reform and California Agriculture, A Year Later.
         California Agriculture 44: 24-27.

  1990b Initial Effects of Immigration on Farm Labor in California. Population
         Research and Policy Review, 9: 255-283.

Martin, Philip L. and Suzanne Vaupel
    1987   Evaluating Employer Sanctions: Farm Labor Contractor Experience.
            Industrial Relations, 26: 304-313.

Mines, Richard and Philip L. Martin
    1984   Immigration Workers and the California Citrus Industry. Industrial
            Relations, 23:139-149.

Pitcher, Brian L., William F. Stinner and Michael B. Toney
    1985   Patterns of Migration Propensity for Black and White American Men:
            Evidence from a Cohort Analysis. Research on Aging, 7: 94-120

Rowe, Corinne M. (Lyle)
1984   Migration Turnaround: Analysis of the Relative Values of Motivators
        Resulting in Migration to Nonmetropolitan Areas. Pullman, WA:
        Washington State University, Ph.D. dissertation.

    1985   Cooperative Extension in Northern Idaho: Who Uses Our Services?
            Moscow, Idaho: University of Idaho Cooperative Extension Service
            Bulletin No. 640.

    1988   Nonmetropolitan County Typologies: Understanding Local Disparities
            of the Mid-1980s.   Presented at the Pacific Northwest Regional
            Economic Development Conference, Boise (April).

    1989   Adapting to Change: Idaho Communities at Crossroads, Preliminary
            Results from a 1988 Study. Moscow, ID: University of Idaho College
            of Agriculture AES Bulletin No. 708 (October).

Rowe, Corinne M. (Lyle) and John M. Wardwell
    1987   Growth in the Inland Northwest. Pullman, WA: Washington State
            University College of Agriculture and Home Economics Agricultural
            Research Center Bulletin No. 0994.

    1988   The Robustness of Residential Preferences. Rural Sociologist 8: 207-
            13.

Seyfrit, Carole L.
    1986   Migration Intentions of Rural Youth: Testing an Assumed Benefit of
            Rapid Growth. Rural Sociology, 51:199-211.

Shearman, Gayle A.
    1983   The Salience of Structural Change as a Factor in the Migration
            Turnaround. Pullman, WA: Washington State University, M.S. thesis.

Stevens, Joe B.
  1983   Economic and Social Consequences of Mill Closures. In Plant Modernization and Community Economic Stability: Managing the Transition. Eugene, OR: Bureau of Governmental Research and Service.

  1984a   Development and Management of Forest Resources for Rural Development in the Pacific Northwest. In Rural Development, Poverty and Natural Resources: Workshop Paper Series. Washington, DC: Resources for the Future, Inc.

  1984b   Objective Indicators, Personal Characteristics, and Satisfaction with Safety from Crime and Violence: An Inter Action Model. Social Indicators Research, 14: 53-67.

  1984c   Satisfaction with Environmental Change: An Empirical Analysis of Attitudes Toward Air Quality by Recent Interstate Migrants. Journal of Environmental Economics and Management, 11:264-281.

  1985   Crime and Prevention (Part One, The US and the West: Facts and Issues; Part Two, Satisfaction with Police Protection in Oregon). Corvallis, OR: Western Rural Development Center, Oregon State University, WRDC Publication No. 28

  1986a   Attitudes and Behavior toward Air Quality in Oregon, With Applications for Contingent Valuation. Presented at American Agricultural Economics Association annual meetings, Reno, NV, August.

  1986b   The Forest Products Industry and Labor Incomes in Rural Areas of the Pacific Northwest. Presented at the First National Symposium on Social Science in Resource Management, Oregon State University, Corvallis, OR, May.

Stevens, Joe B. and Robert Mason
  1988   Agenda Control and Reversion Budgets: Recent Evidence from Oregon School Districts. Presented at Public Choice Society, San Francisco.

Stevens, Joe B. and Linda P. Owen
  1982   Migration and Employment Change: Some New Evidence and New Considerations. Western Journal of Agricultural Economics, 7: 155-67.

Stewart, Christopher
  1991   The Use of School Enrollments as Indicators of Migration Turnover in

Counties of the Northern Rockies. Pullman: Washington State University Environmental Science Program, M.S. Thesis.

Stinner, William F. and Issa Al-Massarweh
   1988   Population Growth and Net Migration in Metropolitan and Nonmetropolitan Areas of Utah. Utah Science 48: 164-68.

   1989   Migration in Nonmetropolitan Utah. Utah Science 50: 143-49.

Stinner, William F., Lydia Baal and Ho-Youn Kwon.
   1984   Growth Trends in Elderly Population in Metropolitan and Nonmetropolitan Utah, 1950-1980.   Logan: Utah Agricultural Experiment Station Report No. 93.

Stinner, William F. and Yongchan Byun
   1990   Transition to Retirement and Geographical Mobility. Presented at the Session on Social Demographic Perspectives on the Life Course, Research Committee No. 41 of the Sociology of Population, XII World Congress of Sociology, International Sociological Association, Madrid, Spain, July.

   1991   Perceptions of Community Quality of Life of Recent Nonmetropolitan Inmigrants and Long Term Residents. Presented at the XXX Congress of the International Institute of Sociology, Kobe, Japan (August).

Stinner, W.F., Y. Byun, S. Chung, and M. Van Loon
   1989   Migration Intentions in Nonmetropolitan Utah. Population Research Laboratory, Utah State University.

Stinner, William F. and Stephen H. Kan
   1983   Patterns of Population Growth and Distribution in Utah: 1950-1980. Utah Agricultural Experiment Station Research Report No. 91. Logan, Utah: Utah Agricultural Experiment Station.

   1984   Newcomer-Returnee Differences in Socioeconomic Standing, Location-Specific Capital and Community Satisfaction and Commitment. The Social Science Journal, 21:135-149.

Stinner, William F. and Mehdi Khosrashahin
   1985   Selectivity Among Nonmetropolitan Bound Male Migrants in the Middle and Later Years. Research on Aging, 7:472-488.

Stinner, William F., Ho-Youn Kwon and Lydia Baal.
   1983   The Growth and Distribution of Utah's Elderly Population. Logan:

Utah Agricultural Experiment Station Report No. 81.

Stinner, William F., Helal Mobasher, Carol McKewen-Stinner and
    Michael B. Toney
  1986 Migrant Status and Public Policy Orientations. Presented at Southern
       Regional Demographic Group, Baltimore, October.

  1987 Do Inmigrants Differ from Natives in Public Policy Orientations?
       Evidence from Utah. Sociology and Social Research 72: 67-70.

Stinner, William F. and H. Y. Nam
  1984 Elderly Migration Patterns in Utah: 1975-80. Utah Science,45: 63-65.

Stinner, William F., Brian L. Pitcher and Michael B. Toney

  1985 Discriminators of Migration Propensity Among Black and White Men
       in the Middle and Later Years. Research on Aging 7: 535-562.

Stinner, William F., Nithet Tinnakul, Stephen Kan and
    Michael B. Toney
  1992 Community Attachment and Migration Decision Making in
       Nonmetropolitan Settings. Pp. 47-84 in Patrick C. Jobes, William F.
       Stinner and John M. Wardwell (eds), Society, Community and
       Migration: Noneconomic Migration in America. Lanham, MD:
       University Press of America.

Stinner, William F. and Michael B. Toney
  1981 Energy Resource Development and Migrant-Native Differences in
       Composition, Community Attachment and Satisfaction, and Migration
       Intentions. Logan, Utah: Utah State University Agricultural
       Experiment Station Research Report No. 52.

Stinner, William F., Michael B. Toney and Keywon Cheong
  1985 Direction of Migration and Occupational Mobility Among Young Adult
       Males in the United States. Presented at International Union for the
       Scientific Study of Population Conference on Patterns of Settlement
       and their Demographic Implications, Florence, Italy, June.

  1992 Direction of Migration and Occupational Mobility among Young Adult
       White Males During the 1970s Nonmetropolitan Turnaround. Pp. 283-
       98 in Patrick C. Jobes, William F. Stinner and John M. Wardwell (eds),
       Society, Community and Migration: Noneconomic Migration in
       America. Lanham, MD: University Press of America.

Stinner, William F. and Mollie Van Loon
   1991   Community Size Preference Status, Community Satisfaction and
          Migration Intentions. Population and Environment, 14: 177-195.

Stinner, William F., Mollie Van Loon and Yongchan Byun.
   1992   Plans to Migrate In and Out of Utah. Sociology and Social Research,
          76: 131-137.

Stinner, William F., Mollie Van Loon, Seh-Woong Chung
          and Yongchan Byun
   1991   Community Size, Individual Social Position and Community
          Attachment. Rural Sociology 55: 494-521.

Swanson, Linda L.
   1984   Changing Patterns of Migration to Growing Nonmetro Areas of the
          Western U.S., 1955-80. Presented at the Population Association of
          America annual meetings, Minneapolis, May.

   1986a The Exchange of Migrants between Nonmetro Areas: A Disruptive or
          Equalizing Process? Presented at the Population Association of
          America annual meetings, San Francisco, April.

   1986b What Attracts New Residents to Nonmetro Areas? Washington, DC:
          US Department of Agriculture Economic Research Service Rural
          Development Research Report No. 56.

   1988   Migration Trends in the Western States Since 1975. Presented at the
          annual meeting of the Rural Sociological Society, Athens, GA
          (August).

Tinnakul, Nithet and William F. Stinner
   1985   Community Commitment and Satisfaction: A Longitudinal Analysis in
          the Context of Nonmetropolitan Turnaround. Utah Agricultural
          Experiment Station Report No. 98. Logan, Utah.

Toney, Michael B.
   1984   Population Profiles of Utah Counties, 1980; Mountain States and the
          United States. Logan, Utah: Population Research Laboratory.

Toney, Michael B., Banu Golesorkhi and William F. Stinner
   1985   Residence Exposure and Fertility Expectations of Young Mormon and
          Non-Mormon Women in Utah. Journal of Marriage and the Family, 47:
          459-465.

Toney, Michael B., Brian L. Pitcher and William F. Stinner
    1985   Geographical Mobility and Locus of Control. Journal of Psychology,
        119:361-368.

Toney, Michael B., Carol McKewen Stinner and Stephen Kan
    1983   Mormon and Non-Mormon Migration In and Out of Utah. Review of
        Religious Research, 25:115-127.

Toney, Michael B., and William F. Stinner
    1990   Population Change: Implications for Villages and Rural Areas.
        Presented at the Rural Villages in the 21st Century Symposium, Logan,
        Utah, July.

Toney, Michael B., William F. Stinner and E. Helen Berry
    1985   Race/Ethnic Differences in Facets of Geographical Mobility. Presented
        at Rural Sociological Society, Blacksburg, VA., August.

Toney, Michael B., William F. Stinner and Elias Nigem
    1981   Life After High School: Long-Term Residence Expectations of Utah's
        1975 and 1980 High School Seniors. Utah Science, Summer: 92-94.

Toney, Michael B. and Roger Swearengen
    1984   Migration Data: Prospects for Research Based on the Youth Cohort of
        the NLS. Review of Public Data Use, 12:211-219.

Van Loon, Mollie and William F. Stinner
    1991   Community Size Preferences, Community Satisfaction and Migration
        Intentions. Presented at the Western Social Science Association annual
        meetings, Reno (April).

Wardwell, John M.
    1982a   The Reversal of Nonmetropolitan Migration Loss. Pp. 23-33 in Don A.
        Dillman and Daryl J. Hobbs (eds.), Rural Society in the U.S.: Issues for
        the 1980s. Boulder, CO: Westview Press.

    1982b   Revitalization of Rural America. Pp. 49-79 in Donald A. Hicks and
        Norman J. Glickman (eds.), Transition to the 21st Century. Greenwich,
        CT: JAI Press.

    1983a   Contributions of Ecological Theory to Understanding Changes in
        Nonmetropolitan America. Presented at the Population Association of
        America annual meetings, Pittsburgh, May.

    1983b   Socioeconomic Forces Affecting Mobility in the 1980s. In Yves Brunet (ed.), Urban Exodus, Its Causes, Significance and Future.   Montreal, Quebec: University of Montreal.

1983c   Theoretical Implications of the Population Turnaround. Presented at the American Association for the Advancement of Science annual meetings, Detroit, May.

1984   The Motivational Salience of Structural Change. Presented at the annual meetings of the Population Association of America, Mpls.

1985   Demographic Similarities between the 1930s and 1970s in the U.S. Presented at the Conference on Culture and Society in the Americas. Rome, Italy: University of Rome, March.

1986a   America in Movement: Implications of Redistribution Trends. Pp. I.95-101 and V.9-22 in United States Internal Revenue Service, Trends Impacting Tax Administration. Washington, D.C.: U.S. Government Printing Office.

1986b   A Demographic Study of the School District by Attendance Areas. Great Falls, MT: Great Falls Public School District.

1986c   Public Policy and Rural Infrastructure.   Pp. 380-387 in New Dimensions in Rural Policy.   Joint Economic Committee of the Congress of the United States. Washington, D.C.: U.S. Government Printing Office.

1986d   Survey of Migration of Families with Children to Cascade County, Montana: Reasons for Moving. Great Falls, Montana: GFPS.

1987   Population Movements in the United States in the 1930s and 1970s. Pp. 153-68 in Gabriella Ferruggia, Paolo Ledda, and Dario Puccini (eds), *Americhe Amare.* Rome, Italy: Bulzoni Editore.

1988   The Resurgence of Rural Growth in the 1980s. Human Services in the Rural Environment II: 20-27.

1989a   Special Education as a Special Problem in Demographic Projections. Presented at the Population Association of America, Baltimore (March).

1989b   Research Opportunities in Nonmetropolitan Population Change. Presented at the Rural Sociological Society, Seattle (August).

1990   Demographic Changes on the Great Plains. Presented at the Canada -

United States Symposium on the Impact of Climate Change and Variability on the Great Plains, Calgary, Alberta (September).

1991   Demographic Change on the Great Plains. Pp. 69-89 in Geoffrey Wall, editor, Impacts of Climatic Change and Variability on the Great Plains. Waterloo, Ontario, Canada: University of Waterloo Press.

1992   The Motivational Salience of Structural Change in Nonmetropolitan Migration. Pp. 85-110 in Patrick C. Jobes, William F. Stinner, and John M. Wardwell (eds), Society, Community and Migration: Noneconomic Migration in America. Lanham, MD: University Press.

Wardwell, John M. and Annabel K. Cook
1982   The Demographic Context of Western Growth. Pp. 1-23 in Bruce A. Weber and Robert E. Howell (eds.), Coping with Rapid Growth in Rural Communities. Boulder, CO: Westview Press.

Wardwell, John M. and Diana L. Cornelius
1988   Enrollment Trends and Projections. Great Falls, MT: Great Falls Public Schools.

Wardwell, John M. and C. Jack Gilchrist

1987   Theoretical Implications of Post-1980 Nonmetropolitan Growth. Rural Sociological Society annual meetings, Madison, August.

1988   Counter-Urbanization in the United States in the 1980s: Trends and Explanations. Presented at the Population Association of America annual meetings, New Orleans (April).

Wardwell, John M. and Dean H. Judson
1990   Cohort Survival Enrollment Projection Refinement. Olympia, WA: Superintendent of Public Instruction (September).

Wardwell, John M. and Corinne M. Rowe (Lyle)
1983   Migration Decision-Making Among Nonmetropolitan Migrants: A Replication Study. Presented at Population Association of America annual meetings, Pittsburgh, April.

1984   Economic Recession and the Satisfaction of Nonmetropolitan Migrants. Presented at the annual meetings of the Rural Sociological Society, Lexington, KY, August.

Wheat, Leonard F., John M. Wardwell and Lee Faulkner

1984   The 1970s Migration Turnaround in Rural, Nonadjacent Counties. Washington, D.C.: U.S. Department of Commerce, Economic Development Administration.

Williams, Anne S. and Patrick C. Jobes.
1990   Economic and Quality of Life Considerations in Urban-Rural Migration. Journal of Rural Studies, 6: 187-194.

Williams, Anne S., Patrick C. Jobes and C. Jack Gilchrist
1986   Gender Roles, Marital Status and Urban-Rural Migration. Sex Roles.

Williams, James D.
1987   New Mexico Population Migration Trends and Patterns. Las Cruces, NM: New Mexico Agricultural Experiment Station Research Report.

Wilson-Figueroa, Maria
1990   The Relationship between Migration Behavior and Poverty Status of Hispanic Youth. Logan, Utah: Utah State University Department of Sociology Ph.D. Dissertation.

Wilson-Figueroa, Maria, E. Helen Berry and Michael B. Toney
1991   Migration of Hispanic Youth and Poverty Status: A Logit   Analysis. Rural Sociology 56: 189-203.

Chapter 2

Population and Economic Change in Metropolitan and Nonmetropolitan Areas of the Pacific Northwest[1]

Annabel Kirschner Cook
Washington State University

Introduction

The nonmetropolitan counties of the Pacific Northwest (Oregon and Washington) participated vigorously in the rural turnaround of the 1970s. Both adjacent and nonadjacent nonmetropolitan counties grew faster than they had in the previous decade, and for most of the 1970s, faster than did metropolitan counties. Nonmetropolitan growth rates slowed dramatically in the 1980s. The recessions of the early part of the decade had a severe impact on the economy of the entire region. However, this impact was greater for nonmetropolitan counties, and as late as 1986 they had showed no signs of recovery. It was not until later in the 1980s that the situation in nonmetropolitan areas began to improve.

This research examines metropolitan and nonmetropolitan growth patterns from 1960 to 1990, and the employment and income changes that are related to these patterns. The issues outlined here are discussed specifically in the context of the economic conditions of the Pacific Northwest. However, these issues also point to some weaknesses with past research and to factors that need to be examined over wider geographic areas in order to better understand the current problems being experienced in nonmetropolitan areas generally, and what the future holds for these areas.

Trends Between 1960 and 1990

In the two decades preceding the 1980s, the population in the Pacific Northwest grew faster than that of the nation, a pattern typical of Western states. Between 1960 and 1970 the area's population increased 19 percent, compared to 14 percent for the nation, but below the 24 percent growth of the Western region. During the 1970s, the Pacific Northwest grew by 23 percent, faster than the West at 21 percent and more than double the 11 percent national growth rate.

That pattern changed in the 1980s. Between 1980 and 1984, the nation's rate of growth slowed only slightly, down to one percent annually, compared to the 1.1 percent per year growth rate of the previous decade. Annual growth in the West slowed somewhat more, from 2.1 to 1.9 percent. But the Pacific Northwest's annual rate of growth dropped substantially, from 2.3 to 0.7 percent, well below the rate for both the region and the nation.

This slowing of growth affected both metropolitan and nonmetropolitan counties in Oregon and Washington, but the impact was much greater in nonmetropolitan counties. As others have noted, the recessions in the early 1980s had a much more severe impact on nonmetropolitan counties throughout the nation (Beale and Fuguitt 1985). This was certainly the case in the Pacific Northwest. The fact that the area's nonmetropolitan counties had shown no signs of recovery by the mid-1980s was even more disturbing, since the second of these recessions had officially ended in the second quarter of 1982.

Table 1 tracks changes in the region's metropolitan and nonmetropolitan areas from 1960 to 1990 (using the 1980 definition of metropolitan). The 1970 to 1980 decade is divided into three periods for comparison with earlier research, which had indicated an ebbing of the nonmetropolitan migration turnaround in the late 1970s. The decade of the 1980s is also divided into three periods. This permits a comparison of patterns of change early in the decade, when there were two recessions,[2] with the immediate post-recessionary period, and the final years of the decade.

During the 1960s, metropolitan areas in the region grew more rapidly than nonmetropolitan areas, as was the case nationally. Even so, the area's nonmetropolitan counties experienced a fair amount of growth, increasing by 8.6 percent and gaining over 100,000 persons. Most of this growth occurred in counties that were adjacent to metropolitan centers.[3] However, even nonadjacent counties grew by four percent during this decade.

Table 2.1 Population Change in the Pacific Northwest, 1960-1990.

Region	1960	1970	1974	1977	1980	1983	1986	1990
Population	4,621,901	5,504,783	5,714,100	6,058,102	6,765,458	6,920,250	7,078,900	7,708,968
Absolute †		882,882	209,317	344,002	707,356	154,592	158,850	630,068
Percent †		19.1	3.8	6.0	11.7	2.3	2.3	8.9
Annual rate †		1.9	1.0	2.0	3.9	0.8	0.8	1.5
Metropolitan								
Population	3,353,362	4,127,341	4,256,950	4,487,300	5,030,385	5,170,750	5,323,850	5,857,802
Absolute †		773,979	129,609	230,350	543,085	140,365	153,100	533,952
Percent †		23.1	3.1	5.4	12.1	2.3	3.0	10.0
Annual rate †		2.3	0.8	1.8	4.0	0.8	1.0	1.7
Nonmetropolitan								
Population:	1,268,539	1,377,442	1,457,150	1,570,802	1,735,073	1,749,300	1,755,050	1,851,166
Absolute †		108,903	79,708	113,652	164,271	14,227	5,750	96,116
Percent †		8.6	5.8	7.8	10.5	0.8	0.3	5.5
Annual rate †		0.9	1.6	2.6	3.5	0.2	0.1	0.9
Adjacent								
Population	808,313	898,693	952,360	1,030,428	1,134,741	1,146,450	1,154,900	1,218,876
Absolute †		90,370	53,677	78,068	104,313	11,709	8,450	63,976
Percent †		11.2	6.0	8.2	10.1	1.0	0.7	5.5
Annual rate †		1.1	1.5	2.7	3.4	0.3	0.2	0.9
Nonadjacent								
Population	460,226	478,759	504,790	540,374	600,332	602,850	600,150	632,290
Absolute †		18,533	26,031	35,584	59,958	2,518	-2,700	32,140
Percent †		4.0	5.4	7.0	11.1	0.4	-0.4	5.3
Annual rate †		0.4	1.4	2.3	3.7	0.1	-0.1	0.9

† Change since prior period.

Sources: U.S. Bureau of the Census 1972, 1981, 1991; Office of Financial Management 1979, 1986; Center for Population Research and Census 1982, 1986.

Note: Using 1980 definition to delineate metropolitan and nonmetropolitan areas. General patterns remain the same with either 1984 or 1970 definitions.

In the 1970s, the area experienced the rural turnaround along with the rest of the nation. Population growth was slower in the early 1970s than in the latter part of the decade. This was due to the recessions of the earlier part of the decade, particularly in aerospace industries located in major metropolitan counties and on which the region is more dependent than would be the case in other parts of the country. In the latter 1970s the aerospace industry rebounded, there was a high demand for timber and agricultural products, international trade was thriving, and the Alaska oil boom and resulting construction provided a number of spin-offs to stimulate the regional economy. Both the metropolitan and nonmetropolitan counties of the region evidenced this pattern of slower growth earlier in the decade and more rapid growth in the later years of the 1970s. Nonmetropolitan counties generally grew more rapidly than metropolitan on a proportional basis, although of course the larger metropolitan counties added more persons in absolute terms.

The severity of the aerospace recession is evident in the slow growth rate of metropolitan areas between 1970 and 1974. In those years these counties accounted for 61 percent of the population added to the region. With the economic recovery, this increased to 66 percent between 1974 and 1977 and to 76 percent between 1977 and 1980. Metropolitan counties added 543,085 persons in this latter period, more than four times as many as they had gained during the first four years of the decade.

Absolute population gains occurring in nonmetropolitan counties during the 1970s were not as substantial. However, the number of persons added to these counties increased with each time period, as did the rate of growth. Nonmetropolitan areas grew by 5.8 percent between 1970 and 1974, by 7.8 percent in the middle of the decade, and by 10.5 percent in the last few years of the 1970s.

To some extent, the nonmetropolitan turnaround in the Pacific Northwest represented a continuation of past urban growth patterns (Johnson and Purdy 1980). The growth of counties adjacent to metropolitan areas can be interpreted in part as the expansion and diffusion of metropolitan services, jobs, and commuting patterns into nearby areas. These areas could then eventually be reclassified as having become part of the metropolitan complex, either because of their ties to the central county, or because they had become metropolitan areas in their own right. This is a pattern of suburban and adjacent growth that has gone on throughout the century. However, in the Pacific Northwest, as was also the case nationally, nonmetropolitan counties which were not adjacent to metropolitan areas also participated in the growth turnaround. Both adjacent and nonadjacent counties experienced increasingly rapid growth through the 1970s, in both absolute and proportional terms.

Others have noted that the slowing of growth of nonmetropolitan counties nationally between 1977 and 1980 foreshadowed the end of the rural turn-around (Engels and Healy 1979; Richter 1985). But in the Pacific Northwest, nonmetropolitan growth did not slow down in this period. Table 1 consistently shows that both metropolitan and nonmetropolitan counties, and both adjacent and nonadjacent nonmetropolitan counties, showed growth rates and increases in absolute numbers increasing as the decade progressed. The turnaround disappeared by the end of the decade in the Pacific Northwest, but not through diminished nonmetropolitan growth as was the case in the nation. Rather, growth in the area's metropolitan counties increased so greatly between 1977 and 1980 that it exceeded the continuing nonmetropolitan growth rates. In this period the metropolitan counties of the region grew

12.1 percent, compared to 10.5 percent in nonmetropolitan counties.

In the 1980s, growth patterns in this region have been markedly different from either those of the 1970s or 1960s. The Pacific Northwest was one of the areas most severely affected by the economic recessions of the early 1980s. The strength of the U.S. dollar at that time reduced demand for the area's timber and agricultural products, as well as for its airplanes. The oil pipeline construction in Alaska came to an end, there was a dramatic decrease in fish production (primarily salmon), and a nationwide slowdown in housing starts, all within a two- to three-year period. The area's rate of growth dropped to just 0.8 percent annually between 1980 and 1986, slower than at any time in the preceding twenty years. The slowdown was particularly dramatic when compared with the boom period of the late 1970s, and it affected both metropolitan and nonmetropolitan counties.

In metropolitan areas, the annual growth rate dropped precipitously from 4.0 percent to 0.8 percent between 1980 and 1983. In the next three years, these areas experienced a modest recovery. Their annual growth rate increased to 1.0 percent, and the population grew by 153,100, compared to 140,365 in the earlier period. While this growth was quite modest when compared to the 1970s, the metropolitan counties of the region were showing signs of recovery in the immediate post-recessionary period.

This was not the case for the nonmetropolitan counties of the Pacific Northwest. The annual nonmetropolitan growth rate had declined from 3.5 percent at the end of the 1970s to just 0.2 percent between 1980 and 1983. Annual growth continued to decline in the next three years, to 0.1 percent. In the post-recessionary period, nonmetropolitan counties grew by only 5,750 persons, compared to an increase of 14,227 between 1980 and 1983.

Both adjacent and nonadjacent counties showed this decline in growth. Adjacent counties however fared better than the more remote nonmetropolitan counties. The growth rate in adjacent counties declined slightly from 0.3 to 0.2 percent between the two periods, and the number of persons added declined from 11,709 to 8,450. Nonadjacent counties, on the other hand, had an absolute decline in population in the immediate post-recession period, something that had not been experienced even in the pre-turnaround decade of the 1960s. Between 1980 and 1983, nonadjacent counties grew by 2,518 persons, an annual rate of 0.1 percent. In the following three-year period they experienced an almost identical rate of loss, declining -0.1 percent annually and losing 2,700 persons.

It was not until the latter 1980s that the Pacific Northwest can be said to have truly recovered from the recessions of the early 1980s. The recovery was more notable in metropolitan than in nonmetropolitan areas. Between 1986 and 1990, metropolitan areas increased 1.7 percent annually, well above the 1.0 percent per year increase in the immediate post-recession period, although still far below the 4.0 percent annual growth rate that had been experienced during the economic boom of 1977-80. The slower growth rate at the end of the 1980s is in part due to the fact that metropolitan counties had a larger base population in the latter period. In the four years between 1986 and 1990 these areas added 533,952 persons, only 9,000 fewer than had been added in the three years from 1977 to 1980.

Nonmetropolitan areas also experienced a substantial upturn in population growth in the late 1980s when compared to the earlier part of the decade. These areas however did not come close either to matching the growth rates of metropolitan counties in the latter 1980s, or to their own previous growth rates in the latter 1970s. Both adjacent and nonadjacent nonmetropolitan counties ended the decade with approximately equal rates of growth, but adjacent counties added nearly twice as many people in the last four years of the 1980s.

Employment and Income Change

In searching for explanations of the turnaround, a great deal of research focused on the possibility of changes in motivations for migration versus changing employment opportunities in nonmetropolitan areas. Community preference surveys of the 1970s routinely showed that most Americans were living in communities larger than they would prefer. Given these findings, many studies of the turnaround focused on the possibility that persons had become more likely to move for quality of life than for economic reasons (Carpenter 1977; Williams and Sofranko 1979; Zelinsky 1974; Zuiches 1982).

At the same time, a number of other studies showed that increased employment opportunities in nonmetropolitan areas were also an important factor in the turnaround (Renshaw et al. 1978; Wardwell and Gilchrist 1980; Williams 1981). Service employment grew as retirees with their higher incomes chose nonmetropolitan counties for their retirement settlement (Beale 1980; Krout 1982). Manufacturing employment decentralized from metropolitan areas in search of lower wages and other costs (Fisher and Mitchelson 1981; Petrulis 1979). In addition there had been some convergence in standards of living between metropolitan and nonmetropolitan areas with highway improvements, telephone systems, network and cable television and other dimensions of social infrastructure (Wardwell 1980).

No data are currently available to ascertain whether people have radically changed their attitudes toward living in the rural Northwest, although Wardwell and Lyle argue in Chapter 9 of this volume that the economic recession of the early 1980s appeared to have had little impact on the residential preferences of people living at that time in rural areas of Idaho and Washington. An analysis of industrial change in metropolitan and nonmetropolitan areas of the Pacific Northwest does provide, however, a partial explanation for the growth trends of the 1980s presented in the preceding section. Between 1970 and 1980, the number of jobs in metropolitan counties grew 47 percent, barely outpacing the rate of job growth in nonmetropolitan areas (43 percent). This in itself could be seen as some support for amenity-based explanations for the turnaround, especially when these areas are also attractive to retirees who are no longer in the labor force. However, it also indicates that, to the extent that employment was a factor in the turnaround, a strong employment base to support future growth was not being formed in nonmetropolitan areas during the 1970s. In addition, the changing industrial composition of the labor force during that time was problematic for future growth.

Table 2 classifies industries into six broad categories, as suggested by Singlemann (1978). The extractive and transformative industries are similar to the earlier classifications of primary and secondary industries. The major difference between these earlier systems and that of Singlemann is that the tertiary, or service, sector is divided into four categories: distributive, producer, social, and personal. This finer detail is provided to better reflect the increasing importance and diversity of this sector.[4]

It is clear that the employment structure of both metropolitan and nonmetropolitan counties changed in the decade, shifting out of extractive and goods-producing industries and into service industries. Wardwell (1980) has suggested that this shift should benefit rural areas since it implies less reliance upon the transportation of raw materials and manufactured goods, which favor urbanized areas and their economies of scale. The increased locational flexibility of service industries and a reliance on communications for doing business could favor more rural areas.

Table 2.2   Metropolitan-Nonmetropolitan Employment
    by Broad Industrial Sectors, 1970-1980 (figures in percents).

Industry	1970 Metro	Nonmetro	Absolute Difference	1980 Metro	Nonmetro	Absolute Difference
Extractive	3.3	10.5	7.2	2.8	9.0	6.2
Transformative	28.7	31.0	2.3	27.3	28.4	1.1
Service:	68.1	58.5	9.6	69.7	62.5	7.2
Distribution	24.9	20.5	4.4	23.8	20.3	3.5
Producer	12.1	6.9	5.2	12.5	7.2	5.3
Social	22.4	21.9	0.5	22.8	23.9	1.1
Personal	8.7	9.2	0.5	10.6	11.1	0.5

Source: See Table 3.

Differences in industrial employment between metropolitan and nonmetropolitan areas lessened between 1970 and 1980. This is consistent with the convergence argument. Table 2 shows that for each broad sector, the absolute difference between metropolitan and nonmetropolitan areas generally declined. But the declines were small and do not indicate rapid convergence in industrial employment between the two areas. In effect, change in nonmetropolitan areas was aimed at a moving rather than a fixed target. Employment in these areas shifted away from extractive and goods-producing activities, but so did employment in metropolitan areas, and from a larger base at only a slightly slower pace.

In addition, the increasing similarity between the two areas in the service sector overall masks an important and persistent difference in producer service employment, when change in the four service categories is examined. Producer services are generally those that are used more by businesses than by individual consumers. A growing body of research indicates that these services are increasingly important to the processing and distribution of raw materials and manufactured goods, and to the economic vitality of an area (Gershuny 1978; Guile 1988; Grubel and Walker 1989; Noyelle and Stanback 1984; Riddle 1987). Between 1978 and 1984, employment in producer services also grew more rapidly than employment in other sectors, including other services, and projections indicate that this trend will continue (Miller and Bluestone 1987; Personick 1987).

As Table 2 indicates, differences between metropolitan and nonmetropolitan areas decreased overall, but there was no decline in the differences in the producer services sector. As these services become more important to the economic vigor of an area in advanced industrial societies, nonmetropolitan areas may find themselves at a disadvantage because of their under-representation in these services.

Many studies of the linkage between employment and population change in nonmetropolitan areas focused on the growth of manufacturing. In an area like the Pacific Northwest, however, consideration of the manufacturing sector as a single broad category can be misleading. The economy of the area is much more dependent on forest products than is the case nationally, but only a small segment of the work that goes on in this industry is classified in the extractive category of forestry.[5] Instead, much of the activity falls in the manufacturing category of furniture, lumber, and wood products. The same is true of the agricultural sector. Here, much of the work falls in the manufacturing category of food and kindred products, although much of this work may be as routine as sorting and grading the wide variety of fruits and vegetables produced in the region.

Table 3 shows the concentration of manufacturing employment in the region's nonmetropolitan areas in these two categories in 1980. Wood products accounted for 59 percent of employment in manufacturing, with another 13 percent in food and kindred products. Only 16 and 8 percent of the metropolitan labor force, respectively, was found in these categories.

Increased employment in manufacturing in nonmetropolitan counties of Oregon and Washington in the 1970s did not result from decentralization from metropolitan centers. Rather it simply represented the continuing exploitation of one of the area's natural resources in the form of milling of timber, and processing of agricultural products. In fact, in 1980, in 39 of the 57 nonmetropolitan counties of the Pacific Northwest, more than 20 percent of employment was in some combination of the basic category of agriculture, forestry, and fisheries, and the manufacturing categories of furniture, lumber, wood products, and food and kindred products. Between 1970 and 1980, employment in these three categories declined as a proportion of all employment, but that was only because the other industrial sectors grew more rapidly. The number of persons employed in these three categories increased 19 percent during the decade, leaving nonmetropolitan areas extremely vulnerable to the boom and bust cycles analyzed by Copp and Knop in Chapter 7, which often characterize resource extraction industries.

Table 2.3   Industrial Change in the Pacific Northwest and Unemployment.

Industry	Metropolitan 1970 Number	Per-cent	Metropolitan 1980 Number	Per-cent	Nonmetropolitan 1970 Number	Per-cent	Nonmetropolitan 1980 Number	Per-cent	West Unemployment Rate 1983
Agriculture, forestry, fisheries	48,340	3.3	62,041	2.8	48,894	10.6	59,278	9.0	16.3
Mining	2,153	0.1	3,763	0.2	1,419	0.3	2,642	0.4	14.4
Construction	91,382	6.2	148,177	6.8	29,457	6.4	47,469	7.2	18.7
Manufacturing	271,186	18.3	372,032	17.0	90,271	19.6	115,374	17.5	11.0
Durable goods	207,964	14.0	286,461	13.1	73,661	16.0	91,806	13.9	10.2
Furniture, lumber, wood products	47,795	3.2	58,300	2.7	60,071	13.1	68,139	10.3	16.2
Metal industries	39,202	2.6	46,360	2.1	6,257	1.4	10,480	1.6	13.8
Machinery, except electric	17,960	1.2	32,327	1.5	2,794	0.6	5,721	0.9	9.6
Electrical machinery	16,604	1.1	28,685	1.3	884	0.2	3,237	0.5	7.4
Transportation equipment	86,403	5.8	120,789	5.5	3,655	0.8	4,229	0.6	7.9
Nondurable goods	63,222	4.3	85,571	3.9	16,610	3.6	23,568	3.6	12.6
Food and kindred products	25,376	1.7	31,575	1.4	11,156	2.4	15,318	2.3	18.6
Textiles	11,135	0.8	13,088	0.6	922	0.2	1,348	0.2	10.4
Printing, publishing, allied	17,696	1.2	29,688	1.4	3,739	0.8	5,862	0.9	6.9
Chemicals, allied products	9,015	0.6	11,220	0.5	793	0.2	1,040	0.2	10.5
Transportation, communication, utiliti	118,643	8.0	176,184	8.0	30,655	6.6	44,569	6.8	7.3
Wholesale trade	85,602	5.8	121,367	5.5	14,805	3.2	23,081	3.5	8.4
Retail trade	255,706	17.3	387,912	17.7	80,668	17.5	118,870	18.0	10.6
Finance, insurance, real estate	93,806	6.3	153,811	7.0	15,501	3.4	28,902	4.4	4.8
Services	430,311	29.1	652,423	29.8	124,469	27.1	185,291	28.1	8.4
Public administration	83,078	5.6	111,805	5.1	23,700	5.2	33,200	5.0	5.3
Total	1,480,207	100.0	2,198,515	99.9	459,839	99.9	658,566	99.9	9.9

Sources: U.S. Bureau of the Census 1972, 1983; U.S. Department of Labor 1984

Note: Unemployment rates for agriculture, forestry and fisheries, and for public administration are national averages; data for West unavailable for these industry groups; see U.S. Bureau of the Census 1986a

In fact, the recessions of the early 1980s, including a steep decline in home building, caused a precipitous drop in both timber harvesting and employment in forestry and wood-based manufacturing. Nonmetropolitan areas have experienced only a slight recovery from this decline.   During the 1980s, timber harvests gradually increased throughout the region, until they peaked above pre-recession levels in 1988. However, the area faced increased competition in manufactured wood products from Canada and the South, and mills responded by retooling, becoming more efficient, and using fewer workers. Thus employment in this manufacturing sector, while above the lowest point in 1982, has never rebounded to the level of the late 1970s (Pacific Northwest Executive 1990). During the 1990s, many timber-based counties in the area will be faced with reductions in harvest levels on U.S. Forest Service land to protect the spotted owl. Thus the dependence upon timber is one factor underlying the economic difficulties experienced by many nonmetropolitan counties, despite a robust economic recovery at the national level.

The situation in agriculture was also problematic for nonmetropolitan recovery. Irrigated acreage increased by more than one million acres between 1969 and 1978, but decreased by almost 400,000 acres between 1978 and 1987. In much of the region, irrigation is essential for transforming rangeland and dryland farming to more intensive uses such as orchards, vineyards, vegetable fields and the like. The products of these uses then become inputs to food processing industries.

As has been the case in the timber industry, automation improved productivity throughout the decade while reducing the need for workers. Thus the value added to the region's agricultural production increased during the 1980s, while employment in food production and processing declined (Pacific Northwest Executive 1990). Although the expansion of food processing has been seen as a viable economic development strategy for rural communities of the region, long-term developments may undermine this strategy. The use of new technologies in food processing and packaging make it extremely difficult for small companies to start operations and the region's food processing is "an increasingly concentrated industry, one characterized by corporate acquisitions and mergers, and large regional facilities owned by food conglomerates from outside the Northwest" (Pacific Northwest Executive 1990, p. 14).

In addition to obscuring important regional differences, use of broad industrial categories poses another problem. The unemployment rates within each industrial sector may vary greatly, and particularly so during recessionary periods. This is indicated in the last column of Table 3, which provides unemployment rates for the West by industrial category in 1983. Unemployment in manufacturing ranged from a low of 6.9 in printing, publishing, and allied industries, to a high of 18.6 percent in food and kindred products. The range was narrower in service-providing industries, but even so, the finance, insurance and real estate category had a low of 4.8 percent, while retail trade had a high of 10.6 percent.

Using these rates, Table 4 provides an explanation of why the recessions of the early 1980s had a much more severe impact on nonmetropolitan counties in the Pacific Northwest. Overall in 1983, the West unemployment rate averaged 9.9 percent. Industries have been classified in Table 4 as having low unemployment rates if they were two percentage points or more below that average (i.e., 7.9 percent or lower), and as high if they were two percentage points or more above the average (11.9 percent or higher). Industries with unemployment rates intermediate between these levels are classified as average.

Between 1970 and 1980, 13.5 percent of the employment growth in metropolitan counties occurred in industries which subsequently had high unemployment rates, compared to 23.2 percent of the employment growth in nonmetropolitan counties. Nonmetropolitan areas had had 20.8 percent of their employment growth in industries which were subsequently characterized by low unemployment rates, compared to 24.0 percent of the employment growth in metropolitan counties. As a result, by 1980, close to one-third (30.9 percent) of all Pacific Northwest nonmetropolitan jobs were in industries that would subsequently experience above average unemployment rates during the recessionary period of the early 1980s, compared to only 16.0 percent of all metropolitan jobs.

**Table 2.4   Employment Growth Between 1970 and 1980
by Industry Unemployment Rates in 1983.**

Industry Unemployment Rate 1983	Percent Employment Growth 1970 - 1980		Percent Distribution 1980	
	Metropolitan	Nonmetroplitan	Metropolitan	Nonmetropolitan
Low	24.0	20.8	22.8	17.6
Average	62.4	56.0	61.2	51.5
High	13.5	23.2	16.0	30.9

Source: See Table 3

Table 5 shows the impact that this differential in the sources of employment growth had on unemployment rates and growth in the labor force during the 1980s. Although unemployment rates were high in nonmetropolitan counties between 1980 and 1983, the increase in metropolitan areas had actually been somewhat higher, 3.9 as compared to 3.2 percent. But between 1983 and 1986, unemployment rates in metropolitan counties declined somewhat more than was the case in nonmetropolitan areas, 2.9 as compared to 2.3 percent. In both types of counties it was not until the end of the decade that unemployment rates dropped below the 1980 levels.

However, focusing only on unemployment rates to judge the economic health of an area can be misleading. These rates take into account only those persons who are actively seeking work. Those who are unemployed over extended periods of time often become discouraged

Table 2.5   Change in Unemployment and Labor Force, 1980 - 1990.

	Region	Metropolitan	Nonmetropolitan
Unemployment Rate			
1980	7.4	6.6	9.7
1983	11.0	10.5	12.9
1986	8.3	7.6	10.6
1990	5.1	4.7	7.1
Number in Labor Force			
1980	3,279,863	2,479,659	800,204
1983	3,410,302	2,593,381	816,921
1986	3,473,335	2,659,169	814,166
1990	3,953,192	3,066,158	887,034
Change in Number in Labor Force			
1980-83			
Absolute	130,439	113,722	16,717
Percent	4.0	4.6	2.1
1983-86			
Absolute	63,033	65,788	-2,755
Percent	1.8	2.5	-0.3
1986-90			
Absolute	479,857	406,989	72,868
Percent	13.8	15.3	9.0

Sources: Oregon State 1980, 1983, 1986, 1990;
Washington State 1980, 1983, 1986, 1990.

and drop out of the labor force altogether (U.S. Department of Labor 1983). When this happens, they are no longer counted as being among the unemployed. Others leave the area and look for work elsewhere. In either case, an area's unemployment rate may decline with little or no improvement in the economy itself.

The bottom half of Table 5 considers changes in the labor force itself, so that growth or decline in the size of the labor force can be compared with changes in unemployment rates. Between 1980 and 1983, the number of persons in the labor force grew in both metropolitan and nonmetropolitan areas, but as in the 1970s, this growth had been greater in metropolitan counties. Between 1983 and 1986, the number of persons in the labor force in metropolitan areas grew at the same time that the unemployment rate decreased. This rate of growth was slower than early in the 1980s, but it did indicate the greater availability of jobs overall for those areas.

By contrast in nonmetropolitan areas between 1983 and 1986, the number of persons in the labor force actually declined at the same time that the unemployment rate declined. Consequently, while decline in unemployment rates in metropolitan areas was due to an expanding number of jobs, the nonmetropolitan unemployment decline was due to persons dropping out of the labor force, through either moving or becoming discouraged and no longer actively seeking work.

It was not until the 1986-90 period that the region's labor force recovered from the recession. Both metropolitan and nonmetropolitan areas experienced substantial growth in their labor forces. The metropolitan labor force grew much faster than did the nonmetropolitan. The metropolitan labor force was also three times larger than the nonmetropolitan in 1986.   Percent changes are biased by the size of the base population. It is much easier for small areas to register large proportional changes than it is for larger areas. Thus the proportional changes described above actually understate the disparity in labor force growth for metropolitan and nonmetropolitan areas. Between 1986 and 1990, metropolitan counties accounted for 85 percent of all growth. For the entire decade, they account for 87 percent of all labor force growth.

Income growth also slumped in nonmetropolitan areas in the 1980s. The income of these areas has historically lagged behind that of metropolitan centers, but the recessions and employment situation of the early 1980s exacerbated the difference. Table 6 shows per capita income and change between 1969 and 1987. Some of the research literature had suggested that income was no longer as important a determinant of migration decisions in the turnaround. Between 1969 and 1979, nonmetropolitan per capita income grew slightly faster than metropolitan: 14.2 percent compared to 14.0 percent. The difference was not great, and metropolitan incomes remained above nonmetropolitan, but at least during the period of the turnaround, income growth in nonmetropolitan areas did not suffer in comparison with that of metropolitan counties.

Between 1979 and 1983, income growth in nonmetropolitan areas did suffer relative to that of metropolitan counties, growing only 4.7 percent, compared to 5.3 percent in metropolitan areas. This disparity continued through the 1983-87 period. Per capita incomes in nonmetropolitan areas had thus grown from 87 to 88 percent of metropolitan averages between 1969 and 1979, but then declined to just 85 percent of metropolitan area incomes by 1987.

Table 2.6   Change in Per Capita Income 1979 to 1983

	Region	Metropolitan	Nonmetropolitan
Income			
1969	$3,277	$3,418	$2,857
1979	$7,872	$8,207	$6,903
1983	$9,507	$9,954	$8,187
1987	$11,738	$12,305	$10,019
Annualized percent change			
1969-79	14.0	14.0	14.2
1979-83	5.2	5.3	4.7
1983-87	5.9	5.9	5.6

Sources: U.S. Bureau of the Census 1972, 1986b, 1990.

Retirement Migration

Although nonmetropolitan counties in the Pacific Northwest lagged behind their metropolitan counterparts throughout the 1980s, there were factors that helped offset the economic difficulties caused by the earlier recessions and by a decade of economic restructuring in agriculture and timber. One of these was retirement migration. Although the Pacific

Northwest is not a retirement mecca as is Florida or Arizona, the 1980 Census showed that Washington had ranked sixth and Oregon ninth in the number of migrants aged 65 and over who had lived in a different state in 1975 (U.S. Bureau of the Census 1984).

Retirement migration to nonmetropolitan areas can be an important factor offsetting job losses in resource based industries. Not only has the number of people aged 65 and older increased rapidly, but the financial well-being of this age group has also improved dramatically since the 1960s. This improvement is due both to expansion of social security benefits and to the rapid increase in real incomes from the mid-1950s to the early 1970s, which had increased the amount of money people could invest.

Retirees who move from an urban to rural area are financially better off than residents at the destination, and generally better educated than their nonmigrant counterparts (Barsby and Cox 1975; Glasgow and Beale 1985). Consequently, growth in unearned incomes (i.e., investment income and transfer payments) has outpaced growth in salary incomes in many nonmetropolitan areas (Bluestone 1979). Retirement related transfer payments helped to dampen cyclical swings in total personal income; these payments can also result in greater employment multipliers than those deriving from the expansion of jobs in manufacturing and agriculture (Hirschl and Summers 1982; Smith 1986).

The recessionary period of the early 1980s had no impact on retirement migration to the nonmetropolitan counties of Oregon and Washington (Cook 1990). Net migration for the total population and the population aged 65 and over for the 1970-80 and 1980-85 periods are compared in Figure 1. As has been pointed out in this chapter, the 1970s were a period of general economic growth for nonmetropolitan counties in the Pacific Northwest. In that decade, 86 percent of all nonmetropolitan counties experienced net inmigration of the general population and 70 percent experienced net inmigration of the population aged 65 and over. In the 1980-85 period, which was one of severe recession for the area in general and for nonmetropolitan counties in particular, only 22 percent experienced net inmigration of the general population. But the proportion of counties that experienced net inmigration of the population aged 65 and over actually increased during this period, to 81 percent (Cook 1990).

Retirement migration varied by type of county. Counties were classified by their economic bases as agriculture, timber, a mixture of the two, and nonresource-based (i.e., counties with a high level of

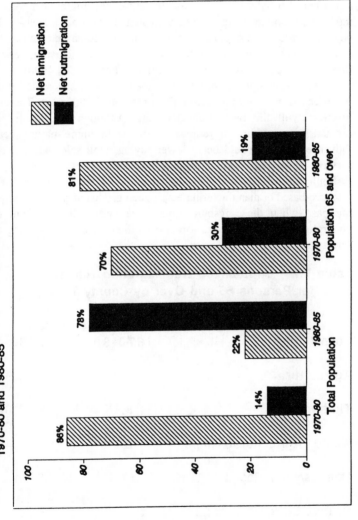

Figure 1. Percent of Pacific Northwest Nonmetro Counties Experiencing Net In- and Outmigration 1970-80 and 1980-85

employment in government and other services). Table 7 summarizes retirement trends by county type for the two time periods. Retirement migration was highest to the nonresource-based counties, followed by timber, mixed and agricultural counties. Mixed resource counties experienced a substantial increase in retiree net migration rates, and agricultural counties experienced a smaller but distinct increase. The slight increase in net migration rates in nonresource-based counties, and slight decrease in timber counties, was probably a fluctuation between these two time periods rather than a different trend (Cook 1990).

Thus, net inmigration of retirees helped offset the severe difficulties experienced by many nonmetropolitan counties in the area. There are problems with this type of development. Although some of the jobs created by an influx of retirees would be in higher-paying health industries, others would be in lower-paying retail sales and personal services industries. Transition into these new types of jobs may be difficult for persons who have spent much of their working life in resource-based or manufacturing employment. This may particularly be the case when those resource jobs have been followed from one generation to the next, as has often been the case in both farming and forestry.

Table 2.7   Annualized Net Migration Rates
for Persons 65 and Over by County Type.

	Time Period	
County Type	1970-80	1980-85
Agricultural	1.9	3.9
Timber	8.8	8.0
Mixed Agricultural-Timber	2.7	6.4
Non-resource Based	11.4	11.6

Source: Cook 1990, p. 92.

Finally, although retirement migration and tourism may offset job losses in basic industries, both have the potential to fundamentally transform the nature of a rural county. Long-term residents may have difficulty adapting and may find themselves socially displaced. In some areas where there are extensive recreation or retirement developments attracting newcomers with higher incomes who can afford more expensive homes, housing values and land prices may escalate to such an extent that long-term residents must leave. That is ironic since they are the very persons who should benefit from such developments. The potential for these conflicts and unanticipated outcomes of rural development are explored in detail by Knop and Jobes in Chapter 5 of this volume, and also by Copp and Knop in Chapter 7.

In the Pacific Northwest, there are now only a few counties in which recreation or retirement developments appear to have dramatically changed the nature of nonmetropolitan counties. However, many other counties stand on the threshold of such a change. If properly managed, these developments can ideally be controlled to contribute to the well-being of both long-term and more recent residents.   Many nonmetropolitan counties however lack the expertise to achieve effective control over the course and consequences of these developments.

Conclusions

The impact of the recession of the early 1980s was more severe in the nonmetropolitan counties of the Pacific Northwest, and these counties showed no signs of recovery in the 1983-86 period. They grew at a much slower rate than they had during even the pre-turnaround period of the 1960s. Nonadjacent nonmetropolitan counties actually lost population for the first time in more than twenty years. It was not until the end of the 1980s that the area recovered, and even then this recovery was at best partial for nonmetropolitan counties.

Changes in employment and income supported these population trends. Pacific Northwest counties experienced substantial employment and income growth during the turnaround decade of the 1970s. Employment growth was slightly less than in metropolitan areas. But the growth that did occur in nonmetropolitan counties made it possible for many persons who lived in those areas to remain rather than having to move to metropolitan areas in search of jobs. The growth also provided employment for persons in metropolitan ares who longed for a more rural way of life.

Nonmetropolitan employment growth also diversified, lessening the traditional dependence of these counties on resource-based industries. This reduction was not enough to offset the high unemployment rates in these industries during the ensuing recessions. The concentration of the nonmetropolitan labor force in timber and agriculture increased unemployment rates in those areas during the recessions of the 1980s, but not more so than in metropolitan areas. Rather, the most adverse impact came between 1983 and 1986 when the nonmetropolitan labor force actually declined. These results confirm the importance of diversification shown by Blevins and Bradely in Chapter 8.

Income growth in nonmetropolitan areas had outpaced metropolitan income growth during the turnaround, but it lagged well behind income growth in metropolitan counties between 1979 and 1986. Consequently, it is not surprising that growth in nonmetropolitan areas has fallen well below that of metropolitan counties during the 1980s. The restructuring of manufacturing in the wood products industries and in the food and kindred products industries, as well as future restrictions on timber harvests on U.S. Forest Service land because of the spotted owl, means that Pacific Northwest nonmetropolitan areas will continue to experience difficulties in population and economic growth and expansion in the near future.

Retirement migration to the area will help offset these and other problems in resource-based industries. But this may not help to decrease the gap between metropolitan and nonmetropolitan incomes, since many of the service jobs created by this new trend will not pay as much as the manufacturing and extractive jobs which have been lost.

Notes

1. This is a revised and updated version of a paper originally presented at the annual meetings of the Rural Sociological Society, Madison, Wisconsin, August, 1987.

2. The first recession began in the first quarter of 1980 and lasted through the third quarter of that year. The second recession ran from the third quarter of 1981 to the fourth quarter of 1982 (U.S. Department of Labor 1983).

3. Several Northwest nonmetropolitan counties, although geographically adjacent to a metropolitan county, are separated from those counties by mountain ranges or large bodies of water, and have therefore been classified as nonadjacent.

4. A more detailed breakdown of each industry is as follows: extractive (agriculture, mining, forestry, and fishing); transformative (construction, manufacturing, and utilities); and four categories of service industries: distributive (transportation, communication, retail and wholesale trade); producer (finance, insurance and real estate, engineering, architectural   business   and legal services, and accounting and bookkeeping); social (medical, welfare,

religious, postal, education, nonprofit organizations, and government); and, personal (domestic, repair, entertainment and recreation, lodging and eating places, repair services, etc).

5. This category is combined with agriculture and fisheries in 1970 county data and Table 3 uses this broad category for consistency.

Chapter 3

Social and Demographic Characteristics of the Mormon Culture Region

Michael B. Toney and William F. Stinner
Utah State University

Youngchan Byun
Korea Institute for Health and Social Affairs

Introduction

While most areas of the United States are noted for their population heterogeneity, some are marked by an identification with a distinct social group. Membership in a particular religious group having unique practices and influences has been one of the significant indicators of regional culture in the United States (Newman and Halvorson 1984). One of the most conspicuous of these is the Mormon Culture Region in the western United States (Meinig 1965; Zelinsky 1961).

The Mormon Culture Region is often perceived as being synonymous with the state of Utah. However, the region actually encompasses territory in surrounding states. The numerical dominance of Mormons, members of The Church of Jesus Christ of Latter-Day Saints, is the primary criterion in identifying the area designated as the Mormon Culture Region.

In his classic analysis of the region, Meinig (1965) maintained that unique customs which prevailed in the area provide the most meaningful justification for concluding that it is the most distinctive religion-based culture region in the country. Their dominance began when Mormon pioneers converged on the area in 1847, after Brigham Young declared, "This is the right place!" as he led the search for a Mormon homeland in the aftermath of the severe persecution which had been experienced in eastern states (Kephart 1982).

At the core of the Mormon Culture Region, Utah is renowned for unusual social and demographic characteristics which tend to be attributed to Mormon influences (Martin et al. 1986). In her article entitled "Unusual Utah," Bernstein (1982) describes a host of demographic differences between Utah and other states. Utah has the highest fertility rate in the nation, for example, despite its high levels of urbanization and educational attainment. Its total fertility rate was about double that of the nation throughout the 1980s.

The literature on cultural regions has traditionally been concerned with the degree of internal homogeneity in terms of various population characteristics. Indeed, some have persuasively argued that detailed examinations of regions usually reveal that heterogeneity on many dimensions should raise serious questions about defining or identifying culture regions on the basis of a single or a small number of such attributes (Poston 1984).

Other researchers emphasize cultural convergence across regions as a consequence of aspects of modernization such as transportation and communication systems. Trepanier (1991) for example notes that French Louisiana is the only remnant of a vast area once dominated by French influences. Similarly, several researchers have noted that many of the characteristics which once distinguished the South from the rest of the United States have disappeared. Thus in focusing on the unique traits of the Mormon Culture Region it is also worthwhile to convey that Mormons do share many basic values and beliefs with the national society. Indeed, Albrecht (1990) maintains that Mormon uniqueness now reflects their higher degree of adopting American capitalist and political ideologies than other groups within the United States.

The Mormon Culture Region has received considerable attention from geographers, sociologists, and other social scientists (Jackson 1978; Meinig 1965; Zelinsky 1961). These writers do not contend that the region is identified solely on the basis of Mormon numerical dominance. Rather, they emphasize the region's unique cultural and social features as their basis for identifying it as a distinct culture region. Francaviglia (1970) also claims that Mormon settlements can be distinguished by the combination of ten visual clues. These include: (1) wide streets, (2) roadside irrigation ditches, (3) barns and granaries within the town itself, (4) unpainted farm buildings, (5) open fields around the towns, (6) the hay derrick, (7) the Mormon fence, (8) I-style homes, (9) more brick dwellings, and (10) Mormon ward chapels.

Meinig (1965) emphasizes that newcomers become aware of Mormon influences on life very quickly, despite the absence of distinctive visual traits such as dress. Visitors report difficulties in purchasing a cup of coffee or unusual liquor laws. The presence of high fertility and correspondingly large families is visibly apparent from the number of children accompanying parents in stores and by the selling of food and other items in larger containers than are typically found in other areas of the country. Bernstein's observation that "Utahans run a higher risk of being run over by a stroller" (1982) points out that visitors to the state are often struck by the number of children they encounter.

The purpose of this study is to describe the degree of sociodemographic heterogeneity within the Mormon Culture Region. While many of the unusual population characteristics of Utah are attributed to its religious composition, the absence of religious identity in census and other data sources on which the region's descriptions are based makes this necessarily a conjecture (Heaton 1986). This study compares counties in the Mountain States which are predominantly Mormon with those which are not, in terms of their sociodemographic characteristics (see Figure 1). The comparisons help clarify the extent to which Utah's unusual attributes are the result of its religious composition.

If counties within the region which are numerically dominated by non-Mormons are more similar to the Mormon dominated counties than to the nation or to other counties in the region in terms of their population characteristics, it may be that other social or environmental factors are more responsible for the unusual sociodemographic characteristics of the region. On the other hand, it has been argued that Mormon influence may also be significant in areas in which they are not numerically dominant because of their organizational effectiveness and cultural traditions (Heaton 1986).

Historical Background

The Mormon religion was founded as a Christian church in New York State in 1830 by Joseph Smith. Despite its turbulent history the Mormon Church has earned a respectable status among other religious groups and many of its members have achieved leadership roles in the larger society (Stark 1984). Although Smith emphasized basic Christian beliefs, the Mormons were not readily accepted by other Christian groups (Larson 1988). Kephart (1982) contends that none of the other twelve hundred religious groups in the United States have had a more tumultuous and controversial history than the Mormons. Belief that the Book of Mormon, which was revealed to Smith, contained divine scriptures just as the Bible did, was one major source of antagonism between Mormons and other Christian groups. Mormons also engaged in practices which antagonized others. Most notable was the practice of polygamy. This was purportedly the major reason for the long and severe persecution of Mormons.

One of the early developments in the church was the announcement of the "gathering doctrine" by Smith (Mulder 1954). This doctrine is particularly important to the geographical settlement and distribution of Mormons because it called upon members to gather into one place. The doctrine is embedded in a context calling for the establishment of a community in which Mormon beliefs and lifestyles would prevail. It suggests that the successful establishment of a Mormon community would result in a culturally unique area.

Prior to their movement into the Rocky Mountains, the Mormons had attempted to establish permanent communities in several eastern states. Their failures resulted largely from persecution by other groups. The bases of early antagonism between Mormons and other groups have been extensively described (Arrington and Bitton 1978; O'Dea 1957). Smith and one of his brothers were murdered in an attack by outsiders in Nauvoo, Illinois. His death and the persistence of conflicts with nonMormons finally provoked the mass movements of Mormons into the Rocky Mountains (Arrington and Bitton 1978).

Mormons have numerically dominated a large geographical area in the Rocky Mountains since their colonization of the Great Salt Lake Basin in 1847 (Bernstein 1982). The Great Salt Lake Basin was selected, in part, on the basis of its isolation from the larger society, and the realization that this would allow the group to practice its beliefs without interference from other groups (O'Dea 1957). Under the leadership of Brigham Young, the Mormons established a thriving community in the Salt Lake Valley. The subsequent successful establishment of Mormon communities at great distances from the original community in Salt Lake marked the beginning of the Mormon Culture Region (Nelson 1952).

The pattern of Mormon settlement is one of the factors that distinguished early Mormon communities from other frontier settlements in the West (Nelson 1952). The fact that their migration and settlement were organized by church leaders is itself a major distinguishing feature. Their movement from the Midwest into the Rocky Mountains represents the largest single group of organized settlers in the entire Western expansion of the nation (Jackson 1978). After leading the mass movement of original Mormon settlers into Utah, Brigham Young, Smith's successor, organized the Perpetual Emigration Fund, which aided in the movement of thousands of Mormons into the Great Salt Lake Valley (Arrington and Bitten 1978). Once there, settlers were organized to establish settlements throughout the region.

In his classic studies, Nelson (1952) explains that Mormon villages differed markedly from villages settled by other groups in all parts of the United States. The primary distinguishing feature was the separation of residence and farm. Farmers lived in the towns rather than on spatially isolated farms. This form of group settlement is credited with the development and maintenance of the Mormon way of life. Living in close proximity with one another and in isolation from other groups contributed to group identity and discouraged the development of divergent life styles.

More recent research indicates persistence of the sociodemographic differences between Mormons and nonMormons. In a detailed comparison of survey data for Utah Mormons with census data for Utah as a whole, Heaton (1986) concludes that differences also exist between the state's Mormon and nonMormon populations. The state's entire population is characterized as having higher rates of marriage, divorce, fertility, and socioeconomic attainment than other states in the region. Heaton's comparison of Utah Mormons and Mormons living in other states did not reveal any significant differences between these groups. Comparisons of more restricted samples of Mormons with other populations also support Heaton's findings (Thornton 1979; Toney et al. 1985).

Data and Procedures

Data for this study come from the U.S. Bureau of the Census 1983 County and City Data Tape and from the Report on Churches and Church Membership in the United States: 1980 (Quinn et al. 1982). Quinn's report provided information on the number of Mormons in counties. The data on membership was provided by the Mormon church as part of a broader survey of church membership. Membership records are considered very accurate because of the emphasis placed on keeping records on members for religious purposes. Information on membership was used in conjunction with census data to compute percent Mormon for counties in the Rocky Mountain States.

Using this information a tripartite classification was developed: (1) Mormon-Dominant are counties where Mormons constitute 50 percent or

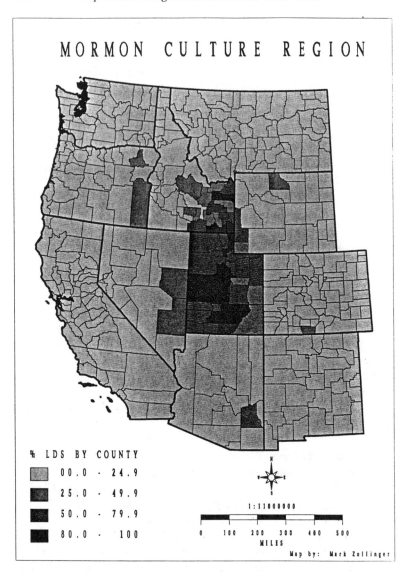

MORMON   CULTURE   REGION

% LDS BY COUNTY

00.0 - 24.9
25.0 - 49.9
50.0 - 79.9
80.0 - 100

1:11000000

0   100   200   300   400   500
MILES

Map by: Mark Zollinger

more of the population; (2) Moderate Mormon are counties where
Mormons constitute between 10 and 49 percent of the population; and, (3)
Mormon Minority are counties in which Mormons constitute less than ten
percent of the population. Discriminant function analysis is employed to

examine the relationship between religious composition and sociodemographic characteristics at the county level. This method reveals the extent to which information about the sociodemographic characteristics can be used to accurately predict whether a county is numerically dominated by Mormons.

Findings

In 1980, there were 2,684,744 Mormons living in the United States, with over 1.5 million of them living in the Mountain States (Table 1). Utah is the only state in which Mormons are numerically dominant (at 67 percent), and had a Mormon population of 985,070. This is 37 percent of the nation's Mormons and 63 percent of the Mormons living in the Mountain States. Yet, Mormons also constitute one-fourth of Idaho's population. In all other intermountain states, Mormons are less than ten percent of the total population, ranging from 8.6 percent in Wyoming to 1.8 percent in Colorado.

Table 3.1. Percent Distribution of LDS in Mountain States, 1980 (summary table)

Area	# LDS	Population	Percent
U.S. Total	2,684,744	226,545,805	1.2
Mountain States Total	1,567,330	11,372,784	13.8
Arizona	139,178	2,718,215	5.1
Colorado	51,884	2,889,964	1.8
Idaho	240,843	943,935	25.5
Montana	26,035	786,690	3.3
Nevada	55,148	800,493	6.9
New Mexico	28,804	1,302,894	2.2
Utah	985,070	1,461,037	67.4
Wyoming	40,368	469,557	8.6

Sources: Quinn et al. 1982; U.S. Bureau of the Census 1983

Mormons were in the majority in 37 of the 278 counties in the Mountain States (Table 2). They constituted between 10 and 49 percent of the population in another 43 counties, and less than ten percent in the remaining 198 counties in the Mountain States. Mormons constituted over half of the population in 26 of Utah's 29 counties, and were in the majority in ten of Idaho's 44 counties. Several Utah counties were over 80 percent Mormon. No Utah county was less than 28 percent Mormon. Mormons were in the majority in only one county in Wyoming, the only other county outside Idaho and Utah with such a majority. Oddly enough, the most Mormon county of all was not in Utah but rather was Franklin County, Idaho, with 94 percent of its population belonging to the Mormon Church.

Table 3.2. Frequency Distribution of Counties by Percent LDS in Mountain States, 1980

States	Total	LDS Dominant (50% +)	LDS Moderate (10-49%)	LDS Low (Below 10%)
Mountain States	278	37	43	198
Arizona	14		5	9
Colorado	63		2	61
Idaho	44	10	20	14
Montana	56		2	54
Nevada	17		4	13
New Mexico	32		1	31
Utah	29	26	3	
Wyoming	23	1	6	16

Sources: Quinn et al. 1982; U.S. Bureau of the Census 1983

As the core of the Mormon Culture Region, Utah is distinct in many ways with respect to sociodemographic characteristics (Table 3). In 1980, half of the state's population was under 24 years of age compared to a median age of 28.0 years for the Mountain States as a whole and 30.0 years for the United States. At that time its crude birth rate was 28.6, compared to 19.9 and 15.9 for the Mountain States and the U.S., respectively. In 1990, the median age had increased to 26.3 but this was still five and one-half years lower than the average of the Mountain States. Similarly, the crude birth rate has dropped to 20.8 but remains well above the Mountain States average of 17.5 (1990 data from Population Reference Bureau 1992).

Consequently, the number of persons per household is larger in Utah and the percent of population under age five higher than for the United States and the Mountain States. Utah's population is much more urban than that of the U.S. or the Mountain States, with 87 percent of its population living in urban areas in 1990. The high proportion of urban residents along with high levels of education and female labor force participation make Utah's persistent high fertility even more unusual.

Table 3.3 Socioeconomic and Demographic Characteristics of United States, Mountain States, and Utah, 1980.

Characteristic	United States	Mountain States	Utah
Percent urban	73.7	76.4	84.4
Percent white	83.4	88.1	94.7
Percent migrant	11.6	23.0	18.0
Percent under age 5	7.2	8.7	13.0
Median age	30.0	28.0	24.2
Persons per household	2.75	2.79	3.20
Percent female head of HHD	14.3	11.5	9.7
Birth rate	15.9	19.9	28.6
Death rate	8.7	7.0	5.5
Marriage rate	10.6	21.3	11.6
Divorce rate	5.2	7.6	5.3
Crime rate	57.5	64.8	53.6
% 12+ years of education	66.5	75.2	80.0
Percent female labor force	42.6	41.3	39.8
Per capita income	$7,298	$7,123	$6,305
% families in poverty	9.6	8.9	7.7
% persons in poverty	12.4	11.9	10.3
% farm population	2.5	2.3	1.3

Sources: Quinn et al. 1982; U.S. Bureau of the Census 1983

It is noteworthy that Utah has lower rates of poverty than the nation or the surrounding states, since Utah's per capita income is low. In a more detailed analysis of the relationship between income and poverty, Fuguitt and his colleagues (1989) also found that few Mormon-dominated counties had poverty rates as high as the average for all counties, despite the fact that the great majority of Mormon counties had lower than average per capita income. They interpret this anomaly as being an effect of the values and class structure common to Mormonism. Their findings revealed that the existence of low poverty levels among counties with lower than average income did not exist outside the Mormon-dominated counties.

Differences between Utah and neighboring states and the nation were not so great nor consistent with respect to social characteristics. One noteworthy exception is the relatively higher percent of the state's population that had completed high school. Of the population of Utah 25 years of age and older, four out of five have a high school diploma, compared to two-thirds of this age group for the nation and three-fourth for the Mountain States. Utah's marriage and divorce rates are quite similar to those for the nation (see Table 3). The Mountain States collectively have higher marriage and divorce rates because of the influence of Nevada on regional statistics.

Table 3.4. Socioeconomic and Demographic Characteristics of Counties in the Rocky Mountains by % LDS, 1980.

Characteristic	LDS Dominant (50% +)	LDS Moderate (10-49%)	LDS Low (Below 10%)
Number of Counties	37	43	198
Percent urban	35.0	36.3	36.0
Percent white **	96.9	89.5	91.1
Percent migrant	16.9	19.4	18.9
Percent under age 5 ***	13.2	10.1	8.3
Median age ***	25.2	27.8	30.1
Persons per household ***	3.20	3.00	2.80
Percent female head of HHD ***	6.7	8.8	9.2
Birth rate ***	28.8	22.1	18.5
Death rate *	7.1	7.6	8.3
Marriage rate	9.7	17.1	19.7
Divorce rate ***	3.6	6.1	6.1
Crime rate	34.6	36.8	39.6
% 12+ years of education ***	76.8	70.0	70.9
Percent female labor force ***	35.5	36.6	38.1
Per capita income	$7,526	$9,062	$9,090
% families in poverty	10.1	12.1	11.4
% persons in poverty	13.2	15.0	14.6
% farm population	7.5	9.4	9.3

Notes:
*   P < 0.05
**   P < 0.01
***   P < 0.001

Sources: Quinn et al. 1982; U.S. Bureau of the Census 1983

Comparisons of the counties in which Mormons are numerically dominant with counties in which they are in the minority reveal differences that parallel those between Utah and other Mountain States

(Table 4). Counties in which Mormons dominate have a higher birth rate and more youthful age structure. Households are larger in Mormon-dominated counties, and the death rate is slightly lower than for the other counties, as would be expected from the lower average age of the county populations. The eleven non-Utah counties in which Mormons are numerically dominant are very similar to the 26 Utah counties in which they are in the majority (see Table 5 and Figure 1). The crude birth rate for the Mormon-dominated non-Utah counties was 27.5, compared to 28.5 for the Utah counties, and only 18.1 for the 198 non-Utah Mountain State counties in which Mormons constitute less than ten percent of the population. Thus, a complete social mapping of the boundaries of the Mormon Culture Region would include several counties in states that are adjacent to Utah.

Table 3.5. Socioeconomic and Demographic Characteristics of Counties by % LDS, State of Utah and Other Mountain States, 1980.

	UTAH		NON-UTAH		
	LDS Dominant	LDS Moderate	LDS Dominant	LDS Moderate	LDS Low
Characteristic	(50% +)	(10-49%)	(50% +)	(10-49%)	(Below 10%)
Number of Counties	26	3	11	40	198
Percent urban	31.4	53.2	36.6	44.9	38.4
Percent white	97.8	95.2	98.3	96.1	95.9
Percent migrant	15.4	15.1	15.5	18.5	17.3
Percent under age 5	13.3	12.6	13.1	9.7	8.2
Median age	24.8	25.9	25.0	28.3	29.8
Persons per household	3.20	3.00	3.20	2.90	2.70
Percent female head of HHD	7.1	9.3	6.1	8.5	8.5
Birth rate	28.5	27.8	27.5	20.7	18.1
Death rate	6.3	6.8	6.5	7.5	8.0
Marriage rate	9.6	8.5	8.0	10.9	11.5
Divorce rate	3.8	5.5	3.1	6.1	5.8
Crime rate	32.9	39.7	28.1	34.1	36.9
% 12+ years of education	77.6	65.8	73.9	70.6	70.3
Percent female labor force	36.6	35.7	35.0	36.3	38.6
Per capita income	$7,206	$8,711	$7,519	$8,951	$8,902
% families in poverty	9.3	10.3	11.6	10.9	10.1
% persons in poverty	12.2	11.0	14.6	13.8	13.6
% farm population	3.7	1.2	14.8	7.4	5.7

The discriminant function analyses presented in Table 6 show the distinctiveness of Mormon-dominated counties with respect to the characteristics considered in this analysis. Of the 18 variables used in the descriptive analysis, seven are identified with a stepwise procedure as important in distinguishing Mormon from non-Mormon counties. These seven variables are percent urban, percent white, percent migrant, birth rate, death rate, percent graduating from high school, and per capita income. The unstandardized and standardized discriminant function coefficients for these seven variables in the stepwise procedure are shown in Table 6. There are two functions in the discriminant analysis because of the use of the three categories (see SPSS 1988).

Table 3.6. Discriminant Function Coefficients for Variables Selected by Stepwise Procedure

Discriminant Function Coefficients

Characteristics	Unstandarized		Standarized	
	Function 1	Function 2	Function 1	Function 2
Percent urban	0.0077	0.0056	0.2462	0.1789
Percent white	0.0456	-0.0061	0.5275	-0.0703
Percent migrant	-0.0459	-0.0441	-0.4026	-0.3864
Birth rate	0.2667	-0.1019	1.0443	-0.3988
Death rate	0.0850	0.1989	0.2280	0.5091
% 12+ years of education	0.0809	0.1301	0.6931	1.1141
Per capita income	-0.0003	-0.0003	-0.6069	-0.6214
Constant	-12.7876	-4.7964		

The numbers of correct and incorrect classifications based on the seven variables are shown in Table 7. Nearly 84 percent of the counties are correctly classified. Only two of the 37 Mormon-dominated counties have characteristics that would lead one to believe that they are not dominated by Mormons numerically. Similarly, only five (2.5%) of the 198 counties in which Mormons constitute less than ten percent of the population have a characteristics profile that would lead one to predict Mormon numerical dominance. The discriminant function analysis misclassifies a larger proportion of the 43 counties which are between 10 and 49 percent Mormon. The majority of these (81.4%) are classified as being less than ten percent, and 7.0 percent are classified as being numerically dominated. This is surprising because of the expectation that strong Mormon identity and organization might generate influences in counties in which Mormons are a sizeable minority. However, the discriminant function analysis is very effective in indicating that the Mormon Culture Region is distinct along several important sociodemographic dimensions.

As a statistical technique which employs linear combinations of variables to distinguish between two or more categories of cases, discriminant analysis shows that Mormon-dominated counties are distinct from other counties with respect to socioeconomic and demographic characteristics (SPSS 1988). The technique shows that 97.5 percent of the

Table 3.7. Classification Results from Dicriminant Function Analysis by Proportion LDS, 1980.

Actual Group	Number of Cases	Predicted Group Membership		
		Group 1	Group 2	Group 3
Group 1 (Low LDS)	198	193 97.5%	3 1.5%	2 1.0%
Group 2 (Medium LDS)	43	35 81.4%	5 11.6%	3 7.0%
Group 3 (High LDS)	37	1 2.7%	1 2.7%	25 94.6%

Note: Percent of grouped cases correctly classified is 83.8.

Mormon-dominated counties do have sociodemographic characteristics distinguishing them from other counties. This is evidence that the forces which have reduced or eliminated the distinctions between the South and the nation as a whole have not eliminated basic cultural differences between the Mormon Culture Region and the rest of the nation.

Summary and Conclusions

The existence of distinct culture regions in modern heterogeneous societies is unusual. The Mormon Culture Region is one of the most conspicuous of these areas in the United States. This culture region began with the mass movement of Mormons into the Great Salt Lake Basin in the mid-1800s. Since then, Mormons have come to numerically dominate a large area of the Rocky Mountains with Utah at the core of the region. The boundaries of the Mormon Culture Region now extend into several counties in adjacent states.

Geographers have noted that the Mormon Culture Region is the most easily mapped area that can be defined on the basis of homogeneity of religious membership (Meinig 1965; Zelinsky 1961). However, its existence as a unique culture region does not rest solely on the basis of the numerical dominance of Mormons. Rather, its identity as a distinct culture region is also associated with social and cultural characteristics which distinguish it from other areas.

This study has shown that there is substantial homogeneity within the Mormon Culture Region with respect to several socioeconomic and demographic characteristics. Counties within the Mountain States which are numerically dominated by Mormons have higher birth rates, lower death rates, a higher percent of high school graduates, a younger age structure, and more persons per household, than counties in which Mormons are in the minority. Mormon-dominated counties not in Utah are very similar to the Utah counties in terms of these characteristics. Multivariate analyses showed that the relationship of religious composition with these characteristics justifies classifying the Mormon counties as distinct from other counties in terms of socioeconomic and demographic characteristics. In essence, the discriminant function analysis indicated that counties which have high percents white, highly educated, urban, with large families, and low income, and with more than an average proportion of migrants and low death rates are almost certain to also be counties that are numerically dominated by Mormons.

The similarity between Utah and non-Utah counties which are also numerically dominated by Mormons indicates that the treatment of Utah as the core of the region is somewhat arbitrary. In their classic work on geographical areas of the United States, Bogue and Beale (1961) point out that most information that is compiled for areas of the nation consists of aggregates of state units that do not functionally form homogeneous regions, and thus relying upon data for states to conduct regional analyses can be misleading.

Between 1980 and 1990 the number of Mormons in the United States increased from 2,684,744 to 4,175,000, a 55 percent growth (Deseret News 1991). In Utah the number grew 32 percent to 1,305,000. Stark (1984) has suggested that there may be more than 250 million Mormons within a century, based on his analysis of their long-term pattern of past growth. His 1984 projections assumed a lower rate of growth than the church has experienced in the 1980s. The rapid growth of this religion, which has unique social and demographic characteristics, could have an important impact on the overall socioeconomic character of larger populations of which they now constitute only a small minority.

Mormons may lose some of their uniqueness as they grow in numbers and as their membership becomes more dispersed. It has already been observed that the Mormon religion is experiencing significant changes and that diversity within the group is increasing along several dimensions (Albrecht 1990; Crapo 1987). Since the extension of full priesthood rights to African-American members in 1987, for example, efforts to recruit them have increased (Jacobson 1991).

Convergence between Mormon and nonMormon ways can also come

about as a result of the larger society adopting practices of Mormons as well as through Mormons adopting the practices of the larger society. The rejection of polygamy symbolized early Mormon adaptation to the marital customs of the larger society. More recently, declines in the use of tobacco and stricter liquor controls in the larger society have diminished some of the differences between Mormons and nonMormons in these practices.

Prospects for persistence of the Mormon Culture Region into the next century seem certain. High fertility rates and patterns of selective migration continue to favor numerical dominance by Mormons. Migration has played a key role in maintaining the area's unique population composition (Stinner and Kan 1983; Stinner and Toney 1981). A majority of the inmigrants to this cultural area were Mormon, while a majority of those leaving were not. Application of survey-based in and outmigration rates to actual migration flows from census data indicated that migration has not been altering the area's religious composition. Survey data collected from Montana support the Utah-based studies by revealing a low preference on the part of nonMormons for destinations within the Mormon Culture Region (Jobes 1984).

It is perhaps of even greater importance that the Mormon Church continues to be highly successful in shaping the lives of its members. Participation in religious activities, group identification, and cohesion are high. It is these forces which underlie the unusual socioeconomic and demographic profile of areas in which Mormons dominate. It may also be these forces which provide the "institutionalist" influence over sociopolitical attitudes analyzed by Stinner and Paita in Chapter 10.

However, there are forces which could alter aspects of this profile. Increased contact with other regions of the nation is one of the more obvious factors which could lead to a larger number of Mormons diverging from Mormon traditions. Political and economic forces which encourage increased involvement of women in the labor force and the increasing costs of raising children might contribute to further declines in Mormon fertility. Continued monitoring of the Mormon Culture Region provides a unique opportunity to contribute to the literatures on social change, assimilation, and the variability of regionalism as an analytical concept.

Chapter 4

Immigration Dynamics and Domestic Labor

Philip L. Martin
University of California, Davis

Introduction

In 1886, the Statue of Liberty was dedicated in New York harbor to symbolize America's openness to European immigrants. One hundred years later, the United States enacted the Immigration Reform and Control Act (IRCA) to stem the influx of Latin American and Asian immigrants. Immigration plays an important but often subtle role in shaping a society's growth and change: in only a few instances have flows of people across national boundaries had definite causes and effects. In most cases, immigration's effects are too subtle, diffuse, and long-term to make causes and effects easy to identify. It is a hotly debated topic, both politically and economically. There is little agreement on the effects of immigrants on the economy and society. This chapter reviews U.S. immigration policies, the major arguments about the impacts of immigrants, and the importance of immigration in California.

Migration across national boundaries for employment and settlement is the exception, not the rule (Martin and Houstoun 1982). Most of the world's more than five billion people never leave their country of birth. Low wages and high unemployment in developing nations, alleged labor shortages in industrial countries, and improved communication and transportation systems have encouraged more workers to cross national borders in search of employment, but the most surprising fact is that so few people do so.

In the United States, persons are either citizens or aliens. Aliens are further subdivided into two subgroups. Immigrants are aliens who are entitled to enter, live, and work in the United States and, after five years, to become naturalized U.S. citizens. Nonimmigrant aliens enter the United States for a specific purpose and time period, to study, to do business, to be a tourist, or in a few instances to work temporarily. Nonimmigrant aliens who are working in the United States illegally are also of two kinds: the majority, who cross U.S. borders surreptitiously, and a minority which enters legally as, for example, students or tourists, but who later violate the terms of their visas by working.

The Select Commission on Immigration and Refugee Policy (SCIRP) divided American immigration history into three phases. Until the 1870s, the U.S. government permitted and often encouraged aliens to immigrate to the United States. Phase 2 began in the 1870s when qualitative restrictions were enacted to exclude certain persons who wanted to immigrate, such as criminals, contract laborers, and the Chinese. In 1921 and 1924, the third phase began with the first restrictions on total immigration and the introduction of annual quotas. Immediate relatives of U.S. citizens have always been exempt from the annual quotas.

Immigration from Western Hemisphere nations was not subject to quantitative restrictions until 1965. In that year a seven-tiered preference system was introduced. (This was reduced to six tiers in 1980.) This system ranked would-be immigrants by their ties to U.S. residents and their work skills, and a world-wide quota was adopted, including 120,000 from Western Hemisphere nations. Hemisphere quotas were abolished in 1978 and replaced with a world-wide quota of 270,000 annually, and the preference system was applied for the first time to peoples from Western Hemisphere nations.

A quota of 270,000 immigrants plus nonquota immediate relatives of U.S. citizens should yield 350,000 to 400,000 immigrants annually, fewer than two for every thousand U.S. residents. However, legal immigration increased rapidly in the late 1970s because the number of immediate relatives exempt from quotas rose, Cuban and Indochinese refugees were admitted, and thousands of would-be immigrants who were waiting in queues for their turn to immigrate to the United States were permitted to become immigrants quickly (U.S. SCIRP 1981). Instead of fewer than 400,000 immigrants annually, legal immigration averaged 600,000 to 700,000 per year during the 1980s.

Apprehensions of illegal aliens or undocumented workers rose along with the number of legal immigrants, prompting Presidents Ford, Carter, and Reagan to assert that the United States had "lost control of its borders" and must enact immigration reforms to reassert the basic right of a sovereign nation to control who crosses those borders. All three

Presidents appointed commissions to examine dimensions and consequences of the surge in legal and illegal immigration. The three commissions reached two similar conclusions: that the United States must reduce illegal immigration to prevent nativist sentiments from halting all immigration; and, that illegal immigration adversely affects unskilled American workers (U.S. SCIRP 1981).

Illegal immigration continued to increase throughout the 1980s. By the middle of the decade, the Immigration and Naturalization Service (INS) was apprehending about two illegal aliens or undocumented workers every minute of the day, 365 days per year, almost two million annually (INS, annual). Apprehension statistics are only a crude guide to the influx and settlement of illegal immigrants in the United States, but they became the major evidence adduced to demonstrate that immigration to the United States was "out of control."[1]

Efforts to reduce illegal immigration have a long history in the Congress of the United States (Congressional Research Service 1987). During the early 1970s, the House of Representatives, at the behest of labor unions, enacted several times a system of sanctions or fines on employers who knowingly hired illegal aliens. Farm employer opposition prevented Senate action each time. This type of control measure which would ultimately be enacted to "close the U.S. labor market" attracting illegal aliens had been accepted by most urban representatives in the early 1970s, when many European nations were also introducing employer sanctions. Rural and farm-oriented representatives, however, opposed employer sanctions.

Immigration reform legislation stalled in Congress because powerful interest groups found that the status quo was their "second-best" option. During hearings on the need to reduce illegal immigration, some Hispanic leaders argued that immigration reforms would reduce the influx of immigrants from Latin America, stopping the Hispanic immigration wave before it influenced American society in the way that European immigration had (U.S. SCIRP 1981). Other Hispanics worried that employer sanctions designed to deter American employers from hiring illegal aliens would increase Hispanic unemployment as employers simply refused to hire any Hispanics in order to avoid fines for hiring illegal alien workers.

The iron fist of sanctions was soon wrapped in the velvet glove of amnesty to make the major instrument of control more acceptable. However, amnesty or legalization for some of the illegal aliens living in the United States was also controversial. Conservatives argued that the

United States should not reward law-breakers with legal U.S. residence. But, many religious and Hispanic leaders argued that the proposed amnesty for aliens who had developed an "equity stake" in the United States was not generous enough, because it might force some illegal alien parents to leave the country with their U.S.-born children who were thus U.S. citizens. State and local governments worried that amnesty would increase their education and service costs, while employers dependent on illegal alien workers were afraid that they could not survive the inevitable adjustment costs of converting to a legal workforce. Farmers argued that they had become uniquely dependent on illegal alien workers and needed legal foreign worker substitutes for these illegal workers.

The debate over the pros and cons of illegal immigration was reduced to three competing arguments by the 1980s (Martin and Sehgal 1980). Those who favored a continuation of the illegal alien status quo argued that the immigrants came to the United States because the United States needed them to fill lower-level jobs. Such immigration was inevitable according to this argument because of the powerful economic pull of the United States and the population and economic pressures abroad. Immigration was also argued to be a safety-valve for important international neighbors.

The counter-arguments were of two kinds: refutations of this "learn-to-live-with" illegal immigration idea; and, concerns about the long-run dangers posed by the influx of unskilled immigrations. Employers always "need" more labor, they argued, but if too much labor is available, employer incentives to develop the labor-saving automation necessary to compete in international markets are reduced. The "immigration-is-inevitable" argument was refuted with evidence that emigration was selective by geographic area; areas abroad that were equally poor sent very different numbers of immigrants to the United States. Further, dependence on illegal aliens varied considerably within industries or occupations in the United States. Finally, anti-illegal-immigrant advocates argued that emigration might be increasing rather than decreasing the dependence of Mexico and other sending nations on the opportunities afforded by the U.S. labor market.

These "first-level" arguments were about need, inevitability and dependence. Second-level arguments involved more profound questions about the nature and future of American society. The major concerns over the influx of unskilled immigrants included the ideas that the availability of these workers would slow the upward mobility of the American underclass, increase inequality within the United States, and would not necessarily act to accelerate economic growth. The debate was not resolved by the immigration reforms of 1986, and it promises to loom larger as the nation continues the argument to further tighten enforcement against illegal immigration and the desirability of admitting large numbers of legal immigrants.

Illegal Immigrants and the U.S. Labor Market [2]

How did the flood of illegal immigrant workers entering the U.S. labor market after the mid-1970s affect the wages and job prospects of U.S. citizens and legal immigrants? There are three major theories of immigrant-U.S. worker interaction: (1) one-for-one displacement assumes that illegal aliens and American workers compete for the same jobs and that the aliens are preferred because they work harder for lower pay, benefits or security; (2) segmented labor market theories assume that illegal aliens and American workers look for different kinds of jobs, so that there is no labor market competition; and, finally, (3) triage theories recognize that some one-for-one displacement occurs, that jobs can be upgraded to attract Americans, and that some jobs exist only because illegal alien workers are available who will take them. After summarizing the three theories, the process of network recruitment and labor displacement will be explained.

In 1978 and 1979, when six million Americans were unemployed, it was sometimes suggested that if the estimated five to six million illegal aliens could somehow be removed from the United States, unemployment would virtually disappear. The presumption for such one-for-one displacement was that unemployed Americans and illegal aliens fill the same job vacancies, and that illegal aliens were hired because they were willing to work at these jobs for low wages and little benefits.

One-for-one displacement suggests that each illegal alien removed from a workplace opens up a job for an unemployed American worker. However, segmented labor market theorists argue that illegal aliens only compete for jobs that American workers shun; unemployed Americans, for example, refuse to apply for hotel cleaning or tomato picking jobs, while illegal aliens seek only such jobs. The segmented labor market theory argues that there is thus no connection between the number of illegal aliens working in the United States and the U.S. unemployment rate. If illegal aliens have any effect on the job and wage prospects of American workers, according to this view, it is positive, since hotel cleaning and tomato picking support better clerk, waiter, truck driver, and food processor jobs for Americans. Segmented theories suggest that the major problem associated with illegal immigration is the frequent violation of labor standards laws in alien-dominated workplaces, and that an alternative to border enforcement efforts is more workplace inspection of wages and working conditions.

One-for-one displacement and segmentation theories occupy the two extreme positions. The familiar triage argument lies between these extremes, with the assumption that for every three jobs held by illegal aliens, one might be filled as soon as it is vacated by an American worker. Another may be filled by an American worker after the employer improves wages and working conditions. The third job would disappear because it would not be worth offering at higher wages; examples include that of the housewife who would do her own cleaning instead of hiring an illegal alien maid, or the farmer who decides that wages are too high to justify repicking a field for the third time. The triage assumption of three responses to removing illegal alien workers suggests too much precision in how the labor market would respond to fewer illegal workers, but it does convey a sense of the complexity of the dynamic adjustment process.

All three theories provide different perspectives on labor market competition, but only triage conveys a sense of the dynamic process through which illegal aliens can eventually dominate in certain occupations. Since most workers find jobs through tips passed along by friends and relatives, the network recruitment system developed by illegal aliens and their employers must be examined in order to understand how illegal aliens displace American workers.

Businesses that depend on illegal alien workers typically experience a high turnover of American workers. A hotel cleaning staff, a light manufacturing operation, or a landscape service may have to hire ten to thirty American workers each year in order to keep ten job slots filled. Many of these jobs pay relatively low wages, are physically demanding, or require work at nights or on weekends. American workers in such jobs rarely develop a career-like attachment to them; they often switch employers if they dislike a supervisor, for example. If the American workers are laid off, they turn to unemployment insurance.

Illegal alien workers from Mexico, Latin America and Asia gained a foothold in jobs of this type in the 1960s and early 1970s. Some were target earners who entered to achieve a savings goal of $1,000 to $5,000, and after reaching this savings target, they returned home. However, some of the successful illegal aliens opened restaurant or garment shops in the United States that employed illegal alien friends and relatives. Other pioneer immigrants found entry-level employment in U.S. hotels, factories, and service firms, and some eventually rose through the ranks to become supervisors.

In the 1970s, two events turned this pioneer immigrant foothold into a dominant presence in many firms. First, the Civil Rights Movement raised the expectations of unskilled American workers, and the programs created by the War on Poverty provided previously unavailable employment and training options for some of the American workers who traditionally had accepted hotel cleaning, restaurant, and light manufacturing jobs. Second, illegal aliens began arriving in greater numbers, and a diverse group of small, labor-intensive businesses expanded after the economy recovered from the 1973-74 energy and food price hikes. Many of these small businesses had pyramid job structures: a few optimistic professionals with a concept or idea employed local clerical and sales workers in the front office and unskilled illegal aliens in the back room warehouse or factory. Other small businesses, such as ethnic restaurants and landscape services, were begun by entrepreneurial immigrants who employed friends and relatives. The proliferation of such small businesses increased the demand for unskilled workers. However, American workers continued to quit low-wage jobs or make demands for higher wages, and some employers turned to the immigrant workers who had persisted, some of whom had acquired legal status, promoting them to supervisory positions and then telling them to recruit new workers. They turned to their friends and relatives to fill vacant jobs. As American workers quit, new employees were increasingly drawn from Mexican villages rather than American ghettos. Small businesses that had suffered from the high turnover of American workers soon realized that immigrant workers gave them the same reliable work forces to which mainstream businesses were accustomed.

The illegal immigrant workers who were hired and supervised by ethnic foremen were a welcome relief to the often shaky businesses that depended on them. A furniture or shoe manufacturer in high-cost Los Angeles could be assured of a virtually unlimited supply of minimum-wage workers who could be trained in one day and supervised closely to assure quality of work. A restaurant or hotel could offer its customers superior service without increasing its production costs, because illegal immigrants proved to be more loyal and dependable than the Americans they replaced. Businesses became dependent on illegal immigrants because they realized they could get the employee loyalty and reliability of high-wage and mainstream businesses even with minimum wages and little or no benefits.

The secret to developing an alien workforce was to turn workforce recruitment and oversight over to an ethnic supervisor who could recruit illegal alien friends, relatives, and compatriots as workers. Once an initial ethnic work crew was assembled, the workers' information network recruited and trained new workers with no advertising, screening, or training costs to the employer.

As illegal immigrants learn more about the U.S. labor market, they are more prone to quit one low-skilled job for another to obtain higher wages or easier work. As settled immigrant workers acquire some of the traits of American workers, employers either upgrade wages and working conditions or tap into a more recent immigrant network. These new arrivals usually require several months or years before they, too, begin to get restless.

Network recruitment and ethnic supervision change the nature of the workplace. The language changes from English to Spanish or Chinese. Most of the immigrant workers are friends or relatives, and the culture of the workplace reflects their shared experiences, such as growing up in a Mexican village. The business owner frequently loses touch with the workers because of inability to speak their language, and the owner becomes dependent on a bilingual supervisor as an intermediary.

The network recruitment and ethnic supervision system is an efficient way to hire workers. New employees can be recruited quickly, trained at little or no cost by friends and relatives who are already employed, and let go easily during business downturns. As long as the ethnic supervisors remain employed, the workforce can be reassembled or a new workforce recruited if business picks up again. If an entire workforce is apprehended or discharged, an employer can pay a "coyote" (labor smuggler) $300 to $1,000 per worker for a new workforce and then establish a new network recruitment system.

Field research confirms the existence of kinship and village networks that educate workers abroad about U.S. jobs and wages (Massey 1986; Mines and Nuckton 1982). These networks provide information and sometimes financing for the trip across the U.S. border and serve as private employment agencies and training schools for new arrivals.

The pioneer immigrants are initially young men who come to the U.S. as target earners, hoping to save enough money for economic advancement back home. Migrant networks "mature" as the pioneer immigrants find better jobs and gradually help friends and relatives move into and up the U.S. labor market. Better U.S. jobs are harder to give up, and some immigrants send for their families. The arrival of women and children extends job networks into new workplaces, encouraging more families to come to the United States.

The pace of network maturation varies considerably. Some networks make the transition from farm to factory within five years, while others continue to link Mexican villages with U.S. farms much as they have for two generations (Mines and Nuckton 1982). However, most field research suggests that more and more illegal workers are bypassing low-wage farm jobs and going directly to urban areas, where immigrant families have gained a foothold, persisted, and now fill vacant jobs in a variety of types of workplaces.

Two decades of this cross-border interdependency have made recruitment networks an integral part of Mexican village economies, and have made Mexican workers key parts of some U.S. industry workforces. As these labor migration networks become more entrenched, the economic impacts of illegal immigrant workers change. Some workers settle with their families in the United States and their attitudes and workplace behavior change. Indeed, it can be asserted that many Mexican villages and U.S. firms depend on a constant migration of new workers across the border, so that remittances continue and migrant workers remain flexible. As European nations discovered with their legal foreign workers, the length of time in residence in the country rather than citizenship or the extension of other political rights to foreigners determines the economic impacts of migrant workers (Martin 1981). Network recruitment not only excludes American workers from certain jobs; it also builds a dependency relationship that requires a constant infusion of new workers. This dependency relationship may prove to be stronger than immigration reforms.

One reason for increased emigration from rural Mexico during the 1980s was that the demand for Mexican labor expanded. There were two phenomena at work. First, Mexicans replaced U.S. workers in rural labor markets which ranged from North Carolina tobacco to Idaho sugar beets. By 1991, a nationwide farmworker survey found that 73 percent of all workers employed in U.S. crop production were foreign-born, and that 90 percent of the foreign-born farmworkers were Mexican (U.S. Department of Labor 1989). Reliable data for earlier years are not available, but a 1981 survey found that only 32 percent of U.S. fruit and vegetable workers at that time were Hispanic.

The revolving door through which entry-level immigrant farmworkers entered the U.S. labor market turned faster in the 1980s because U.S. farm wages fell and working conditions worsened. Real farm wages fell during the 1980s, making nonfarm jobs more attractive to farm workers with the language, skills, and contacts to get them. Second, the current oversupply of farmworkers, many of whom have fraudulent documents, means that seasonal farm work gets done quicker, so that the annual earnings of many workers has dropped as they experience longer spells of unemployment. Third, farm employers in the 1980s began to hire more workers indirectly via farm labor contractors (FLCs) to avoid even the small risk of fines for hiring illegal aliens. FLCs generally do not provide free housing for workers, and often charge workers for rides to the fields, so that a worker earning $200 weekly during the peak of the season may have to pay $50 for housing and transportation, lowering take-home pay by 25 percent.

In addition to replacing U.S. workers, more Mexicans found jobs in rural America as labor-intensive agriculture expanded. The fruit, vegetable and horticulture sector of U.S. agriculture increased its sales by 63 percent between 1980 and 1989. Data to determine how much more farmworker employment was generated by this expansion are not available, but there were relatively few labor-saving breakthroughs in agriculture during the 1980s which would have reduced the need for farmworkers, so in most crops increases in sales mean that more workers were required.

How Many and Which Immigrants?

The United States gains immigrants through the six-tier preference system alluded to earlier in this chapter. The system limits immigration to 270,000 annually through a non-quota admission of 100,000 to 200,000 spouses and minor children of U.S. citizens, and through special adjustment-of-status programs such as those for Cubans and Haitians in the early 1980s and the legalization programs created by the 1986 Immigration Reform and Control Act (IRCA). These programs generate 500,000 to 600,000 immigrants annually. This is equivalent to over half of the worldwide total of about one million legal immigrants accepted annually in all 165 nations.

Legal immigrants to the United States thus gain admittance because of family ties, special skills, or refugee status. Illegal immigrants by contrast are primarily persons with few skills. There is little disagreement that the United States benefits by being an open society which admits several hundred thousand relatives and skilled immigrants annually. The debate is over how many unskilled immigrants to admit.

Most of the people who would like to migrate to the United States do have relatively low levels of skills so that upon entrance into the U.S. labor market, they fill the lower rungs of the job ladder. However, they usually catch up in income with similar U.S.-born workers. A 35-year-old, Mexican born worker with a third-grade education typically earns less in the U.S. than does a 35-year-old U.S.-born worker with a third grade education for about 15 years, but then the Mexican-born worker's earnings catch up with and surpass those of his native U.S. counterpart (Chiswick 1980). It is important that these immigrant earnings studies compare earnings profiles of similar foreign- and U.S.-born workers, in terms of equivalent age, education, and work experience.

Does the United States "need" another wave of low-skilled immigrants similar to that which took place in the early 20th Century? The arguments for another wave of such immigrants stress that (1) their earnings do catch up with the incomes of similar U.S.-born workers, (2) their children enjoy upward mobility, and (3) they accelerate U.S. economic growth. The arguments against more unskilled immigrants are that the American society and economy have changed throughout the 20th Century: the U.S. economy no longer needs waves of unskilled immigrants, and American society has erected a social safety net which may prove attractive to immigrants whose U.S. earning potential is limited. This counter-argument further asserts that jobs like sewing, picking and dishwashing will be mechanized or exported whether immigrant workers are available or not, so that admitting them into dead-end jobs compounds the labor displacement problems that inevitably result (U.S. SCIRP 1981).

It is hard to evaluate these arguments, but the weight of evidence seems to show that another wave of unskilled immigrants is not necessary for the health of the American economy and may indeed aggravate U.S. economic and social problems. Unskilled immigrants are often employed in industries which produce goods that are traded across national borders, and some of the U.S. industries most dependent on alien workers are also industries that are most likely to ask for legislative protection from imported goods. These industries include garment and apparel firms, and fruits and vegetables. This suggests that the jobs immigrants fill cannot be preserved indefinitely under any circumstances. Employers who assert that they would go out of business without low wage immigrants are likely to go out of business eventually even if they employ these immigrant workers.

Low-wage immigrants do create and preserve service jobs in hotels and restaurants, in gardening, and in other service industries, but there are many other ways to create service jobs, if that is the goal, such as reducing or eliminating the minimum wage. The evidence suggests that most illegal immigrants come to the United States to work, not to collect welfare, but California data indicate that there is a substantial minority of immigrants who are illegally collecting social safety net payments (U.S. SCIRP 1981). Finally, the Japanese economy is proof that immigration is not necessary for economic growth. Japan is one of the societies most closed to immigration, yet it has had one of the world's most rapid growth rates.

NAFTA and Immigration in the 1990s [3]

The North American Free Trade Agreement (NAFTA) is unprecedented. Never before have countries whose per capita GNPs differed by 9 to 1 entered into serious negotiations to free trade and investment between them. In contrast to European efforts at economic integration, NAFTA is a much narrower effort aimed at creating a common market for goods and investments in Canada, the United States, and Mexico.

Labor migration is not formally a component of NAFTA, but the Mexican and U.S. governments have expressed the hope that NAFTA will eventually reduce Mexico-to-U.S. migration. Mexico would much rather export goods than people. In the long term more trade and investment has the potential to reduce Mexican emigration, but disruptions and displacement associated with restructuring the Mexican economy are likely to increase emigration during the first decade of the agreement. In particularly, NAFTA is likely to add more immigrants to the U.S. farm workforce in the 1990s and up to half of any additional immigrants from Mexico will come to California.

How will NAFTA affect the demand-pull, supply-push and network factors that govern migration flows? First, NAFTA is not likely to decrease rural Mexican migration to the United States during the 1990s because a still-expanding U.S. labor-intensive agriculture should continue to pull Mexican workers into the United States. These demand-pull pressures are augmented by the continued departure of U.S.-born workers from the rural workforce and their replacement with rural Mexicans.

Second, Mexican supply-push pressures should remain high in the 1990s. They may even increase as Mexico's rural economy is restructured as a result of land reforms, NAFTA, and the further opening to world trade of the Mexican economy. Third, the sophisticated networks in place bring rural Mexicans legally and illegally to the United States, and they will guide some of the one million or more farmers, farmworkers and their families who are expected to be displaced from Mexican agriculture each year in the 1990s to the United States (Tellez 1991).

This expected displacement can be put into perspective by comparing it to past displacement from U.S. agriculture. During the 1950s over one million people left U.S. farms each year. The Southern U.S. states lost 40 percent of their farm population in the 1950s through mechanization, farm consolidation, and the availability of urban factory jobs. Mexico, with a population half the size of that of the U.S. in 1960, is expected to experience a similar level of displacement from agriculture. The prospect of twice the proportionate volume of displacement from agriculture in Mexico, and the strong ties that already link Mexican and U.S. labor markets, practically guarantee more Mexico-to-U.S. migration in the 1990s.

Thus demand-pull, supply-push and network dynamics will sustain or even increase Mexican migration to the United States in the 1990s, but it is important to recognize that NAFTA will primarily affect the supply-push factors which encourage emigration. NAFTA may not even be the most important factor pushing Mexicans out of agriculture: land reforms and Mexico's unilateral lowering of trade barriers may be responsible for displacing more Mexicans from agriculture and propelling them north to the United States than NAFTA. This means that migration from Mexico to the United States is likely to remain high and perhaps increase during the 1990s with or without NAFTA.

NAFTA will not halt Mexico-to-U.S. migration quickly, but it is the best hope for the economic growth and jobs that should eventually encourage more Mexicans to stay at home. The reason for embracing NAFTA despite its potential to increase emigration in the short-term is simple. The United States during the 1980s received about nine million immigrants, including three million Mexicans. Without a NAFTA-inspired trade and investment boom in Mexico, the United States is likely to accept a large number of Mexican immigrants in the 1990s, and then also look forward to another large number in the following decade. NAFTA, on the other hand, should accelerate the economic development in Mexico that can diminish both the demand-pull and supply-push factors that increased Mexican migration to the United States throughout the 1980s.

Models of NAFTA's effects on migration agree that free trade in farm products will spur additional migration from Mexico because it will displace far more Mexicans than Americans. Mexican farmers are likely to be displaced by cheaper imported corn and other grains. Since most rural Mexicans have friends and relatives in the U.S. labor market, a quick transition to free trade could make corn farming unprofitable for many of the six to eight million workers currently employed in Mexican agriculture. This poses a dilemma for the United States. A quick move toward free trade in corn, which benefits Midwestern farmers, might also increase Mexican immigration and depress wages and increase unemployment in Los Angeles. Mexico wants to move toward free trade in agriculture very slowly, and these models support the Mexican position.

NAFTA will not change the most important features of the farm labor market: agriculture is likely to remain an industry in which 2.5 million workers work on average half the year for poverty-level incomes. The conditions of U.S. farmworkers have pricked the nation's conscience since The Grapes of Wrath in the 1930s. During the 1960s, the federal government launched a series of programs designed to help farmworkers and their families as part of the War on Poverty. Most of those programs initially served only migrant farmworkers who crossed state lines, but they have since been expanded to assist seasonal farmworkers and nonfarm workers employed in the food processing industry.

Farmworker service programs will assume a new importance as NAFTA speeds up the entry and flow of immigrant workers through the farm labor market. These programs now operate in the shadows of other programs because they are relatively small and have unique federal administrative structures. But the challenges facing this system are likely to grow under NAFTA, making it imperative that the programs which are likely to serve one-fourth of the adult immigrants to the United States during the 1990s are structured and funded in a manner that will permit them to provide the services needed to give farmworkers and their children a chance to climb the U.S. job ladder.

Social Scientists and Immigration Policy

For over a decade, Congress was warned that immigration was out of control, that immigrants were displacing American workers and depressing wages, and that the social service costs for the immigrants were or would become a drain on government revenues. There was no legislative action to reform immigration policies despite these warnings, partially because other voices argued that the estimates of illegal immigration were exaggerated, that immigrants did not displace domestic workers or depress wages, and that immigrants workers paid more in taxes than they withdrew in social services or other benefits.

Some policy debates can be resolved after social scientists step forward with analyses that support one or another of the conflicting assertions. Unfortunately, the immigration debate does not appear to be one that additional social science knowledge can resolve. Instead, the menu of competing analyses permits partisan advocates to select "hard evidence" from eminent researchers to support the entire spectrum of policy positions on immigration.

Immigration research involves inadequate data, few widely-accepted models, and often emotionally involved researchers. Policy makers have learned that much of the immigration scholarship is weak; hence, social scientists have not played a dominant role in the immigration reform debate. For example, Senator Simpson complained that the voluminous social science materials assembled by the Select Commission on Immigration and Refugee Policy in 1979-81 were of little use in the Congressional debate; in the end, illegal immigration was declared to be bad public policy because it was "illegal in a nation of laws."

The United States never thought it necessary to coordinate immigration and other labor market policies because immigrants added only a small fraction to labor force growth in the 1950s and 1960s (Briggs 1984). However, the immigration reforms of 1965 and illegal immigration in the 1970s increased the number of immigrants in the American workforce so much that legal and illegal immigrants and refugees now contribute perhaps half of the nation's net labor force growth (U.S. Department of Labor 1989).

The immigrants who now loom so large in labor force growth have different legal statuses and impacts. Legal immigrants tend to be professionals; illegal or undocumented immigrants concentrate at the low-wage end of the job ladder. Since economic theory predicts that an infusion of workers will increase unemployment or depress wages, illegal immigrants should adversely affect low-wage American workers, who are often of minority status. These are the same workers that employment and training programs are designed to assist, and these programs may be undercut by illegal immigration. The concentrated and negative impacts of illegal immigrants justifies efforts to stop illegal immigration and to coordinate immigration and labor market policies, in the view of many social scientists (U.S. Department of Labor 1989).

Other social scientists, however, have analyzed Census of Population data and found that immigrant workers play an unusual role in the U.S. labor market: instead of displacing American workers, immigrants increase the usefulness of adult U.S. men so much that male wages rise and new jobs are created. Indeed, a variety of tests with census data finds no negative impacts of immigrants on the wages or unemployment rates of adult U.S.-born men (U.S. Department of Labor 1989). These results suggest that a growth-oriented society should welcome more immigrants.

Conflicting research results such as these permit policy makers to defend whatever position is seen as satisfying their constituents or their personal convictions. Given such conflicting research claims, policy makers can more easily fall back on their own beliefs or on those of their constituents. Thus social scientists have less impact on immigration policy than might be expected.

Immigration and Population Change in California [4]

California's current population of some 30 million (see Table 1) is a far cry from its two million inhabitants in 1909 when, upon visiting the state, Lord James Bryce, the Ambassador from the United Kingdom to the United States, asked: "What will happen when California is filled by fifty millions of people, and its valuation is five times what it is now?...There will be more people--as many perhaps as the country can support--and the real question will be not about making more wealth or having more people, but whether the people will then be happier or better than they have been hitherto or are at this moment."

Rapid population growth driven by immigration has long been a concern in California. Several years ago, a Lieutenant Governor of the state, Mervin Dymally, expressed a related kind of immigration and population concern. He predicted that by 2000 a majority of the state's population would have Third World or minority ethnic origins. There is a growing consensus that whatever occurs in California will happen sooner or later to the nation. This concern has been particularly well expressed by the poet, Richard Armour (as cited in Bouvier and Martin, 1985, p. 1):

So leap with joy, be blithe and gay, or weep my friends with sorrow.
What California is today, the rest will be tomorrow.

California is the nation's most urban state with 95 percent of its population living in cities. Fully 60 percent of the state's nearly-30-

Table 4.1.   Population of California 1860 to 1990
(in thousands)

Year	Population	Percent Change
1860	379	
1870	560	47.8
1880	864	54.3
1890	1,213	40.4
1900	1,485	22.4
1910	2,377	60.1
1920	3,426	44.1
1930	5,677	65.7
1940	6,907	21.7
1950	10,586	53.3
1960	15,720	48.5
1970	19,971	27.0
1980	23,667	18.5
1990	29,760	25.7

Source: U.S. Bureau of the Census

million people live in Los Angeles and adjacent counties. The state's second largest urban center is the San Francisco Bay Area, comprised of nine counties which contain 5 million people, 22 percent of the state's population.

With more than 15 percent of its population foreign born, California's cultural diversity cannot be overstated. The evolution of the state's heterogeneity began in the 1840s, when Chinese immigrants and Americans from other states came to find work and fortune in the gold fields. They joined the Native Americans and Hispanics already in California, and they were later joined by Japanese immigrants. Early in the 20th Century, Mexicans streamed into California as civil unrest in their country pushed them out, and a demand for unskilled labor pulled them over their northern border. African-Americans did not reach the state in great numbers until the Second World War, when the California economy boomed with the production of war goods.

Migration from other states contributed to California's population growth until the 1970s. However, in that decade more people left the state than moved into the state. A recent Urban Institute publication on the impacts of immigration notes that: "Although immigration to California has soared since 1970, net internal migration to this region has virtually stopped because there is a decreasing propensity for people to move to California coupled with a rising tendency to leave for other states" (Muller and Espenshade 1985). This report further notes that: "Net migrants to California from other parts of the nation tend to be better-educated professional workers, whereas there has been a net outmigration of the less educated, unskilled, blue-collar and service workers." Net domestic migration had again become positive in the 1980s. In the early 1990s, California is second only to Hawaii in its net international migration rate (Population Reference Bureau 1992).

Immigration from Asian and Latin American countries has contributed significantly to the state's growth in both size and cultural diversity. Because of changes in Census of Population definitions, comparisons by race over time are not always accurate. Nevertheless, since 1970 there appear to have been significant shifts in the state's racial composition.

Substantial inmigration and differential fertility among ethnic groups have contributed to a reduction in the Anglo, or non-Hispanic White, proportion of the population in California. In 1970, about 77 percent of Californians were non-Hispanic Whites; in 1980, this group constituted only two-thirds of the state's population. The proportion of African-Americans in the population changed little during the 1970s; most of the population growth of minorities in California's population occurred among Asians and Hispanics.

Since 1970, the proportion of Californians of Asian origin--at that time only three percent--has climbed each year. About one-fourth of Asians are Filipinos, and another one-fourth are Chinese; about one-fifth are Japanese. Latin Americans are even more prominent: Hispanics, of which 80 percent are of Mexican origin, make up 20 percent of the population of the state and numbered 4.5 million in 1980. Fully one out of every four foreign-born persons living in the United States resides in California. The foreign-born population in California includes nearly one-third of all Hispanics and close to 40 percent of all Asian-Americans in the United States.

Both past and current immigration have led to cultural diversity in California and have sustained a relatively young age structure. Internal movement has brought mobile young adults from all states, especially the North Central and Southern states between 1975 and 1980. At the same time, an influx of young immigrants with large families and relatively high fertility rates has skewed the age distribution so that California's median age remains somewhat lower than the nation's. The median age has edged up, however, from 28 in 1970 to 30 in 1980 and 31.5 in 1990. The proportion elderly (65 years and older) rose to ten percent in 1980 from nine percent a decade earlier, and stood at 10.5 percent in 1990 (data for 1990 from Population Reference Bureau 1992).

California's economy was expected to add over five million jobs by 2000 and perhaps another five million by 2030, thus continuing to attract newcomers. However, in 1990 the state began to experience an economic recession, which by early 1993 had led to the loss of one million jobs. Falling tax revenues and rising social service costs led to state budget deficits. The continuing influx of needy immigrants was identified as one reason for California's fiscal woes.

In January 1993, California Governor Pete Wilson submitted a bill for $1.45 billion to then-President-Elect Clinton to cover state costs of providing services to legal immigrants, refugees and illegal aliens. California estimated that the state was spending $4.8 billion on immigration-related services, including $1.7 billion on services for illegal aliens. The largest single cost item was the estimated $3.6 billion spent on K-12 educational services for immigrant children.

The $1.45 billion bill sent by California to the federal government included $534 million for Medi-Cal, $350 million of this to provide health care services to undocumented aliens. It also included $324 million for other state services for those legalized under IRCA, $250 million for incarcerating illegal aliens, $290 million for AFDC payments to U.S.-citizen children of undocumented parents, $31 million for Medi-Cal services for these children, and $104 million for refugee resettlement services.

Clinton reported to the California economic summit on February 16, 1993 that he was working on a plan to provide California and other states that are "overwhelmed by immigration problems" with more federal aid. California could expect to receive about $500 million of the $900 million available. The receipt of these additional funds would require "complex and controversial" changes in federal law, in the view of some representatives.

It seems clear that California's job structure and workforce are changing. In the past the structure of jobs and workers was diamond-shaped: most jobs were semi-skilled or unskilled, and most workers had only high school educations. This structure is being replaced by an inverted triangle, with most new jobs requiring more education. The distribution of education for the immigrants who account for about half of the state's job growth, however, has more of an hourglass shape: these workers tend to be better or less well educated than the average resident of the state.

Immigration patterns will affect the number and types of jobs and workers in California, and thus affect the distribution of wages and incomes. Legal immigrants, especially from Asia, tend quickly to catch up to American education and earnings levels. Illegal immigrants, especially from Mexico and Central America, lag behind. Immigration patterns will have important effects on the evolution of the labor market. The large increases projected for the Hispanic and Asian workforces suggest a continuation of the emerging two-tier economy, with Asians and the better educated non-Hispanic Whites and African-Americans competing for the more prestigious occupations while poorly educated Hispanics and African-Americans scramble for lower status jobs.

Conclusions

The United States is a nation of immigrants unsure about the role that immigrants should play in U.S. society. Since 1970, the United States has experienced large-scale illegal immigration. For 15 years, social scientists and policy makers have debated what to do about such immigration and, finally in 1986, the nation enacted immigration reforms meant to reduce the influx of illegal immigrants. The ability of these reforms to actually reduce the immigration in the face of continuing strong push and pull forces is not yet clear. There is some discussion that, if reforms cannot halt illegal immigration, they should be scrapped, because the immigration is largely beneficial to the U.S. economy and society. The counter argument that unskilled immigrants hurt underclass Americans and distort economic growth has equally strong adherents. These opposing positions are likely to frame the 1990s debate over immigration.

The debate has a special significance for California because the state absorbs one-fourth to one-third of all immigrants. Most are Asians and Hispanics and most settle in urban areas of the state. However, Asian and Hispanic immigrants have fared differently in the state's economy. Many Asians have experienced upward mobility while many Hispanics remain trapped in lower-tier jobs. Current immigration and absorption patterns thus foster the creation or enlargement of a two-tiered society.

Notes

1. INS apprehensions are "events," not unique individuals. Thus, a person apprehended five times in one week becomes five apprehensions in the INS data.

2. This section is based on Martin 1986, which includes references to the major proponents of each theory.

3. This section is excerpted from Martin 1992.

4. This section is based on Bouvier and Martin 1985.

Chapter 5

The Myth of Rural Stability: Population Turnover in Nonmetropolitan Communities in Colorado and Montana

Edward Knop
Colorado State University

Patrick C. Jobes
Montana State University

Introduction

Questions raised by changes in rural-urban migration flows and by the consequences of these shifts remain unresolved (Beale 1975; Brown and Wardwell 1980; Zelinsky 1977). Explanations include a higher value placed on social and natural amenities (Blackwood and Carpenter 1978; Christenson et al. 1983; Heaton et al. 1981), rural and urban convergence (Dillman 1979; Marans et al. 1980; Wardwell 1977), disillusionment with the strains of urban living (Ilvento and Luloff 1982; Williams 1981), employment growth in rural areas (Beale 1980; Summers 1977; Wardwell and Gilchrist 1980), increased mobility with advances in transportation and communication (Carpenter 1977; Schwarzweller 1979; Wardwell 1982), and related factors (Cook 1987; DeJong and Fawcett 1981; Swanson 1986; Uhlenberg 1973).

Many areas grew during the 1970s after decades of stability or decline (Fuguitt 1985; Johnson and Purdy 1980). Smaller, remote areas that combined natural amenities with social or economic attractions grew rapidly and had significant adjustment challenges (Morrison and Wheeler 1976; Price and Sikes 1975; Stinner and Toney 1980; Zuiches 1982).

Growing communities faced a subtle problem. Attracted by natural amenities, new residents had limited experience in small towns. They did not fully understand what small town life involved (Long and DeAre 1980; Williams and Sofranko 1979; Yepsen 1987). Nor did some of the more established residents understand or appreciate local processes and the consequences of migration (Dailey and Campbell 1980; Ploch 1978).

It is this dimension that provides the emphasis in this chapter. The focus is on turnover migration: people moving to a community and then leaving, and people moving in and staying but with consequences that cause others to leave. Many more people are involved in migration than appear in net growth or decline statistics. Their movements have consequences and call for community management options beyond those implied only by changes in total population size (Jobes 1980; Knop and Bacigalupi 1984).

The turnover perspective on migration processes and consequences is analogous to the changes in a ponded stream. Stream flow into and out of the pond affects the amount of water within the pond at any point, but the dynamics of the flow and its consequences are partly separate from the effects on pond level. Much water can flow through without changing that level, but not without some erosion. Channels of more rapid flow through portions of the pond can agitate and muddy the waters, sometimes drawing water at the quiet edges into the flow. Variable in-and-out flows also often bring about variations in pond level, compounding their consequences.

In this study, the comings and goings of people have been tracked in four types of western mountain communities. These include a small, traditional, agricultural service town; a small but well-known recreational and cultural center; a medium-sized regional service, transportation and extractive industries center; and, a large nonmetropolitan community combining several community functions with the presence of a state university.

The general questions posed in the analysis include: What are the relative numbers of people involved in turnover migration, compared with net migration, in different type of smaller communities? What are the patterns in local citizens' early and later evaluations of community conditions and migration consequences, under differing local circumstances? How do these patterns help explain who comes, who stays, and who moves on?

This research began in Montana in 1972, when data were collected from a random sample of residents of Bozeman to investigate the expectations of newcomers and prior residents, and their levels of satisfaction (Jobes 1987). A high proportion of the initial sample had moved away during the early study. The proportion was so high and the movement in and out so rapid that the phenomenon was labeled "spin-around" migration. Subsequent research substantiated that finding and added details on its dynamics (Williams and Jobes 1990; Williams, Jobes, and Gilchrist 1986). The research evolved to include repeated interviews with panels of residents in 1976 and 1982, analyses of secondary data, and collection of additional information from people to facilitate a fuller contextual analysis of the migration data.

In the early 1970s, a Colorado project surveyed several different types of communities to better understand the consequences of migration (Knop and Bacigalupi 1984). Telephone listings were sampled to trace the appearance, continuance, or disappearance of residential entries over a ten-year period (1970-1980). These tracking data in combination with decennial surveys conducted in the communities enabled comparable analyses of Colorado and Montana communities. The Colorado research was modified to include the study of population turnover.

Case Analyses: Turnover Proportions and Patterns

Bozeman, Gallatin County, Montana
The Setting. Bozeman is the largest city in Gallatin County, on the eastern edge of the Rocky Mountains in southwestern Montana. The city and county have grown continuously since 1900. Growth spurts took place in the 1940s, 1960s, and 1970s, due largely to inmigration (see Table 1). In 1980, Bozeman reached 21,645, an increase of 62 percent in the prior two decades, while the county was 42,865 (65 percent greater than in 1960). Between 1980 and 1990, growth slowed as the percentage of poverty-level residents increased, setting the stage for even higher rates of outmigration.

The region is largely farming and ranching country. Timber and mining are limited. The area is well known as an outdoor recreation and tourist center. Bordering Yellowstone National Park, it has numerous wilderness areas and trout streams. It also has two ski areas and many dude ranches, wilderness outfitters, and other developed facilities catering to tourists.

Montana State University is the largest single employer in the county. Employment in education increased nine-fold between 1950 and 1980. Since 1970, the growth in tourism-related employment has been greater

Table 5.1   Selected Demographic Characteristics,
Bozeman and Gallatin County, Montana, 1950-1980.

Characteristic	1950	1960	1970	1980	1990
Population:					
Gallatin County	21,902	26,045	32,505	42,865	50,463
Bozeman	11,325	13,361	18,670	21,645	22,660
Rural Population:					
Gallatin County	10,577	12,684	13,835	21,220	24,392
Percent rural	48.3	48.7	42.5	49.4	48.3
Percent change from prior decade	10.1	19.9	9.1	53.4	14.7
Bozeman population:					
Percent change from prior decade	30.7	18.0	39.7	15.9	4.5
Percent in same house 5 years		32.2	29.5	24.4	29.7
Percent born in Montana		59.9	57.2	48.6	48.6
Employment:	4,403	1,968	6,985	9,391	11,353
Agriculture	136	152	200	218	344
Educational services	387	1,098	2,443	2,700	2,620
Percent Nonwhite	0.0	3.7	1.3	2.6	3.5
Percent below poverty level			6.3	9.5	25.2

Sources: U.S. Census of Population, Montana, 1950, 1960, 1970, 1980, 1990

than in education. Bozeman and the county have been attractive to migrants, drawn by the natural and social amenities of the area.

Study Methods. Data were collected through personal interviews in 1972, 1976, and 1980. Questions dealt with household demographic characteristics, recent residential and migration histories, reasons for and evaluations of moves, and satisfaction with selected community characteristics. Respondents were randomly selected from the most recent community directories and were included if they had a permanent address, a telephone, were not college students, and indicated they intended to remain.

New samples were drawn for each of the surveys. Respondents from the 1972 and 1976 samples who were still in the area were re-interviewed in subsequent years. Table 2 provides the number of respondents who participated at each phase, and notes some of their demographic characteristics. The response rate of initial participants varied from 83 percent of those successfully contacted in 1972 to 76 percent in 1980.

Selected Preliminary Findings. The first noteworthy finding came in the process of data collection itself. The directories used were only six months old at the time of the first survey (1972), but 27 percent of the numbers sampled had already been canceled or belonged to new residents. This led to a study to determine that turnover was indeed very high: less than one-fourth of the respondents in the 1972 study were still living in

Table 5.2   Sample Numbers and Percents for Survey Years,
            and Selected Demographic Characteristics

A. Numbers in Panels for each Set of Interviews:

Year	First	Second	Third	Total
1972	146			146
1976	107	60		167
1980	80	31	17	128

B. Selected Demographic Characteristics (percents):

	1972	1976	1980
Grew up in Montana	63.0	53.0	61.0
Raised on farm or in small town	63.0	65.0	68.0
Lived in Bozeman 15 years or more	47.0	68.0	65.0
Married	71.0	75.0	75.0
College graduate	39.0	44.0	46.0
White collar occupation	53.0	51.0	48.0
Children away from home	21.0	35.0	51.0

Bozeman just eight years later. Three times as many people left as remained. Table 1 indicates that this is consistent with the percent of residents occupying the same address in Bozeman in 1985 and 1990.

Comparable figures from prior censuses showed that this high rate of turnover had changed little since 1965. While college towns are to some extent special cases, the finding suggested that the phenomenon of high turnover might also be related to the amenities-attractive nature of the community and the area, and not due solely to the high turnover normally associated with a college population. The studies conducted in Colorado provided the comparative base needed to assess this.

Bozeman was thus not a community composed predominantly of the same persons, preferences, and social patterns over any extended period of time (Jobes 1987). Rather, it was a settlement in which a larger number of persons moving in and then out is superimposed upon a smaller core of long-term residents who are responsible for cultural continuity in the community. Some newcomers settle, invest in the community, and in time join this core. Most are less prepared to make that investment and move on. Many of the prior long-term residents also leave, often for similar reasons. Bozeman lacked much of the essential permanence, familiarity, and stability many inmigrants and established residents seemed to expect.

Three Colorado Communities

Research on consequences and patterns of migration had been underway in nonmetropolitan Colorado communities since 1970. Del Norte, Craig and Aspen were the focus of a longitudinal study.

Del Norte is a small (1,674 in 1990), traditional service center located in the high, semi-arid, remote San Luis Valley of south central Colorado. Its economy is based largely on farming and ranching, with some retail trade, limited tourism, and natural resource and social service administration. The area has long been one of the poorest and most Hispanic in the state. Del Norte experienced a steady population decline, with a high rate of net loss, until the 1970s when a modest growth began (see Table 3). Recent inmigrants were a mixture of former residents

Table 5.3   Size and Change of Population in Colorado Communities and Counties, 1970 to 1980.

	Population Size		Percent Change		Percent Change
	1970	1980	1970-80	1990	1980-90
Del Norte, town:					
Population	1,569	1,709	8.9	1,674	-2.0%
Occupied houses	521	576	10.6	611	6.1%
Occupancy rate	3.01	2.97	-1.3	2.74	-7.7%
Rio Grande County:					
Population	10,494	10,511	0.2	10,770	2.5%
Occupied houses	3,070	3,522	14.7	3,930	11.6%
Occupancy rate	3.42	2.98	-12.9	2.74	-8.1%
Aspen, town:					
Population	2,437	3,678	50.9	5,049	37.3%
Occupied houses	846	1,782	110.6	2,551	43.2%
Occupancy rate	2.88	2.06	-28.5	1.98	-3.9%
Pitkin County:					
Population	6,185	10,338	67.1	12,661	22.5%
Occupied houses	2,069	4,519	118.4	5,877	30.1%
Occupancy rate	2.99	2.29	-23.4	2.15	-6.1%
Craig, city:					
Population	4,205	8,133	93.4	8,091	-0.5%
Occupied houses	1,561	2,947	88.8	3,005	2.0%
Occupancy rate	2.69	2.76	2.6	2.69	-2.5%
Moffat County:					
Population	6,525	13,133	101.3	11,357	-13.5%
Occupied houses	2,095	4,578	118.5	4,178	-8.7%
Occupancy rate	3.11	2.87	-7.7	2.72	-5.2%

Sources: U.S. Census of Population and Housing, 1970, 1980, 1990.

returning, and new settlers attracted by the small town atmosphere, ruggedly attractive Western setting, traditions of personal independence, and the low cost of living.

Craig is a medium-sized (8,091 in 1990) regional service center in northwestern Colorado's arid foothills and valleys. It was chosen in 1970 as a stable control community. Two years after data collection began it had a major growth boom as the result of coal mining and an electricity generating plant, doubling the local population in the process. (See similar examples of this phenomenon in Texas, discussed in Chapter 7.)

A subsequent bust in the early 1980s cost the community surprisingly few people, services, or spirit, although most shared in economic hardships. The town has historically been shaped by successive waves of inmigration related to ranching, railroading, coal mining, regional commerce and, more recently, light industry and tourism. Patterns of flexible accommodation to change developed during its history to produce a modern service center that copes creatively with periodic challenges of growth and retrenchment.

Aspen had a permanent population of 5,049 in 1990 and a reputation as a winter sports and year-round cultural and artistic center. It is located high in the west central Colorado mountains, with a large hinterland linked by employment, identity, and social participation. It has been among the fastest-growing communities in the region since its resurrection from the remains of a mining town in the early 1950s. It grew by roughly 1,000 in each succeeding decade. It is a part-time home for many more people than appear in the census, and hosts up to 100 times its permanent population in visitors each year. In addition to a variety of service occupations related to tourism, the area has substantial employment in construction and resource management. Most of the area's considerable wealth originates outside and is brought in by visitors, newer residents, or local artists, athletes, writers, executives, and consultants, all of whom primarily serve outside clienteles.

Lifestyles are intense in Aspen. Devotion to recreation, art, ecological activism, and political liberalism is combined with a mixed spirit of personal autonomy and commitment to the collective good. It's an exciting, awkward, unclear blend of characteristics which ultimately demand consideration and compromise from its citizens. The extended community is ostensibly open, but full participation is informally restricted to those who diligently and patiently work their way into what are actually rather closed inner circles. The difference in image and reality has clear implications both for inmigrants and the established citizens who maintain continuity and control in the flux of population turnover (Clifford 1980).

Study Methods.   Techniques included mailed questionnaires, interviews with a panel of informants, analyses of census data, compilation and analyses of a range of other documentary information, and an assessment of turnover migration obtained through tracking a sample of households over the course of a full decade. Turnover was measured annually by selecting a sample of alphabetic sections of local telephone directories. The sample varied from 7 to 14 percent, depending on community size. All households within the sample sections were tracked yearly from 1970 through 1980. A summary was made of the names which disappeared from the listings, those added, and those which remained. A record was also kept of the cumulative years of appearance for each household from 1970 or from first appearance.

While local phone books have advantages, they also have disadvantages. They list households rather than people, although estimates can be made of the equivalence of the two concepts. They do not distinguish part-time from full-time residents. Nor do they separate names dropped due to death, marriage or conversion to unlisted numbers from those dropped as a result of movement. Listings could be added through divorce, movement of youth out of the parental home into a separate residence within the community of origin, as well as through inmigration. Although migration is the major component of the causes of changes in listings, use of telephone directories would generate an inflated estimate of both inmigration and outmigration.

Correction factors were established for the non-migration components of change. In Craig and Del Norte, four percent of the base was subtracted from the number disappearing from annual listings, and five percent of the numbers appearing in each new listing. The greater dynamic in Aspen required an initial 14 percent reduction in 1970 base numbers to account for part-time residents who maintained telephones, and a seven percent reduction thereafter to new names in the annual listings.

When 1970 and 1980 population and net migration estimates were compared with the censuses and with annual figures generated by the Colorado State Demographer's Office, there was little evidence of any systematic bias in the data, as adjusted and employed in this research. Table 4 provides the approximate annual percents of in- and outmigration and net gains and losses due to migration for each community. The total household net gains for the decade in each community correspond closely to the population net gain figures from the census as shown in Table 3.

Table 5.4 Households Gained and Lost in Three Colorado Towns, 1970-1980 (figures in percents).

	Del Norte			Aspen			Craig		
	Lost	Gained	Change [*]	Lost	Gained	Change [*]	Lost	Gained	Change [*]
1970-71	7	11	4.3	15	23	8.5	4	7	3.3
1971-72	9	11	2.5	20	32	12.2	9	11	1.6
1972-73	6	8	2.4	17	35	18.6	6	8	2.3
1973-74	10	10	0.0	20	26	5.7	8	18	10.3
1974-75	7	6	-0.8	29	35	6.1	15	22	7.2
1975-76	6	9	3.1	26	34	7.7	16	23	7.4
1976-77	11	12	0.7	25	30	5.0	14	22	8.5
1977-78	9	8	-0.7	14	19	4.5	22	48	25.4
1978-79	11	14	3.6	16	19	2.4	17	20	3.7
1979-80	8	12	3.4	12	16	3.5	13	21	7.4
Arithmetic total:			18.5			74.2			77.1
Compounded total: [**]			20.5			104.9			112.2
Percent of 1970 sample remaining in 1980 [**]			56.0			34.0			52.0
Percent of 1980 sample remaining from 1970 [**]			46.0			17.0			25.0
Ratio A: Σ in/out net change [***]			9.76			6.25			4.23
Ratio B: out/1970 base [***]			1.89			4.95			7.32

Notes:

[*] Percent change calculated from absolute numbers.

[**] Calculated from telephone tracking data, adjusted as described in text.

[***] Ratio of total movement to net gain (Ratio A) or 1970 residents (Ratio B), from tracking data.

Selected Findings. In Del Norte through the 1970s and Craig until 1973, the rate of turnover migration was substantial, averaging between five and ten percent annually. The ratio of total moving households to the number of households at the start of the period indicated that almost two households turned over for each one that had been present in 1970.

As the inmigration rate increased, so did outmigration. Net gain or loss drastically understated the flow of people. More rapidly growing communities had as many as 20 to 35 percent of the households new each year, with net growth of ten percent. Aspen had a ratio of five turnover households by 1980 for each household present in 1970. In Craig it exceeded seven to one. The ratio increased regularly with net growth.

Integrating newcomers while adjusting to turnover migration presented a dual challenge. Few long-term residents worked at managing migration consequences. Political power shifted away from established residents who sought to preserve local traditions and continuity. In Del Norte and Craig, only about one-half of the original 1970 households remained a decade later. In Craig this was equivalent to just one-fourth of the 1980 population. In Aspen, only one-third of the base 1970 population was left by 1980, or about one-sixth of the number of households in 1980.

Dynamics of Community and Migration Assessments
Montana

Responses to a series of perception items were compared for Bozeman newcomers and oldtimers. The items addressed the effects of migration expectations on community evaluations and compared changes over time in expectations and evaluations. Newcomers were defined as persons who had lived in the county less than five years when they were first contacted. They are compared with oldtimers, and continuing residents are compared with each other, between each pair of time periods. Successive cohorts of newcomers and oldtimers are also compared over time.

The community perceptions fall into four categories. The first includes indicators of general satisfaction. The other three include assessments of basic public services, private goods, services, and opportunities, and opinions about planning and community management processes. Summary data are presented in Table 5 with appropriate tests of significance. Lower mean scores indicate greater agreement with questionnaire items, which may indicate satisfaction or dissatisfaction, depending on item wording.

Table 5.5   Mean Satisfaction for Selected Topics, Montana Panels and Subsamples.

Panel or Subsample	N	A. General Satisfaction			B. Public Service Satisfaction:		
		Overall	Helpful	Growth	Schools	Roads	Garbage
Oldtimers	246	2.08	2.63	2.69	2.08	3.31	2.27
Newcomers	59	2.56	2.96	2.43	2.64	4.05	2.63
t =		2.00*	1.1	1.02	2.80**	2.96**	2.77**
1972 Panel	145	2.35	2.84	2.51	2.44	3.71	2.75
1976 [2nd]	60	2.02	2.75	2.75	2.08	3.43	2.22
1980 [3rd]	17	1.76	2.35	2.51	2.48	3.13	2.03
F =		2.38**	1.86*	0.68	0.27	2.43**	3.04**
Oldtimers:							
1972	107	2.26	2.82	2.58	2.11	3.41	2.46
1976	96	2.04	2.60	2.73	2.06	3.40	2.26
1980	71	1.82	2.45	2.77	2.07	3.10	2.06
F =		4.27**	2.56**	0.33	0.08	1.78*	4.30**
Newcomers:							
1972	39	2.59	2.92	2.56	2.79	4.23	2.89
1976	11	2.64	3.27	2.41	2.18	3.72	2.27
1980	9	2.33	2.71	2.37	2.55	3.66	2.00
F =		0.21	0.77	0.42	2.19**	2.50**	4.41**

		C. Private Services			D. Planning		
		Good Shopping	Need Health	Need Jobs	Oppose Scientific	Favor Local Only	Oppose State/Fed
	N						
Oldtimers	246	2.46	2.75	2.14	2.30	2.30	3.01
Newcomers	59	2.80	2.67	1.85	2.03	2.45	3.34
t =		1.13	0.88	3.22**	1.36	4.24**	2.66**
1972 Panel	145	2.83	2.51	1.90	2.22	2.60	3.35
1976 [2nd]	60	2.54	2.86	2.25	2.14	2.30	3.24
1980 [3rd]	17	2.19	2.79	2.19	2.12	2.06	2.75
F =		5.36**	4.11**	4.08**	0.29	1.93*	2.17*
Oldtimers:							
1972	107	2.62	2.51	1.91	2.40	2.60	3.24
1976	96	2.57	2.86	2.33	2.28	2.29	3.07
1980	71	2.12	2.87	2.14	2.23	2.01	2.73
F =		5.23**	4.70**	4.16**	2.18*	6.85**	4.26**
Newcomers:							
1972	39	2.90	2.59	1.77	2.05	2.95	3.79
1976	11	3.09	2.55	1.91	2.07	2.32	3.42
1980	9	2.00	3.25	2.13	1.96	2.08	2.80
F =		3.71**	2.50**	0.55	1.28	5.63**	5.89**

Notes:
* p < .05; ** p < .01
Likert scales range from strongly agree (1) to strongly disagree (5).

Responses to general satisfaction items indicated that oldtimers perceived more personal happiness between 1972 and 1980, and that residents had become more helpful during that period (Panel A). Newcomers felt less favorable than oldtimers, and were less likely to identify significant change. Oldtimers were more positive about the community than newcomers (Panel B). Newcomers saw more positive changes in public services. Each wave of newcomers reported that school operations, road maintenance, and garbage collection were better than had the last wave. Except for the latter, oldtimers did not sense significant service improvements.

The responses concerning private goods, services, and opportunities again showed oldtimers more satisfied than newcomers (Panel C). Some differences, however, were not statistically significant. Newcomers who remained through the period also gave more positive evaluations by the time of the 1980 survey.

The final set of items pertained to community planning (Panel D). Residents were not favorable toward planning and became less so throughout the study period. No consistent differences emerged between oldtimers and newcomers. Each group significantly reduced support for scientific planning. Both new and established residents grew increasingly opposed to external state and federal planning for the local area, while increasing their support for local control.

The majority of comparisons between groups in Table 5 show significant differences. Theoretically and statistically, if no differences existed in the expectations of oldtimers and newcomers, and if no changes had occurred either in actual characteristics of the area or in the ways that respondents perceived the communities over time, no differences between categories would be expected. How then should the differences be interpreted?

Oldtimers generally viewed community conditions more favorably than newcomers. Since they live in the same place, the perceived differences are primarily due to differing expectations. If there were convergence over time between oldtimers and the then-longer-term newcomers, it would suggest that inmigrants were becoming assimilated. Alternatively, it might suggest that those who persisted in their differing perceptions were among those more likely to have left. In fact, the data do show a convergence over time with particular patterns that support both of these complementary explanations. Newcomers who redefined conditions and expectations to resemble oldtimers were more likely to be satisfied with the community and remain. Those who were not were more likely to leave.

This process of accommodation and assimilation was not a one-way street. If each subsequent group of newcomers had shown relatively more satisfaction with the community than prior cohorts, it would suggest that local conditions were becoming more consistent with their general expectations. This in turn would argue that newcomer orientations were also influencing the community and its oldtimers.

The data in Table 5 show this pattern. Evidence of newcomers affecting oldtimers is found in the oldtimer time-series data. A pattern similar to that of the newcomers, which showed growing satisfaction over time among oldtimers, implies both that local changes were occurring and that at least some newcomers had influences agreeable to oldtimers. This is indicated, with the same magnitude of change among oldtimers as with subsequent groups of newcomers and with retested members of the 1972 panel.

Colorado

The findings from Colorado complement those from Montana. The data came from a 1981 survey mailed to a random sample of households in the three communities and their hinterlands. Sample proportions ranged from 7 to 14 percent, with the smaller towns having the higher sampling frames to balance for statistical analyses. In Craig and Del Norte, respondents were drawn from the most recent phone books, none more than seven months old. These directories included home mailing addresses. A random sample of active post office boxes was drawn for Aspen.

Questionnaires were mailed with a postcard to be checked and returned if the household were no longer in the community, were part-time, or chose not to participate. Those indicating they had moved away from the area, and those returned as undeliverable, were tallied and deleted from the sample, as were responses obtained from part-time residents. After follow-up mailings, completed questionnaires were received from between 60 and 65 percent of the households remaining in the study sample.

Table 6 provides salient sample features for comparison with the Montana research. Seven to nine percent of the households in the two towns sampled from phone books were no longer in the community. In Aspen, 21 percent of the boxholders had moved by the time of the survey. While these average less than the 27 percent which could not be contacted in the Montana research, they still indicate that the phenomenon of spin-around migration was also present in Colorado.

Newcomer-Oldtimer Migration Dynamics. The Colorado sample was also divided into newcomers and oldtimers, using the same five-year residence criterion. Responses concerning evaluations of the community and community issues were compared. Tests of statistical significance were conducted within communities, between communities, and for all communities pooled, on variables that complemented the Montana study.

The full data are available on request from the authors. These include the proportions of newcomers and oldtimers who indicated that they were

Table 5.6   Selected Colorado Community Survey Mailing and Sample Characteristics.

A. Mailing Details	Del Norte	Craig	Aspen
Percent:			
undeliverable/moved	7	10	21
declining participation	10	9	6
no response	25	29	34
Final Sample sizes	52	106	65
B. Sample Characteristics			
Origin (where born):			
Percent in same town	31	9	3
Percent same region	12	4	2
Percent other Colorado	12	28	6
Percent metropolitan	20	40	73
Length of residence:			
Five years or less	15	44	31
Six to fifteen years	27	19	34
Percent married:	67	80	52
with children at home	31	42	17
with children away	50	31	23
Percent college graduate	42	35	69
Percent occupied as			
manager or professional	38	37	46

considering a move.   These data permit comparison of migration intentions with results reported in other related research.

Reasons for moving were classified as (1) predominantly economic, (2) balanced between economic and social or natural amenities, (3) primarily social or natural amenities, and (4) primarily personal ties or other idiosyncratic responses. Responses varied significantly. Craig had the highest proportion reporting primarily economic reasons (38 percent as compared to 23 and 7 for Del Norte and Aspen). Del Norte had more reporting personal reasons (34 percent, compared to 19 and 12 percents for Craig and Aspen). Aspen had the highest proportion reporting primarily amenities reasons, at 55 percent, compared to only 17 and 13 percent in Craig and Del Norte.

In comparing old and new residents' reasons for moving, only Aspen showed a significant difference, with slightly more old than new residents having come primarily for amenities (59 and 47 percents, respectively), and many more new residents having come for mixed economic and amenities reasons (47 percent of new compared to just 17 percent of old), and fewer for personal reasons (five percent of new and 15 percent of old). The greatest proportion who gave primarily amenities reasons came between 1968 and 1977, after which the preponderance came for mixed economic and amenities reasons. This was most distinctive in Aspen but present also in the other towns. Among those oldtimers who had arrived prior to 1967, very few even in Aspen came primarily for amenities; most gave economic or personal reasons. It is mostly "midtimers" of 6 to 14 years residence that affect the oldtimer-newcomer difference in importance of amenities.

No statistically significant patterns were found when reasons for moving were compared to intentions to leave, among either oldtimers or newcomers. Post-arrival adaptations make new considerations more relevant than original expectations in explaining inclinations toward another move. Two patterns stood out: (1) among newcomers, those who came primarily for economic reasons, particularly to Del Norte or Craig, were most apt to be thinking of leaving; and, (2) among both new and old residents, those least inclined to leave had come primarily for amenities.

No differences between communities were found in terms of the proportion who were thinking of leaving. About 40 percent of each sample said that they were considering moving away. Since the proportion of newcomers was greater in Craig and Aspen, it had been expected that more people would be considering another move, on the assumption that newcomers were more mobile. It was further expected that Aspen would have the highest proportion who were thinking of leaving.

In Montana a high proportion of newer residents had come primarily for natural amenities and became discouraged by the practical realities of economic conditions (Williams 1982). The situation in the Colorado towns was more complicated. Newcomers were not more likely than prior inmigrants to have come primarily for amenities, although this consideration was important. Practical limitations (such as community conditions and economic opportunities) would have been more apparent in the Colorado communities, since they are smaller and less diverse than Bozeman.

Del Norte is the most limited in both amenities and jobs and it was the only one to show a significantly higher proportion of older residents considering a move: 75 percent of the new residents and 34 percent of older residents were considering moving. When all towns are pooled, there is a significant tendency for more newcomers to be thinking of leaving. Just under half the newcomers and more than a third of oldtimers were considering a move. The potential for movement was great for both categories.

To complicate matters further, the Bozeman interviews had shown that many residents who had not indicated any inclination to leave sometimes suddenly did so. This was particularly the case among more recent arrivals. This rapid change is likely to be more typical of newcomers who have less integration with and investment in the community than oldtimers.

Demographic Characteristics. Background information on the age, education and income of the respondents in the Colorado communities shows that each variable differed significantly between the towns. Del Norte had the highest proportion of older adults, followed by Aspen and Craig. Aspen had the highest level of education, with two-thirds of the sample having a bachelor's degree or more, and also the highest level of income, with almost half of the families making more than $30,000, in 1980. Craig ranked second on these characteristics with Del Norte a distant third.

There were neither surprises nor many differences when oldtimers and newcomers were compared. Migrants to all places tended to be younger than those already there. Significant differences in education and income were less consistent. Only in Del Norte were newcomers better educated. Only in Aspen were newer inmigrants less well-to-do than established residents. When communities were combined a significant curvilinear relationship with income emerged: newer residents were most likely to have middle incomes, with oldtimers more apt to earn either more, or less.

Community Satisfaction Patterns. Table 7 provides summary measures across communities and across residents. Aspen data reflect orientations typical of an area high in recreational and cultural amenities, while Craig reflects those of a larger regional service center that had recently experienced a growth boom, and Del Norte reflects those of a small, traditional, and poor community. Responses reflect relative expectations as much as objective facts of the community's attributes. Data show no difference in satisfaction with public service offerings, although objectively Craig's were superior and Del Norte's quite limited. Aspen respondents were the most satisfied with commercial and professional services, while Craig actually possessed the fullest range of these services.

Table 5.7 Summary of Colorado Satisfaction Differences and Preferences among Towns and between Newcomers and Oldtimers. [Date in Appendix Table A]

Satisfaction with:*	Differences Between Towns	Newcomer-Oldtimer Differences
Quality of Life and Social Climate		
B1 Overall	Aspen most satisfied, others similar	No significant difference
B2 Helpfulness, friendliness	No significant difference	No significant difference
B3 Feel "at home" in community	Aspen and Del Norte most satisfied	Newcomers slightly less satisfied
B4 Wholesome for children	Aspen least, Del Norte most satisfied	Del Norte: newcomers less satisfied
Local Infrastructure		
C1 Public services	No significant differences	Craig: Newcomers less satisfied
C2 Safety/Security	Craig least, Aspen most satisfied	Craig: Oldtimers more and less satisfied
C3 Teacher quality	No significant differences	No significant differences
C4 Recreation/Entertainment	Aspen most satisfied, others similar	Craig: newcomers less satisfied
C5 Commercial/Professional services	Aspen more, Del Norte least satisfied	Craig: newcomers less satisfied
C6 Local cost of living	Craig least, Del Norte most satisfied	Newcomers less satisfied in all towns
C7 Job opportunities	Del Norte least satisfied, others similar	No significant differences
Political Processes		
D1 Ease of local agreement	Aspen least, Craig most satisfied	Aspen: Oldtimers less satisfied
D2 Closed/Oligarchic decision-making	Craig less, Aspen most satisfied	Craig: newcomers less satisfied
Management practices		
E1 Appreciation of planning processes	Craig most, Del Norte least supportive	Aspen: Newcomers more supportive
E2 Improved local information flow	Craig most agreement, others similar	Craig: Newcomers more agreement
E3 Need to change power distribution	Aspen most, Del Norte least agreement	Craig, Del Norte: Newcomers more
E4 Population growth limitation	Aspen most, Del Norte least supportive	Newcomers slightly more supportive

Notes:

*   Indicates topic and item number in Appendix Table A

**   Significance level noted under item in Appendix Table A.

Aspen residents appeared to have the specialized services they most wanted (acupuncturists, gourmet restaurants, specialized sport and art supplies, for example). They did not expect, perhaps did not even want, many typical local services such as discount stores, fast-food chains, full service building supply centers, and the like. Aspenites were apparently content to go outside the community for such services. While specific patterns of helpfulness and friendliness differed between the communities (for example, Craig residents were more outgoing and Aspenites valued privacy), the data show no significant differences between them in these aspects of general satisfaction with the communities.

Newcomer-oldtimer data show patterns consistent or complementary with those observed in Montana. While Colorado showed fewer significant differences between groups, this was partly for conceptual and partly for methodological reasons. In general, the data in Table 7 show newcomers to be somewhat less satisfied with those aspects of their community that are emphasized by popular conceptions. It is likely that the differences reflect their respective expectations, which appeared to be more idealistic among newcomers than oldtimers.

Community size, for example, is one basis for expectations. Del Norte newcomers seemed more disappointed with the community as a place to raise children than did oldtimers, but objective indicators would suggest that it offered at least as wholesome an environment as did the other communities. Newcomers to Craig were less satisfied than oldtimers with public, commercial and professional services, recreation, and entertainment, while objectively Craig's facilities in these respects were superior to the other two. Craig's reputation as a multi-state regional service center, and the improvements during its boom period (which newcomers lacked the perspective to appreciate), help explain these differences.

While newcomers were somewhat less satisfied with their communities in some regards, there were not many large differences within or across the communities. The ones which bear mention occurred most often in Craig, the largest of the three and not known as a high-amenities town. Aspen showed few differences. These data suggest that inmigrants who remained long enough to have been included as newcomers (in contrast with what the locals called "transients") had brought or acquired more realistic expectations, and so did not differ greatly in their evaluations.

Outmigration Inclinations. This study was oriented by the expectation that community conditions for which newcomers' expectations had been most unrealistic would be most prominent in outmigration inclinations. Newcomers are more likely to be uninformed or misinformed about local conditions, and to have less opportunity to change them to their liking. It was thus expected that newcomers would be more dissatisfied and more likely to be thinking of moving. This should particularly be the case where there were clear newcomer-oldtimer differences. The evidence was mixed, suggesting qualifications to assumptions and relationships between expectations, satisfactions, and future migration intentions.

The Colorado data showed that almost half of those newcomers were thinking of leaving, but more than one-third of longer-term residents were also. These data indicate that dissatisfaction had little bearing on migration intentions, and that newcomers and oldtimers showed different patterns in this regard. Table 8 summarizes migration intentions patterns.

Among newcomers, two categories of variables explained most of the variation in migration intentions: dissatisfaction with various aspects of the social amenities of the community, and local income or cost of living. Those who were least satisfied with the social climate of the community were from two to three times more likely to be thinking of moving on than were those who were most satisfied. Those least satisfied with economic conditions were twice as likely to be thinking of leaving.

The degree of satisfaction with local structural considerations such as service offerings, political processes, or even job opportunities, did not make much difference in newcomer's thoughts of leaving. They behaved as though such conditions were givens, and there were more important matters, such as amenities or their own niche in the community's future. Such community attributes as public and commercial services, safety, and job opportunities were apparent and likely to be accurately perceived by inmigrants very quickly.

Local political processes were presumably accepted by newcomers as mainly the prerogative of established residents (but, see Stinner and Paita's analyses on this point in Chapter 10). The exception concerned the flow of information about community conditions, which is both a social and political concern. Newer residents who were least satisfied with this aspect were also least likely to be thinking of moving. It may well be the case that they had made a commitment and knew that they needed access to information if they were to eventually become active and responsible participants.

There were some clear differences in the effects of levels of satisfaction on migration intentions. Oldtimers and newcomers who were

Table 5.8   Summary of Differences in Migration Intentions by Personal Characteristics and Community Evaluations between Newcomers and Oldtimers.   [Date in Appendix Table A]

	Newcomers	Oldtimers
Demographic Characteristics		
A3 Age	No significant difference	Younger twice as likely to consider move
A4 Education	No significant difference	No significant difference
A5 Family income	Lowest twice as likely to consider move	Middle income most likely to consider move
Quality of Life and Social Climate		
B1 Overall	No significant difference	Lower slightly more likely to consider move
B2 Helpfulness, friendliness	Least 3 times more likely to consider move	Least twice as likely to consider move
B3 Feel "at home" in community	Least twice as likely to consider move	Less satisfied 3 times more likely
B4 Wholesome for children	Least 3 times more likely to consider move	Least twice as likely to consider move
Local Infrastructure		
C1 Public services	No significant difference	Least 4 times more likely to consider move
C2 Safety/Security	No significant difference	Least twice as likely to consider move
C3 Teacher quality	No significant difference	No significant difference
C4 Recreation/Entertainment	No significant difference	Least twice as likely to consider move
C5 Commercial/Professional services	No significant difference	Least 4 times more likely to consider move
C6 Local cost of living	Least twice as likely to consider move	No significant difference
C7 Job opportunities	No significant difference	No significant difference
Political Processes		
D1 Ease of local agreement	No significant difference	Least twice as likely to consider move
D2 Closed/Oligarchic decision-making	No significant difference	Least twice as likely to consider move
Management practices		
E1 Appreciation of planning processes	No significant difference	No significant difference
E2 Improved local information flow	Least twice as likely to consider move	No significant difference
E3 Need to change power distribution	No significant difference	Most 3 times more likely to consider move
E4 Population growth limitation	No significant difference	No significant difference

Note:

* Indicates topic and item number in Appendix Table A

dissatisfied with the social climate were several times more likely to be thinking of leaving, but there the similarity ends. Among established residents, middle-income and younger citizens were more likely to have been contemplating leaving. While their views of local living costs and job opportunities seemed unimportant to them, these issues were significant to newcomers.

Perceptions of community services were a major consideration among the oldtimers. Longer-term residents who were least satisfied with public and commercial services were four times more likely to be thinking of leaving than were the most satisfied oldtimers, and further dissatisfactions with public safety and recreational opportunities made them several times more inclined to move. Strong dissatisfaction with ease of obtaining agreement, oligarchic decision-making, and power allocations, left oldtimers two to three times more likely to contemplate leaving than those who were most satisfied on these dimensions. None of the views on these issues showed any significant influences on the outmigration inclinations of newcomers.

The reasons for these differences are probably based more on differing expectations and circumstances than on differing evaluations of local conditions. The patterns do not correspond to significant differences in newcomer-oldtimer satisfaction. Newcomers who survived initial experiences may have become more realistic about what they felt they had a right to expect than did many more-established residents.

Regression Analyses. Multiple regression controlled statistical interactions and conceptual overlap effects while examining the relative importance of these variables in explaining the differences in outmigration inclinations of newer and older residents. With listwise deletion of missing data, stepwise inclusion of independent variables was the first step, with forced entry of the remaining variables in order of their ability to explain the variance remaining. Several variables had to be recoded to give response categories a consistently logical order. Reasons for moving were changed to an economic-mixed-amenity emphasis, with natives and those coming for personal reasons assigned to the mixed category.

Table 9 summarizes the regression results. The single most important variable influencing newcomers' migration intentions was their view that the community was not very helpful and friendly, followed by relatively low income. These two variables together explained about 26 percent of the variance in migration intentions. All other variables in combination added another 26 percent to the explained variance. In order of their

Table 5.9   Multiple Regression Summary of Intentions for Moving
with Main Explanatory Variables for Colorado Newcomers and Oltimers.

A. Newcomers

Variables	Multiple Regression Entry Method	Beta	t - sig	R*	R2*
Satisfied with helpfulness, friendliness	Stepwise: 1	-0.38	0.002	0.39	0.15
Income	Stepwise: 2	-0.32	0.009	0.51	0.26
Satisfied with wholesomeness	Forced: 3	-0.20	0.10		
Use of improved information	Forced: 4	-0.17	0.16	0.72	0.52
Feel at home	Forced: 5	-0.17	0.19		

[plus remainder, Beta < 0.15 and/or p > 0.20]

B. Oldtimers

Variables	Entry Method	Beta	t - sig	R*	R2*
Feel at home	Stepwise: 1	-0.22	0.0001	0.42	0.17
Satisfied with commercial and/or professional services	Stepwise: 2	-0.23	0.009	0.50	0.25
Change who holds power	Stepwise: 3	0.19	0.02	0.54	0.29
Age	Stepwise: 4	-0.20	0.02	0.57	0.32
Reason for moving to community	Stepwise: 5	-0.19	0.02	0.60	0.36
Satisfied with wholesomeness	Forced: 6	-0.14	0.11		
Better use of planning	Forced: 7	-0.13	0.14	0.65	0.43

[plus remainder, Beta < 0.10 and/or p > 0.20]

Note:
   Each subsequent item value includes contribution of previous item(s).

contribution these secondary variables include: concern with community wholesomeness; perception of the importance of good information flows in the community; and, not feeling at home in the community.

Among the oldtimers, thoughts of leaving were associated first with not really feeling at home in the community, followed by dissatisfaction with commercial and professional services, perceptions of the need for change in the community power structure, being younger, and having originally come for economic reasons. These variables together explained 36 percent of the variance in oldtimers' outmigration inclinations. Other variables increased the explained variance only to 43 percent.

Oldtimers who were thinking about leaving appeared to feel that they were not as well integrated as they would like to have been, that they were disappointed with community services, or, for some, frustrated with the economic promise they had envisioned when they moved. Oldtimers who were thinking of leaving did not indicate disappointment with the other general amenities of the community, nor in the faster-growing places did they seem to be bothered by most of the changes that had taken place (as had been the case in the Montana studies).

Discussion of Comparative Findings

These data suggest that at first, newcomers are primarily consumers of the community. They expect basic services and the ability to support themselves. They also hope for particular natural and social amenities, including personal acceptance and a sense of of belonging. If disappointed, they are inclined to move on. But if their basic needs are satisfied and they feel accepted, they increasingly contribute to the community's welfare and identify with it. Their influence may come in religious, athletic, or other voluntary associations, or simply through friendships in neighborhoods or workplaces. In the process, their understanding of and accommodation to local conditions grow with their sense of control over their circumstances and satisfaction in the community (Bellah et al. 1985; Toney et al. 1985).

As this occurs, many inmigrants make a commitment to the community and their future in it. As they make adaptive concessions, the community responds to their influences. Those who feel insignificant may be compensated by specialized consumption benefits. Some adjustments of personal expectations are also likely. Many may not be able to avoid disappointment with their acceptance, influence, or access to community benefits, and consider leaving. With any precipitating event, such as divorce, graduation, or a job change, they are set in motion.

These dynamics favor high-amenity smaller communities in some ways, and larger nonmetropolitan cities in others. A spirit of openness, acceptance and responsiveness is an important social amenity which, when coupled with a good natural setting and recreational opportunities, creates the potential for a satisfying life, even in the absence of full-scale private and public service structures (Brooks 1974; Corbett 1981; Louv 1985).

To the extent that social and natural amenities are locally limited, larger towns have the advantage of being able to offer compensating public and private services. Both high-amenity smaller towns and larger service centers are likely to have reputations which less distinctive smaller towns lack. These reputations serve both to encourage selective inmigration and provide basic early orientations for newcomers. Migrants believe that they can more or less know what to expect of the community.

Large service centers and high-amenities smaller towns attract disproportional numbers. Their unrealistic expectations contribute to the high volume of spinaround migration that characterizes these communities. That many people leave so quickly indicates a relative absence of cohesion, though it also clarifies what is necessary for those who wish to settle. Other types of towns may have ambiguous or particularistic expectations of their citizens, and thus suffer an image disadvantage. They may attract few optimistic people but at a higher marginal cost. Local mediocrity, ambivalence and ambiguity are thus sustained as the human capital moves on.

Conclusions

Nonmetropolitan places may experience substantial inmovement and outflows well beyond what is apparent from net population change. Turnover migration often involves the movement of from four to ten times as many people as would be indicated by net migration data. When net migration exceeds five percent a year, this likely results from as much as one-fourth of the community's population being newcomers, and one-fifth outmigrants, in any given year. Even in ostensibly stable communities and times, the turnover rates may often involve more than ten percent of the total population gained and lost annually.

There is little reason to doubt that most of those who come and go quickly are people disappointed with their choice, perhaps because expectations had been unrealistic. The data in this chapter were derived from those who stayed long enough to begin settling in. Newcomers and old-timers saw the local situation differently at first, but a convergence process began through which old and new residents influenced each other. This produced both community change and adaptation on the part of newcomers, as they redefined the local situation.

The Bozeman data suggested that many who came with unrealistic expectations had chosen on the basis of social and natural amenities. While most people must eat to enjoy life, many recent inmigrants are probably more interested in enjoying life. If they have even a modest meal and after-dinner pleasures await, they may be satisfied. Assuming that basic living needs are met, those most oriented to the social and natural amenities of a place will be most satisfied and least likely to be thinking of leaving.

Longer-term residents also want to feel at home in their community, but they expect, in addition, a voice in community affairs, and to a greater extent than do newcomers. Lacking this, they want good private and public services. When deprived of both, they thought in terms of leaving.

Although there were differences in rates of flow, characteristics of people, and levels of satisfaction between types and sizes of communities, the differences were less than might be expected. Within each type there was evidence that newcomers and oldtimers alike expected the comfortable, accepting, mutually supportive human processes associated with the social climate of nonmetropolitan communities. These considerations became less important as community size increased.

Life in smaller communities involves economic and service tradeoffs for access to desired social and natural amenities. This tradeoff makes such towns reasonable places to live for those who are prepared to accept this reality. If not, they were more likely to have moved on. Basic sustenance and socioemotional benefits appeared to be both a reality and an ideal for smaller town residents, whether of a traditional agricultural service village, a regional service center, a small city famed for its natural, social, and cultural amenities, or a larger city combining these attributes.

Chapter 6

Reasons for Nonmetropolitan Moving to the Inland Northwest and North Central States[1]

John M. Wardwell
Washington State University

Corinne M. Lyle
University of Idaho

Introduction

In Chapter 2, Cook demonstrated that rural and nonmetropolitan county growth through net inmigration continued well into the early 1980s in Oregon and Washington, long past the time when the nonmetropolitan migration turnaround had come to an end nationally. State growth in the Pacific Northwest is dominated by population change on or near the coast, where more than three-quarters of the population is located. This chapter describes the processes of nonmetropolitan migration into the Inland Northwest region of the Northern Rockies, and specifically within an area of northern Idaho and eastern Washington that lies on the western edge of the Rocky Mountains (see Figure 1). Migrant motivations and perceptions in this high-amenities area are compared with those found in rapidly growing nonmetropolitan counties of the North Central States. Perceptions of the preferred future rates and patterns of economic growth for the region are then also compared to similar research conducted in states of the North Central Region, by (1) metropolitan-nonmetropolitan origins of migrants, (2) selected background traits, and (3) reasons for moving to the respective nonmetropolitan destinations.

Growth Trends

Consistent with Cook's findings for the Pacific Northwest, population growth in nonmetropolitan Idaho and Washington slowed dramatically after the 1970s. All but one of the counties in this study had net outmigration for the 1960s and subsequently displayed the classic turnaround pattern in the 1970s (Table 1). Collectively the Idaho counties grew from a net migration rate of +2.9 in the 1960s to an astonishing rate of 49.3 in the turnaround decade, dropping back to +5.9 in the early 1980s. The corresponding counties in Washington changed from net outmigration ranging from -7.7 to -18.7 in the 1960s to positive net migration rates between 32.8 and 56.9. Two of these counties subsequently experienced net outmigration in the first half of the 1980s (data in Table 1).

Table 6.1   Population Growth and Net Migration, Inland Northwest, 1960-1985.

Area	Population Size		Population Change			Net Migration		
	1980	1985	1960-1970	1970-1980	1980-1985	1960-1970	1970-1980	1980-1985
Idaho	943,935	1,005,000	6.9	32.4	6.4	-6.3	15.4	-0.2
Benewah	8,292	8,600	3.2	33.1	3.7	-5.6	26.5	-1.6
Bonner	24,163	26,000	-0.2	55.3	7.6	-4.7	41.2	2.5
Boundary	7,289	7,700	9.7	14.4	5.6	-11.2	25.7	-0.1
Kootenai	59,770	67,200	19.5	69.2	12.4	11.5	60.2	7.8
Subtotal	99,514	109,500	9.9	59.0	10.0	2.9	49.3	5.1
Washington	4,132,204	4,384,100	19.6	21.1	5.8	8.7	11.4	1.7
Ferry	5,811	6,100	-6.0	59.0	4.8	-14.3	45.7	-1.2
Pend Orielle	8,580	9,100	-12.9	42.2	5.7	-18.7	32.8	2.8
Spokane*	170,535	182,200	20.9	45.8	6.8	* *	* *	* *
Stevens	28,979	30,100	-2.7	66.5	3.7	-7.7	56.9	-1.4
Subtotal	213,905	227,500	14.9	48.5	6.3	* *	* *	* *
Study Area	313,419	337,000	13.2	51.7	7.5	* *	* *	* *

Notes
* Spokane County, exclusive of City of Spokane;
   for comparison, the population data for Spokane City are as follows:
         171,300   172,100   -6.1   0.5   0.5

** Net migration data cannot be separated for Spokane City and the remainder of the county. The very low population growth rate for the city (0.5 percent) indicates that natural increase for the city is barely offsetting substantial net outmigration. Accordingly, the reported county net migration was probably accruing entirely to the non-city portion. If this is correct, the resulting rate of 19.1 for 1970-80 and -0.3 for 1980-85 underestimates net migration to the remainder of the county, because migration from the city of Spokane may also be adding to the population in the remainder of the county.

The slowdown and reversals in population growth rates came about through a reduction in migration to nonmetropolitan counties that was part of the nationwide trend (Beale and Fuguitt 1985) and an increase in movement from nonmetropolitan counties. At the national level these changes are generally attributed to the recession of the early 1980s, which hit nonmetro counties harder, leading to slower growth of incomes and higher unemployment (Beale and Fuguitt 1985; Engels 1986). Little research was conducted in the Northwestern States after the late 1970s (Cook 1986; Swanson 1984, 1986). Even less research was done in the Inland Northwest region of Washington and Idaho (Campbell 1986; Leon 1984).

Study Design [2]
The Context of Migration
In the spring of 1982, the survey on which this chapter is based was conducted in the eight rapidly growing counties of the Inland Northwest (see Figure 1). It focused on recent migrants to that region, and on a smaller control group of long-term residents. Because the economic recession was extreme in those counties at the time of the study, the survey included questions designed to determine if reasons for moving had changed since earlier research was conducted in North Central States, in 1977 at the height of the nonmetropolitan migration turnaround. Those questions may now shed some light on the unexpected slowdown of population growth in the study counties and in the nonmetropolitan Northwest generally. Since rural and nonmetropolitan areas are once again struggling in the midst of a second chronic recession, these results may also provide insight into the motivational dynamics accompanying movement to areas that have subsequently experienced lower levels of prosperity than had been anticipated.

Regional Character
The Inland Northwest is integrated as an agricultural and natural resource area by the city of Spokane. It is the only city of over 50,000 within or close to the region, and the only metropolitan area of its size or larger in the northern United States between Minneapolis and Seattle, a distance of over 1,500 miles. Spokane serves as a trade center and transfer point for an area of more than 70,000 square miles with a population of just over 1.7 million. People moving through and goods being shipped into and out of the region, or between Seattle, 300 miles to the west, and points east generally pass through Spokane. One additional

Figure 6.1   Inland Northwest Study Area

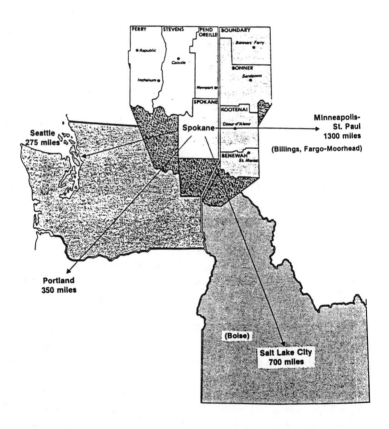

small metropolitan area, Boise, lies 390 miles to the south; Salt Lake City, 700 miles southeast of Spokane, is the next larger metropolitan area. Spokane thus serves as the dominant metropolitan center for a vast area.

This is an area of natural scenic beauty and abundant recreational land. Parts of six national forests are located within the area. The economy is based on natural resources, centering on lumber and wood products, some agriculture and mining, and recreation-tourism. Recreational opportunities are available in the forests and mountains as well as in the four large lakes within the area and the numerous smaller lakes, rivers and streams. Hunting, fishing, boating and swimming, whitewater rafting, skiing and snowmobiling during the four seasons are within easy reach of all who live in the area, and to vacationers and tourists from outside the region.

Objectives

The primary purpose of the study was to understand why the population of the Inland Northwest had grown so much more rapidly during the 1970s than could be justified on the basis of employment and other economic opportunities in the region. As Adamchak (1987) has argued with respect to the North Central States, to which results in this chapter are compared, the Inland Northwest is a high-amenities region in which noneconomic motivations should be prominent in accounting for the unexpected growth.

Documenting the reasons for population growth through migration in the Inland Northwest was a primary purpose of the research, and is discussed in this chapter. The primary purpose however was to compare these reasons with those found in other rapidly growing regions of the country. This comparison is essential to assessing the national character of the migration turnaround and to an identification of the conditions under which renewed growth may once again come to characterize rural and nonmetropolitan America. It will also better identify the distinctive character of the Inland Northwest by examining the differences in the reasons people gave for movement to this region. This is the principal object of this chapter.

Data Collection

The study design used a two-part sampling frame. The first consisted of a telephone screen to locate migrants from outside the area who had moved into the area within the past 10 years, and a small sample of longer-term residents. They were asked to participate in a telephone interview designed to collect information on their residence and migration history and reasons for moving to (or remaining within) the Inland Northwest. The telephone interview was then followed by a mail questionnaire. The Total Design Method developed by Dillman (1978) was followed throughout, resulting in a final return rate of 85.5 percent for the mail questionnaire.

A systematic sample of nearly 6,000 was first drawn from published telephone directories of each community within the eight-county region, excluding the city of Spokane. The sample was divided in half, and just over 3,000 calls were made. Of these, 1,496 resulted in businesses, wrong numbers, disconnected numbers, persons physically unable to participate, or no answers. This left 1,512 eligible households. We interviewed each recent migrant and one out of every six long-term residents. From those eligible, 117 refused to be interviewed and another 26 refused the mail questionnaire. All who had moved to the area since 1972 and who agreed to participate were interviewed (563); 134 people were interviewed of the 806 long-term residents contacted. These 697 households were then asked to fill out and return a written questionnaire in addition to the telephone survey.

Thus, 697 (of 840), or 83.0 percent, of the eligible households completed the telephone survey and agreed to accept the written questionnaire. Of these, 596 (85.5 percent) returned the questionnaire. This high rate is due to the prior telephone agreement, to the use of a carefully designed and systematically pre-tested questionnaire, and the rigorous follow-up procedures prescribed by Dillman (1978). Because of the necessity of matching telephone responses with mail questionnaires, the study sample is reduced to that for which both are available. Of this final sample, 481 (81 percent) are defined as migrants and the balance (115) are long-term residents. Slightly over one-half (53.4 percent) of the migrants came from a metropolitan location, and the rest from another nonmetropolitan area. Migrants and residents are equally divided between the two states.

Migrants were younger, better educated, and had higher incomes. Consistent with national trends (Beale 1980), they worked in professional services, public administration, manufacturing, and trade. Residents were more apt to be employed in extractive industries, although a high percent of residents have also found employment in the rapidly growing services, trade, manufacturing, and public service sectors (data in Table 2).

Table 6.2 Sample Characteristics (figures in percents).

Characteristic	Metro Origin	Migrants Nonmetro Origin	Residents
Age			
Under 35	44.5	46.9	13.2
36 to 59	45.0	40.7	48.1
Over 60	10.5	12.4	38.7
Education			
High school graduate	91.1	89.5	76.8
College graduate	26.6	28.5	12.5
Sex and Marital Status			
Male	50.4	44.1	47.7
Married	86.3	79.9	71.1
Type of current residence			
Farm	10.8	8.7	14.4
Nonfarm acreage	47.2	35.9	34.2
Other, country	11.7	17.9	14.4
Town or city	30.3	37.4	36.9
Employment status			
Employed full or part time	62.6	55.2	44.8
Unemployed	19.1	26.4	14.0
Retired	15.3	12.9	38.6
Industry (labor force only)			
Professional	24.2	21.1	19.8
Manufacturing	15.3	13.5	12.3
Wholesale or retail trade	13.0	10.8	17.9
Admin, finance, ins, real estate	16.7	16.8	12.2
Constr, transp, comm, utilities	14.9	14.6	5.6
Agriculture or other extractive	4.2	7.6	28.3
Income in 1981			
Over $15,000	62.1	64.8	53.9
Prior residence			
Pacific Northwest	46.5	70.5	n.a.
California	35.0	2.5	n.a.
Other, West	7.8	15.7	n.a.
Other region in U.S.	10.7	11.3	n.a.

Migration to the Inland Northwest: Reasons for Moving

Most of our understanding of the causes and consequences of recent nonmetropolitan migration patterns comes from research conducted in other regions of the country. The survey on which this chapter was based is the only research of this nature conducted in the Inland Northwest region (Rowe 1984; Kershaw 1985; Shearman 1983; Rowe and Wardwell 1987). Similar surveys were employed in the Ozarks (Dailey and Campbell 1980), New England, Pennsylvania (DeJong and Gardner 1981;

DeJong and Sell 1977), the Southeast (Christenson et al. 1983), and the North Central States (Sofranko and Williams 1980; Voss and Fuguitt 1979). Few national studies were conducted (Fuguitt and Zuiches 1975; Long and DeAre 1980). As noted, very little research was done in the West, and virtually none in the Pacific Northwest (Wardwell and Cook 1982). The survey instruments used in this research were specifically designed to replicate research in the North Central States, where the most detailed and precise measures of the complexity of migrant motivations had been developed (Sofranko and Williams 1980; Voss 1980).

Quality of Life Motivations

Research conducted in other parts of the country had shown that noneconomic reasons for moving seemed to have been more important than economic reasons (Williams and Sofranko 1979). In most studies, when asked why they had moved, recent movers from metropolitan areas were more likely than nonmetropolitan movers to give noneconomic reasons for their decision to move. These included factors related to their families and friends, physical environments, or community structure and characteristics, and other aspects of the quality of life.

This difference by origin was particularly important in accounting for the nonmetropolitan migration turnaround. The turnaround took place because of an increase in the movement from metropolitan to nonmetropolitan areas (as well as because of a decrease in nonmetropolitan outmigration). Changes in movement between nonmetropolitan counties could not have had an effect upon the relative growth rates of nonmetropolitan and metropolitan categories, because it is only a form of movement within one of the two categories.

The economic context of migration changed radically in the early 1980s. The nation sustained the worst economic recession since the Great Depression. From 1978 to 1983, median household and family income declined (U.S. Bureau of the Census 1988). Even in families in which the wife was in the paid labor force, constant dollar income declined from 1975 to 1982. The impact was more severe in nonmetropolitan areas than in metropolitan areas in both employment declines and real income declines (Beale and Fuguitt 1985; Fuguitt 1985).

Noneconomic factors had been most frequently cited to explain the appearance of the nonmetropolitan migration turnaround (Dillman 1979; Zuiches and Price 1980). However, the turnaround from population loss to population gain through positive net migration in rural areas occurred in nearly all subregions of the country and all sizes of counties, and for most categories of migrants (Beale 1975; Wardwell and Brown 1980; Zuiches and Rieger 1978). The pervasiveness of this change across types of places and migrants suggested that structural convergence between urban and rural areas had gone far enough to sustain an equilibrium in movement patterns between them (Long 1981). Opportunities for employment and economic advancement had become more similar. As a result, movement from one type of place to the other was being roughly balanced by an equal movement in the opposite direction. This situation would persist until further change upset the balance of economic opportunities (Williams 1981). The recession played just that role in the migration trends of the 1980s.

In a situation of economic equilibrium, patterns of greater movement from one type of place to another would have to be explainable by noneconomic causes. This is the essence of the "deconcentration hypothesis" as set forth by Frey (1988). If convergence had developed among places with respect to economic determinants, other factors related to quality of life and residential preferences would become more important in influencing the decision to move and the choice of location (Zuiches 1980).

Residential and other lifestyle preferences are one set of noneconomic motivations for migration (Dillman 1979; Zuiches 1981). This component includes accessibility to parks and recreational facilities, convenience to work, low risks of crime, good air and water quality, childraising considerations, and cost of living (DeJong and Sell 1977). These were associated with community size in the minds of migrants and expressed in the form of preferences for communities under 50,000 in size (Dillman and Dobash 1972; Fuguitt and Zuiches 1975).

It is for this reason that by far most of the effort devoted to explaining the nonmetropolitan migration turnaround of the 1970s concentrated either on the role of changing residential preferences, or on the role of changes in the social infrastructure of smaller communities and unincorporated areas. Both approaches also noted the importance of growth in employment opportunities and the removal of other economic constraints upon migration to smaller-sized destinations, and some noted as well the effects of income growth on migrants' hierarchies of values (Brown and Wardwell 1980; Hawley and Mazie 1981; Williams 1982). However, interactions between income levels or income growth, and migration motivations, were not emphasized in the explanation of a phenomenon that appeared to be primarily noneconomic in nature.

As a consequence, Williams (1982) was one of the few who

made any attempt to identify the economic conditions under which the nonmetropolitan migration turnaround could or would continue through the 1980s. The continuing importance of economic motivation was recognized by all. Most of the attention was simply devoted to documenting and understanding the motivations of those who had given noneconomic factors as the most important reason for the move they had made.

There were thus no deductions drawn as to what the impact of a deep economic recession (which, in fact, would be felt more severely in rural and nonmetropolitan areas) would be on the direction and volume of net migration flows between metropolitan and nonmetropolitan areas. Given that the economic recession gripped the Inland Northwest as it did much of the nation by the time of this research, there was thus a strong interest in the extent to which changes in reasons for moving that might be attributed to the recession could be observed. For that reason, the survey instruments were designed so as to be able to replicate surveys of nonmetropolitan migration that had been conducted earlier, prior to the onset of the recession and during the peak of the net migration movement to nonmetropolitan areas.

Prior research had also shown that when respondents were asked two questions about their move rather than one, they frequently gave quite different answers to these questions. In the past, researchers had asked only the question, "Why did you move?" Since the onset of the migration turnaround, respondents have been given the opportunity to separately answer, "Why did you choose to leave your prior residence?" and, "Why did you choose this place to live, rather than other places to which you could have moved?" Long-term residents have still been asked the single question, "Why have you chosen to stay in this area?"

In the present study, the answers given to reasons for leaving prior residence, choosing current residence, and remaining in current residence, were obtained in the telephone survey and coded into 65 categories, which were then grouped into six major classifications. This part of the research replicated the procedures used in a study conducted in the North Central States in 1977 (Sofranko and Williams 1980; Williams and McMillen 1980).

The findings were similar to those reported in the prior research, but important differences were also found. These data are presented in Tables 3 and 4. With respect to the value of asking two questions rather than one, the results strongly confirmed the conclusions of the prior research (Williams and McMillen 1980). In that study, 45 percent of migrants to nonmetropolitan counties in the North Central Region gave different kinds of answers to the two questions of reasons for leaving prior residence and reasons for choosing present location. In this study, 58 percent did so. Significant information on the total decision-making process would be lost if only the single, "Why did you move?" question had been asked.

The relative importance of employment-related and other economic reasons compared to quality of life reasons for moving was also similar. Nearly one-third of the migrants to the Inland Northwest cited employment or other economic reasons, both for leaving their former community (31.9 percent) and for selecting their current location (29.5 percent). While these figures were higher than found in the North Central study (25.8 and 20.9 percent, respectively), the two studies were similar in that in both cases only a minority of respondents gave economic reasons for their move (data shown in far right columns of Table 3).

Slightly more respondents in the Inland Northwest study cited either social or physical aspects of the environment as reasons for leaving their place of origin, both in the general sample of migrants (36.8 percent compared to 30.6 percent in the North Central study) and in the subsample of working-ages only (40.3 compared to 36.0). This difference was greater that that for reasons for choosing destination (38.0 and 26.1 for the general sample, 38.0 and 26.2 for the working-ages subsample). The difference contrasted with the results found for social ties to family, friends in the destination area, or to a previous residence in that area. These reasons were more important in the North Central study (47.7 percent) than in the Inland Northwest (26.0 percent).

The corresponding data for residents are not shown in Table 3 in order to reduce detail in the table. For comparison, 19.1 percent of residents gave employment and other economic reasons when asked why they had decided to remain in the region. One-fourth cited social ties, and over half (53.9 percent) identified aspects of the environment of their communities as their primary reasons.

With respect to the effect of type of origin upon reasons for moving, this research confirmed the findings of prior studies and also shed additional light on the distinctive nature of migration to the Inland Northwest. These data are shown in the four columns to the left of Table 3. In both studies, migrants from metropolitan areas were significantly less likely to give employment-related reasons than quality of life reasons, and they were less likely to give economic reasons than were migrants from other nonmetropolitan areas. This difference, however, was more pronounced in the North Central study.

Table 6.3 Reasons for Leaving Prior Residence, and for Choosing Current Location, by Type of Migrant and Type of Origin, North Central Region, 1977, and Inland Northwest, 1982.

A. Reasons for Leaving Prior Residence

	Metro Origin		Nonmetro Origin		Both Origins	
	North Central	Inland Northwest	North Central	Inland Northwest	North Central	Inland Northwest
Reasons:			All Migrants			
Economic	24.4	22.8	46.4	42.4	25.8	31.9
Social ties	7.4	14.6	13.0	10.2	17.9	12.4
Environment	40.2	44.7	19.3	28.8	30.6	36.8
Retirement	17.2	6.9	9.7	9.3	14.0	8.4
Other	10.8	11.0	11.6	9.3	11.7	10.5
Total	100	100	100	100	100	100
N = ( )	(500)	(247)	(208)	(215)	(708)	(462)
			Migrants Aged 18-59 Only			
Economic	34.6	27.0	56.6	46.6	41.8	36.2
Social ties	6.3	12.2	8.2	8.6	6.9	10.5
Environment	43.7	48.0	20.1	31.6	36.0	40.3
Retirement	4.2	3.1	1.9	5.7	3.5	4.3
Other	11.2	9.7	13.2	7.5	11.8	8.7
Total	100	100	100	100	100	100
N = ( )	(332)	(196)	(159)	(174)	(491)	(370)

B. Reason for Choosing Destination Location

	Metro Origin		Nonmetro Origin		Both Origins	
	North Central	Inland Northwest	North Central	Inland Northwest	North Central	Inland Northwest
Reasons:			All Migrants			
Economic	21.4	29.0	41.5	31.4	20.9	29.5
Social ties	45.4	29.9	31.4	22.4	47.7	26.0
Environment	29.8	35.7	21.8	41.7	26.1	38.0
Retire/Other	3.4	5.4	5.3	4.5	5.3	6.5
Total	100	100	100	100	100	100
N = ( )	(500)	(238)	(208)	(211)	(708)	(449)
			Migrants Aged 18-59 Only			
Economic	30.3	31.5	50.3	35.1	36.4	33.2
Social ties	38.5	27.9	24.0	18.4	33.4	23.5
Environment	27.6	33.5	20.7	43.1	26.2	38.0
Retire/Other	3.6	7.1	5.0	3.4	4.0	5.3
Total	100	100	100	100	100	100
N = ( )	(333)	(197)	(159)	(174)	(492)	(371)

The Natural Environment and Community Ties

The most significant difference between these results and those of prior research had to do with the relative importance to migrants of ties to their community of destination compared to the importance of characteristics of the natural environments around that community. Migrants to the Inland Northwest were far more likely to cite environmental factors as important to their moves than were migrants to nonmetropolitan counties in the North Central States, particularly with respect to reasons given for choice of destination: in the Inland Northwest data, about 40 percent of nonmetro-origin migrants identified aspects of the environment, in both the general and working-ages samples; the corresponding proportions in the North Central States ranged between one-fifth and one-third. Social ties were consistently more important to migrants to nonmetropolitan counties of the North Central States than to migrants to the Inland Northwest.

The issue of the relative importance of various reasons was addressed by asking whether selected factors had "a lot" or "a little" or "no importance" to their decision to move to the area. These data further indicate the great importance of aspects of the environment to people of the Inland Northwest. More than 75 percent of the migrants and 91 percent of residents indicated that scenic beauty had "a lot" of importance in their decision to move to (or remain in) the area; 60 percent of migrants indicated that lifestyle and leisure opportunities had a similar level of importance for them (as did 75 and 72 percent of residents, respectively).

Relationships Among Reasons

Table 4 presents the reasons given for choice of destination by reasons for leaving the prior residence, for both this study and the study of migration to the North Central States. In both studies, the data are restricted to those who gave separate reasons for the two decisions. In analyzing the importance of asking two questions, the interest is in those who did not give the same reason for both questions. For those who did give the same reason, it can be argued either that they in fact only made one decision, or that there would be no loss of information if only one question had been asked.

Consider the individual who explains leaving because of a company transfer, and then says that the destination was determined by the company. The only decision made was to accept the transfer: no choice of destination separate from the decision to leave was made. Some individuals had left their origin because they were frightened of crime, bothered by air pollution, or that the pace of life was uncomfortable. Some then indicated that they had chosen their destination because of lower crime, cleaner air, or a quieter, slower pace of living. These individuals also can be said to have moved for a single reason. The interest here is in those who made two separate decisions, and thus the analysis in Table 4 is restricted to those who gave different answers to the two questions.

Table 6.4   Reasons for Destination Selection by Reasons for Leaving Origin,
North Central States, 1977, and Inland Northwest, 1982.*

Reasons for leaving origin	Reasons for Destination Selection						
	Employ-ment	Social ties	Environ-ment	Retire/Other	Total	N	%
Employment							
North Central	55.8	32.4	11.8	0.0	100	63	13.8
Inland Northwest	37.9	15.3	42.0	4.8	100	124	29.6
Social ties							
North Central	n.a.	n.a.	n.a.	n.a.	n.a.	3	0.7
Inland Northwest	11.1	33.3	51.1	4.5	100	90	21.5
Environment							
North Central	12.4	40.8	42.0	4.8	100	215	47.2
Inland Northwest	29.0	26.6	39.1	5.3	100	169	40.3
Retire/Other							
North Central	2.0	58.2	26.5	13.3	100	175	38.3
Inland Northwest	5.6	44.4	44.4	5.6	100	36	8.6
Total							
North Central	11.7	46.6	32.4	9.3	100	456	100
Inland Northwest	25.7	26.3	43.0	5.0	100	419	100

Note
*   These data are presented only for those who did not give the same exact reason
    for leaving place of origin and for choosing destination. The procedures followed
    to remove simultaneous decision-makers are identical to those employed
    in the North Central research (see Williams and McMillen 1980).

Employment. Migrants to the Inland Northwest who were motivated to leave their place of origin for employment and other economic reasons were significantly more likely to cite environmental factors as reasons for choosing this area than were those in the North Central study (42 percent and 11.8 percent), and only half as likely to identify social ties to their destination (15 percent and 32 percent in the North Central study). Thus, for migrants who were primarily oriented toward leaving for economic reasons, the ties-environment difference between regions was sharply accentuated, when reasons for destination choice are examined.

Social Ties. Too few respondents in the North Central study gav e ties as the reason for leaving to permit a comparison (N = 3). In the Inland Northwest study, environmental factors weighed even more heavily in the destination choice of migrants who gave social ties as their reason for leaving, with about half (51.1 percent) giving reasons related to the environment of their current residence as the primary explanation for their choice of a community.

Environment. Only 7 percent of the migrants in the North Central study who mentioned aspects of the environment of their community of origin as their reason for leaving identified employment-related or other economic reasons for choice of destination. In the Inland Northwest research, 29 percent did so. In the North Central States, 41 percent of these migrants identified social ties as most important to their choice of destination, whereas in the Inland Northwest, 26 percent of these migrants gave social ties as their primary reason for destination choice.

Retirement and Other Personal Motivations. Once again, social ties were less important and environmental reasons more important in the Inland Northwest than in the North Central study. Among people who gave retirement as their reasons for leaving, equal numbers (44 percent) gave ties or environment reasons, but in the North Central study, these proportions were 58 and 26 percent, respectively. However, the frequency on which the Inland Northwest proportions are based is too small ($N = 36$) to permit reliable conclusions with regard to differences between the two regions by these reasons for leaving places of origin.

Discussion of Migrant Motivation Findings

The differences observed in the two studies between environmental and reasons related to social ties are consistent with differences in the settlement histories of the two regions. Metropolitan origin migrants to North Central nonmetropolitan counties are more likely to have social ties in those destinations, because the urban centers of the region were more likely to have been settled by within-region, rural-to-urban migration. Metropolitan centers in the West, by contrast, were more likely to have been settled through interregional, intermetropolitan migration. Western metropolitan-origin migrants to nonmetropolitan destinations within the Western Region have fewer opportunities to define their search space on the basis of pre-existing social ties. In the West, the choice of a destination within the region may preclude the possibility of choosing on the basis of family and other ties to a rural community, because those ties are less likely to exist.

It is likely that distance also plays a role in mediating the influence of social ties on destination choice. Prior research indicates that economic factors are more likely to predominate in long-distance migration. Data from the North Central study (Roseman and Williams, personal communication; Sofranko and Williams 1980) stress the short-distance intrastate and intraregion origins of the majority of metropolitan to nonmetropolitan migrants in their research. In the Inland Northwest, only one-half of the migrants originated in the same or an adjacent state, and one-fourth moved from California; one-sixth of the migrants came from another region of the country. The distances involved in these latter two categories are greater than would be involved for the vast majority of North Central migrants in the earlier study.

Migration and Orientations Toward Future Economic Growth

Attitudes toward economic growth are an important subject in their own right, and are further explored in Chapters 8 and 9. They can have much to do with residential satisfaction following the move and thus with future mobility intentions. An area's ability to retain its recent migrants may depend in part on the fit between the way those migrants view the subject of economic growth and the subsequent economic experience of the area, as was emphasized in Chapter 3 on the Mormon Culture Region. The research on which this chapter is based also sought to replicate findings with respect to relationships between reasons for moving to a nonmetropolitan region and migrant orientations toward subsequent economic growth of that region. Earlier research on this relationship had also been conducted at the peak of the nonmetropolitan migration turnaround in the North Central States.

The Gangplank Syndrome

There is a widespread belief that recent migrants to nonmetropolitan areas, such as the Inland Northwest, which are high in natural amenities and recreational opportunities are opposed to economic growth and expansion in the future, particularly if it would bring in more new people. As the American Society of Planning Officials described this view,

> Each new resident hopes he will be the last one. Called the "gangplank" or "last-one-in" syndrome, these early arrivals want to pull in the gangplank and shut the door on further growth and development, realizing that if others follow, the amenities which they sought may be endangered (Quoted in Voss 1980, p. 86).

It is commonly believed that the "gangplank" syndrome is particularly true for those moving from metropolitan centers, and for those moving primarily to gain greater access to the natural environment and other desired attributes associated with low population density. Voss critically examined this hypothesis with data gathered from recent migrants to and long-term residents of rapidly growing nonmetropolitan counties in the Upper Great Lakes Region, in a survey that was also conducted in 1977.

He found that the data did not support the hypothesis. Recent migrants were no less likely to favor continued economic growth than were residents, and migrants did not differ in their economic growth orientation by type of origin. In fact, while differences between groups were not statistically significant, migrants consistently were slightly more likely to favor growth than were residents. Nonmetropolitan-origin migrants were more likely to be more strongly pro-growth than were either metropolitan-origin migrants or long-term residents (65.2 percent, compared to 54.0 and 51.2 percent, respectively).

These slight differences by origin persisted across controls for education, employment status, and income. That is, while each of these variables may have had an independent effect on growth orientations, they did not fully account for the effects of origin. For example, both higher income migrants and residents were more likely to be strongly pro-growth than were lower income respondents, but higher income nonmetropolitan-origin migrants were still more likely to strongly favor growth than were either higher income metropolitan-origin migrants, or higher-income long-term residents.

Voss did not report growth orientations by reasons for move. In both the North Central States such as those of the Upper Great Lakes and in the Inland Northwest, reasons vary significantly by origin [see Table 3]. It is thus possible that differences by origin in growth attitudes may be due to the associated differences in reasons for moving.

Findings

In Table 5, several indicators of economic growth attitudes for categories of migrants and residents are examined. While very few respondents wanted either rapid or no economic growth, far more preferred moderate growth to slow growth: 61 percent of migrants (and 54 percent of residents) said they favored moderate economic growth, compared to only 28 percent and 34 percent of the two groups who favored slow economic growth.

Thus in both the the Inland Northwest and the Upper Great Lakes, well over half of the samples were moderately-to-strongly pro-growth (66 and 59.6 percent respectively). Recent migrants were slightly more likely to be pro-growth than were long-term residents. In Panel B of Table 5, responses to six items tapping growth orientations are compared for metropolitan and nonmetropolitan-origin migrants and for residents, with

Table 6.5 Economic Growth Attitudes of Migrants and Residents.

| | Migrant Origins | | Long-term |
	Metropolitan	Nonmetropolitan	Residents
A. Economic Growth Rate Preferred			
Rapid	7.0	4.2	1.8
Moderate	58.4	62.6	54.1
Slow	28.0	27.6	34.2
None	6.6	5.6	9.9
Total	100	100	100
N = ( )	(243)	(214)	(111)
Chi square not significant			

| | Migrant Origins | | | | Long-term | |
	Metropolitan		Nonmetropolitan		Residents	
B. Percent favoring: *						
New businesses	69.9	(77.8)	74.7	(79.0)	73.0	(74.7)
Urban expansion	42.6		48.4		51.3	
Sounder economic base	36.9		41.9		43.5	
New people, new ideas	63.9	(62.7)	65/4	(77.0)	48.7	(68.6)
More jobs	40.2		44.7		45.2	
People with liberal ideas	30.9	(35.9)	18.9	(36.9)	27.8	(29.8)

Note: figures in parentheses are corresponding percents
from Upper Great Lakes study (Voss 1980).

C. Pro-growth score	2.84	2.94	2.90
F not significant			

comparisons to the Upper Great Lakes research results presented where available. An index of these responses was obtained by summing across response categories to obtain pro-growth scores; these scores are presented in Panel C.

None of the differences between groups in Panels B and C were statistically significant. Three of these items, dealing with new businesses and new people, were sufficiently similar to three of the five items that Voss scaled to allow us to compare results. The similarities are striking, as is shown in Table 5. These data offer no support to the gangplank hypothesis. Newcomers to remote nonmetropolitan areas, whether in the Inland Northwest or the Upper Great Lakes, showed no strong tendency to want to be the last ones in, and tended to favor moderate economic growth to about the same extent as did long-term residents of the areas.

Table 6 compares scores on the pro-growth index for migrants and residents by social and economic status and by satisfaction with the move. Education made no difference. Employment status had some effect, with the employed having a slightly stronger pro-growth orientation. Income also had an effect, with higher income groups of both migrant and resident categories showing the higher scores. These results are also consistent with those reported by Voss (1980, p. 106).

Table 6.6   Pro-growth Scores by Selected Characteristics of Migrants and Residents.

Characteristic	Migrants	Residents
Education		
Less than high school	2.85	2.97
High school or more	2.88	2.73
Employment status *		
Employed	3.02	3.00
Unemployed	2.90	3.19
Not in labor force	2.42	2.74
Income *		
Less than $15,000	2.73	2.77
$15,000 - $25,000	2.94	2.56
More than $25,000	3.20	3.70
Regrets at making move?		
Yes	2.75	2.89
No	2.91	3.38
Was move considered:		
Temporary	2.98	n.a.
Permanent	2.88	n.a.
May return to origin?		
Yes	2.82	n.a.
No	2.92	n.a.

Note
  * F significant at $.01 < p < .05$

None of the three indicators of satisfaction in Table 6 showed significant relationships, although there was a consistent pattern of more satisfaction with higher scale scores. This was most notable in the resident column, with those who had no regrets at having stayed showing a higher pro-growth score (3.38) than those who did regret their decision (2.89). While much weaker, the pattern was also present for migrants who had no regrets (2.91) and who did not anticipate a return to their place of origin (2.92). This pattern was also found in the Voss data, in response to a question as to whether the respondent planned to move again (1980, p. 107).

Finally, the interaction between growth attitudes, origin, and reasons for moving is examined in Table 7. Economic growth attitudes differed with reasons for moving, but not significantly. Those giving economic reasons placed more emphasis on moderate or rapid growth, regardless of origin (77 percent), than did those moving either for noneconomic (62 to 65 percent) or mixed reasons (70 percent). In the mixed reasons category the largest difference was in preference for slow growth by origin. The difference was in the opposite direction from that suggested by the gangplank hypothesis: nonmetropolitan origin migrants were more likely to prefer slow growth (37.8 percent) than were metropolitan origin migrants (23.3 percent).

Table 6.7 Growth Attitudes by Reasons for Moving and Type of Origin.

Reasons for Moving:

Economic growth rate preferred	Economic		Mixed		Noneconomic	
	Metro Origin	Nonmet Origin	Metro Origin	Nonmet Origin	Metro Origin	Nonmet Origin
Rapid	2.9	1.9	13.3	2.7	6.7	5.7
Moderate	74.3	74.1	56.7	56.8	55.6	59.3
Slow	20.0	24.1	23.3	37.8	30.3	26.0
None	2.9	0.0	6.7	2.7	7.3	8.9
Total	100	100	100	100	100	100
N = ( )	(35)	(54)	(30)	(37)	(178)	(128)

Chi square not significant

Pro-growth score

	3.27	3.27	3.00	3.05	2.73	2.76

F significant at $.01 < p < .02$

The slight preference for rapid growth on the part of those moving for economic reasons was also evident when comparing pro-growth scores:

a monotonically increasing score from noneconomic through mixed to economic reasons is shown in Table 7, with the differences moderately significant (F < .02). Origin made no difference within reasons categories. Newcomers were supportive of economic growth regardless of origin and largely regardless of reason for moving. These findings thus contradict the gangplank hypothesis of nonmetropolitan migration growth in the popular view, and support the findings reported for the Upper Great Lakes region.

Conclusion

The findings reported in this chapter have an indirect bearing on the equilibrium hypothesis that has guided the research (Wardwell 1977, 1980). This hypothesis argues that the turnaround took place more because of then-increasing similarities between rural and urban places than because of their residual differences. That in turn has implications for the motivations of migrants moving to more remote areas. If, as the "gangplank syndrome" suggests, these migrants were moving primarily to escape from the conditions of urban living (Blackwood and Carpenter 1978), they would be expected to be resistant to future social and economic expansion. If, on the other hand, the turnaround was due more to the extension to rural areas of urban forms of social organization (Hawley 1971), we would expect recent migrants to be more supportive of the continuation of those conditions that made it possible for them to move to their nonmetropolitan destinations.

That is what this chapter has sought to demonstrate, first with the data on the relatively nonchanging priority given to noneconomic quality of living reasons for moving, and then with data on the support for new businesses, further urban expansion, more new people with new ideas, and the other correlates of moderate economic growth in the future. Thus, these data lend further, albeit indirect, support for the equilibrium hypothesis.

It thus seems essential to seek to maintain the social infrastructure developed over the past few decades in rural areas in order to retain current residents and to attract newcomers, when economic circumstances once again allow residential preferences free sway over migration decisions. This research, and that in other sections of the country, has shown that people had been moving to smaller-sized towns and cities and into the open countryside in large part as an expression of their desires for the qualities and unique attributes found in rural America (Christenson et al. 1983). But they were doing so in the belief that it was not necessary for them to give up the basic material qualities of living found in the larger society.

If the social infrastructure were allowed to deteriorate, so that roads and highways no longer offered safe and convenient access to work, shopping, and outdoor recreation, or if modern telecommunications were to cause rural areas to once again fall outside the mainstream of modern society, as Dillman (1985) has argued, or if the variety of goods and services available in nonmetropolitan America were once again to become secondary and inferior to those available in metropolitan centers, Americans would once again respond to those differences by moving back into or near to those centers. Retention of population growth gained in the 1970s thus requires attention to the social infrastructure of rural communities as well as to the number and mix of employment opportunities.

Unexpected findings have been reported in other research with these data (see Chapter 9), indicating that reasons for moving had more of an effect on perceived gains and losses associated with the move than did the effects of the economic recession. These findings also have a strong bearing on the future migration trends affecting nonmetropolitan America. Mobility data from the Current Population Survey of the U.S. Bureau of the Census (1988) indicated that significant net outmigration from nonmetro areas was once again occurring at a rate comparable to that of the 1960s or even the 1950s. It is widely believed that this was primarily due to the lingering rural recession. The results reported in this chapter support this belief, but these results also have important implications for both the perceived quality of living of the new nonmetropolitan outmigrants in their most recent metropolitan destinations, and for the future of migration patterns when economic conditions once again change.

The results suggest that even during the depth of the economic recession in 1982, respondents who had moved to the study area for primarily quality of living rather than economic reasons chose to emphasize the gains they felt they had made in access to and characteristics of the physical environment, social aspects of the community and personal lifestyle.

These findings correspond to other indications that the changing economic and population trends in the 1980s are closely linked. There have been suggestions that the reduced growth of rural and nonmetropolitan areas, and the return of net nonmetropolitan outmigration were in part due to another shift in residential preferences and values. It has been suggested that some portion of the slower nonmetropolitan growth is due to a process by which newly-arrived metropolitan movers discover that conditions in smaller communities and in the open countryside of unincorporated areas are not to their liking, and return to more urban locations.

These alternative explanations are undoubtedly true of some individuals and families. However, the results reported in this chapter do not support the suggestion that, since the late 1970s, there has been any widespread or general shift in values. Rather, they suggest that the downturn in growth is due to changing economic conditions. They suggest that values supporting residential preferences associated with the nonmetropolitan migration turnaround have persisted, while reduced economic opportunities were constraining the ability of migrants to implement those values by remaining in or continuing to move to nonmetropolitan destinations.

This in turn implies that the emphasis of research on rural and nonmetropolitan living in the remainder of the 1990s should be on the conditions under which economic fortunes may shift in favor of smaller-sized places rather than divert scarce research resources toward additional surveys of current residential preferences. This research has demonstrated that so-called noneconomic migration motivations are in fact heavily dependent upon the context of economic opportunities. It appears that the economic context will have more to do with the vitality of rural and nonmetropolitan America through the remainder of this century than will possible changes in the values and preferences of urban and rural dwellers.

Notes

1. The research reported in this chapter was supported by Project 0354, Washington State University College of Agriculture and Home Economics, Agricultural Research Center, and by Project R-871, University of Idaho College of Agriculture, Agricultural Experiment Station, contributing projects to Western Regional Project W-118.

2. For a full description of the research methods and study area, see Rowe and Wardwell 1987.

Chapter 7

Social Change in Resource Development Communities

James H. Copp
Texas A&M University

Edward C. Knop
Colorado State University

Introduction

Resource development communities are particularly susceptible to boom and bust cycles over which they have little control. Cycles are generated by national, and now international, variations in supply and demand. Some may be locally induced by the rapid exploitation and early exhaustion of a resource, most dramatically oil. Mineral resource depletions proceed more slowly, while other resources are renewable with careful management, such as timber, rangeland, agricultural land, fisheries, or outdoor recreation sites. Variations in resource development can have severe community impacts, including massive inmigration imposing scarcities of facilities and services, followed by outmigration and the resulting excess capacities, demoralized leadership, and apathy.

In this chapter, a number of resource-based communities are examined, communities which have undergone growth or decline in response to varying patterns of resource exploitation. Three kinds of resource development, oil and gas, coal (with and without associated electric generating plants), and tourism, are contrasted with no development, in a control community. The communities impacted by oil and gas are in Texas, while those impacted by coal and tourism are in Colorado and Montana. The control communities with no resource development are in Texas and Colorado.

The focus of the study is on the community and institutional context within which migration flows take place in response to externally initiated resource developments. This is in contrast to Chapter 5, where the focus was on population turnover and its impacts on community stability. While the study communities do not represent a systematic sampling of resource communities in the West, their conditions may be generalized to similar communities located throughout the semi-arid regions of Wyoming, Utah, Idaho and New Mexico, as well as in Colorado, Montana and Texas.

Contrasts in the Impact Process

Resource development impacts vary with the resource being exploited. Oil and gas developments are largely unplanned. They occur when new fields are discovered, or when prices encourage exploitation of known fields. Much exploration takes place in a trial and error fashion, and at the beginning of an oil boom, no one knows anything certain about the amount or disposition of the resource. Impact analyses are not required. Production potentials and findings are private or are unknown. Developments proceed in an abrupt, boom or bust fashion, in as little as a few weeks and rarely over more than a few years. Community excitement is high and rumor is rife. Rational planning is difficult and restraint gives way to excitement. It is easy to sustain the illusion of good times (Olien and Olien 1982).

Coal development involves fewer uncertainties. Exploration can be very exact, particularly with strip mining. Amounts and locations are known. Social and economic impact analyses are generally required. The demand tends to vary with the business cycle and interacts with the price of alternative fuels, such as natural gas. Development proceed deliberately. There may be lay-offs and shutdowns, but in general there isn't the unpredictability nor the high excitement that accompanies oil and gas developments.

Power plant development responds to the demand for electricity. Development issues concern not "Whether?" but rather "When?" If demand flags, building may be postponed for years or decades, but once the plant is built it will operate in a sustained fashion. The cost of the physical plant is so great that it can hardly be idled. As with coal development, power plants require social impact analyses before construction. Feasibility analyses are also conducted because of their exceptionally high cost.

The most significant community aspect of power plant building may be the contrast between the boom employment of a brief construction phase and the much lower level of employment throughout the longer operational phase. Construction typically involves over a thousand workers, many relatively unskilled, while operations extend over a period of thirty years and require only a few hundred workers, many of whom are technicians. These contribute a stabilizing, relatively affluent element to the community (Murdock and Leistritz 1979).

Tourism and recreation involve controlled resource exploitation oriented toward promoting and preserving the touristic attraction. Tourism and outdoor recreation are only somewhat responsive to the business cycle. Sites compete in a national and even international complex of markets. The demand may be sustained for decades. Sustained long-term demand is dependent on consumer tastes and preferences, and on community moral attitudes toward such attractions as gambling and drinking, or other recreational forms defined as deviant by local communities.

Stagnating communities present a more problematic situation. They typically manifest an indifference to attempts to mobilize development (Copp 1984c). Leaders appear frustrated in their attempts to mobilize community resources, with much activity remaining privatized within institutional spheres such as the family, church, or profession. Cooperation seems to be the exception rather than the rule. Gradual, protracted decline is the general tendency. The process is made harder to reverse by the absorption of accumulated physical capital and resources and the difficulty in retaining talented, ambitious residents.

The type of resource must thus be controlled in comparing impacts across communities, because consequences are highly differentiated by type of resource. At the same time, some impacts of boom and bust cycles may be relatively invariant across types of resource developments. These impacts must be particularly noted since they would be helpful in projecting the expected effects of resource developments other than oil and gas, coal, or tourism, on migration flows into and out of rural communities in the West.

The Impacted Communities
Oil and Gas Boom Towns

Caldwell and Giddings are small towns in central Texas about 35 miles apart. Both are county seats and were largely dependent on agriculture prior to the oil boom of the late 1970s. They had been the same size until the 1940s, when the greater proximity of Caldwell to

Bryan and College Station, home of Texas A&M University, favored it over Giddings as a trade center. Both communities grew over the next forty years, with Giddings growing a little faster.

The oil boom impacted Giddings first, in 1975, and its growth rate has exceeded Caldwell's, which did not feel the impacts until three years later. Oil service companies placed their headquarters and field offices in the Giddings area. The population of Giddings was 3,950 in 1980 while that of Caldwell was 2,953. At the peak of the boom, Giddings' population rose to about 5,000 and Caldwell's to about 3,700, 80 and 60 percent, respectively, above their 1970 levels. Since that peak, the population in both has declined to 1990 levels of 4,093 and 3,181 (Murdock and Hogue 1992).

Thus in the past decade, Giddings' population has increased 3.6 percent and Caldwell's 7.7 percent. But if the period prior to the boom is used as the base for calculating growth, the percent increase to 1990 for Giddings is 47.1 and for Caldwell, 37.8.

The rapid influx of population put severe demands on public services in Giddings. Before the boom, it had a very closely controlled, fiscally conservative and traditional leadership, and little excess capacity for public services (Ballard et al. 1981). When the boom arrived, the water system was inadequate, the sewers malfunctioned, the electrical system was obsolete, the streets needed improvement, police and fire protection were virtually nonexistent, municipal records were chaotic, traffic was congested, and the sidewalks and business places were peopled with "strangers." The pressures on community leaders were so great that they either withdrew in despair at what had happened to "their" community, or resigned from public service and took advantage of new business opportunities in the oil industry. Giddings experienced an almost complete turnover in leadership (Ballard and Copp 1982).

Quite a different situation prevailed in Caldwell. Caldwell had also shared some of the growth from Texas A&M University, but it had had a history of progressive leadership and a local tradition of rapidly incorporating new people into the leadership structure. Caldwell had planned excess capacities in place for many public services when the oil boom suddenly arrived. The water system was more than adequate throughout the boom period, and the sewage treatment system had just been enlarged and proved to be adequate to subsequently increased demands. Electrical distribution systems and streets and roads were well maintained. Close cooperation characterized the City Council, Chamber of Commerce and Industrial Foundation. The Caldwell leadership experienced very little turnover through the oil boom, in part because many of the key leaders were younger and had had experience in larger communities. The contrasts between Caldwell and Giddings show that an oil boom need not be a revolutionary experience for small community citizens, leadership and institutions (Copp 1984b).

Effects of the Boom on the Communities

Housing. Acute housing shortages developed in both communities. With insufficient motels, apartments and homes, people slept in cars, makeshift housing, or commuted long distances. Some of the tight supply was subsequently relieved with mobile homes, located in the open country. Caldwell and Giddings had fairly effective ordinances regulating trailer housing within the city limits. Outside those limits there were no land use controls other than those governing sanitation, and County Health Officers could not effectively implement even the sanitation regulations.

Response to the housing shortage was slow (Copp 1984a) and both communities eventually had excess motel capacity. Caldwell now has about four times the number of motel rooms needed. Apartment buildings began appearing somewhat later in both communities, and occupancy now runs at about 50 percent, with the better apartments enjoying higher rates. New construction of detached homes did not begin until the end of the boom and the supply never outpaced demand to the extent that occurred with motels and apartments. As residents associated with the oil industry left, their homes were occupied by commuters and retirees.

Physical Structures. Both communities have greatly improved their physical infrastructure. Construction began with the erection of oil service industrial buildings and moved next to financial institutions, then court houses and city halls, to fraternal organizations, shopping malls, and churches. Shopping malls were opened after the booms ended, while church buildings lagged about five years behind the boom. As a result of the oil boom, both communities have greatly improved physical plants. Many of the new industrial buildings, no longer used for their original purposes, may now be used as garages, business offices, or fraternal lodge halls. Many others stand vacant because of quality, location or aesthetics.

Public Services. Water, sewer and electrical systems, as well as streets, telephone services and cable television, experienced similar improvements (Copp 1984a). Municipal parks were improved. Police and fire protection are much better. Health care delivery systems are better, but underutilized because of restructuring among health care providers. Neither community had a motion picture theater before the boom and neither has one now; video tape rentals are big business in both communities.

Economic Organization.   The oil boom had paradoxical consequences for local businesses. The high volume of sales during the boom attracted outside entrepreneurs and chain stores. Both communities now have shopping malls and WalMarts, and both have chain groceries, franchised hardware and auto supply stores.   These new businesses provide a variety of goods and services and often at reduced prices. As a result, the economic situation of local merchants may be much worse. Shopping is better for the consumer, but competition is more intense for local merchants.

Quality of Life. Local residents are thus living in better communities after the boom, in most respects. Community infrastructure and service quality have greatly improved. Both cities are now well governed and maintained. Those who gained wealth from new businesses or from oil and gas royalties handled their money conservatively, gradually improving their homes and cautiously investing. New families have become prominent in the social structure, but older, landowning families are even more wealthy. Some families victimized by the bust moved on. Very little of an underclass was left behind. Public welfare caseloads did not increase appreciably in either community (Copp 1987). Even the spirit of the social communities has been helped more than hurt, as expressed in positive attitudes of optimism. Patterns of neighboring and social sensitivity have not suffered.

Coal Boom Towns

Many communities in the West have been impacted by coal development, as prices for oil and gas rose precipitously in the 1970s. Two communities are reported on in this chapter, Craig, Colorado, and Decker, Montana. Craig was also included among the communities in Chapter 5 in which population turnover was examined. Craig was a small city of 4,200 in 1970; its population grew 80 percent in five years. Several coal mines have been developed nearby and a large electricity generating plant was constructed. Decker was a small ranching village of less than 200 people in 1972. In subsequent years it was adversely affected by strip mining of coal and its population declined by 30 percent in ten years.

The effects of coal development depend on whether a community is a place of residence for new workers or only the site of the mining itself

(Murdock et al. 1981). A generating plant is a more stabilizing influence than is coal mining alone. Craig profited from more jobs, although there were dislocations. The city and adjacent areas, now with about 10,000 people, have shopping, entertainment and city services. Surveys taken before and after the growth showed little change in residents' evaluations of community life (Knop 1982). Community morale seemed to be high after the rapid growth, and much was learned about managing problems that has continued to benefit the town (Knop and Bacigalupi 1984).

Decker had the opposite experience. New workers lived in Sheridan, Wyoming, a city of 25,000 only 20 miles away. The strip mining involved five operations employing a total of about 1,400 workers, and disrupted local ranching (Jobes 1986). Land was taken out of production, community conflicts erupted over the coal developments, road congestion exploded, and environmental amenities were reduced by noise and dust. Social interaction and the sense of control over events declined sharply as the development changed the close primary character of Decker (Jobes 1989).

Physical Structures and Public Services. Craig's boom occurred in two stages over seven years, with plant construction followed by operations. The first phase was sudden and came after a decade of relative population stability. Craig was already a major regional service center when the boom began, with a diversified economy and substantial tax base. It had had some surplus capacity in public and commercial services, although a shortage of housing quickly developed. Motels became crowded, rooms were rented in private homes, houses were subdivided, and new trailer spaces were developed.

Although new arrivals strained public utilities to some extent during the first several years, Craig's problems were far less than those that had been experienced earlier in boom towns such as Rock Springs, Green River, and Sheridan, Wyoming. The boom in Craig was accompanied by state and industry front-end funding, various legal standards for planning and preventative actions. Craig had also gone through prior boom and bust cycles and had gained some experience in dealing with them.

When newcomers began arriving in Craig in 1973, the expansion of public services was assumed to be the prerogative and responsibility of city and county officials, with help from the energy industry and from the State. Local officials had only to maintain positive relations with the new industry and with the State, to coordinate available resources, and to be responsive to the concerns of citizens. An official rather than an informal approach to migration management was thus taken in Craig. Political and professional personnel resources administered the adjustment process rather than local citizens. The importance of local responses appeared in social integration and adjustment patterns, particularly as the boom gained momentum and became a sustained phenomenon.

In Decker, the community infrastructure was sparse prior to the development, although residents reported high levels of service satisfaction. There was no local law enforcement, medical services or high school before the boom, and there remained none of these services after the boom. A highway was widened, a railroad spur line installed, and power lines were built. A resident deputy sheriff was assigned to the area (Jobes 1989).

Economic Organization. The economy of Craig expanded through the boom rather than changing significantly. Increased jobs and wages in construction and services imposed some hardship on businesses that had to adjust to the loss of clerks, waiters and bartenders, but there was also some reserve local labor in housewives, older persons and adolescents, all with relatively low levels of labor force participation. Vacant positions in local businesses were absorbed by this reserve labor pool when pay and working conditions proved attractive. In addition, existing laborers responded with part-time work in second jobs.

Private sector service adjustments were thus left largely to the marketplace, although some attention was given to recruiting needed professionals and specialty businesses. As in the oil communities, more outside chain stores and franchised restaurants appeared, as did discount stores and specialty businesses. Established local and chain retail outlets and services expanded to remain competitive. Some merchants suffered short-term losses and some went out of business rather than upgrading operations and facilities. Expanding opportunities led to substantial diversification of specialty retail and professional services, and of leisure industries.

Competition among suppliers and the increased volume of business held down price inflation except in housing and public utilities; the latter sectors imposed a burden on people living on fixed incomes. As in the Texas oil and gas communities, expansion of some services was judged less critical and lagged behind other sectors. Churches, lodges and public recreation took longer to catch up with rapidly expanding demand, but in the long run the community benefited from improved facilities.

Craig also developed a surplus of motels and apartments as the boom ran its course. Attractive suburban residential developments accompanied the freeing of older middle-income housing for people moving in or moving up. Public schools and playgrounds were added and the community college got a well-designed campus. Roads and public utilities were improved and new shopping areas were added at the edge of town. Public recreation areas and community parks were built or improved.

The economy of Decker changed from locally controlled ranching to an externally controlled economy dominated by strip mining. All workers were outside the area and all decisions and transactions took place beyond the community. In Craig, the dominant influence was the electric generating plant, which provided long-term operational, technical and professional employment for workers living in the community. Unlike Decker, workers in Craig had no alternative larger city in which to reside within 100 miles.

Quality of Life. Officials, citizen organizations, and individuals in Craig combatted negative effects of rapid growth on quality of life (Freudenburg 1982), such as disorderly conduct, child neglect, depression and alcoholism. Professional services dealt with these problems, supplemented by primary community interest and integration. Craig had long been a railroad center and mining town, was larger, and had had a less distinctive character than do many Colorado towns. It had also experienced previous growth crises. Less attention was thus given to preserving an established local culture and image. Craig managed its boom so well that population turnover during the boom did not exceed rates of previous decades, as was shown in Chapter 5. In the bust period, a high proportion of the more recent newcomers chose to stay, despite limited local economic opportunities. They behaved as though they had found a comfortable new "home town."

Craig maintained standards, public utilities and order. Citizen groups such as the Chamber of Commerce, Trout Unlimited, and service clubs enhanced or preserved natural and leisure attractions. Citizens held out a welcome while maintaining a watchful eye through churches, service clubs and fraternal groups. The combination seemed to have worked well.

The quality of life in Decker declined. Surveys of Craig residents in 1981 showed that they were generally as optimistic and positive about their community and its services as they had been in 1971 (Knop 1982). The same cannot be said of the social change in Decker. Interpersonal relations in Decker declined with diminished neighboring and mutual helpfulness and increased alienation. Degradation of the physical environment and destruction of primary community feelings accompanied

Decker's resource developments (Jobes 1989). Social impacts thus varied by size of community, prior infrastructure and amenities, attraction and retention of new residents, the kinds of jobs created by the resource development, and the maintenance of the perception of control over community change.

A Tourist Community

Aspen is the county seat of Pitkin County in western Colorado. Itself at an elevation of 7,850, Aspen is surrounded by mountains reaching 12,000, making it an outstanding skiing and scenic area. Aspen is also known for its education and research institutes, music festivals, and summer cultural events. The permanent population grew 51 percent in the 1970s, from 2,437 to 3,678, and another 37 percent in the 1980s, to a 1990 population of 5,049. While growth slowed in the 1980s, it has continued at about half the rate of the previous decade, and has shown more consistent growth than Craig, with a history of rapid growth over several decades (see Chapter 5).

Housing. Given its attractiveness, limited private land, and the need for tourist accommodations, living costs in Aspen are high, particularly for housing. While many are quite wealthy, many are not. Aspen has been overbuilt with condos and despite the presence of over 20,000 units, the major concern of inmigrants is the ability to enjoy attractive amenities after meeting the costs of housing and associated services. Pay scales are quite high compared with other towns of the same size, and special adaptations have emerged to ease living expenses. It is common for a number of people to share a house or apartment, to house-sit for a series of part-time residents, or to take lodging or meals in exchange for limited service labor.

Public Services. While mass merchandising, retail sales and franchised services are limited in Aspen, they are nearby and are generally not valued by local residents, compared to the range of specialized shops and services, boutiques, ethnic restaurants, natural foods, sports, art galleries and music. Public services are excellent for a town of its size, consistent with Aspen's image, large number of visitors, and tax base. While Aspen did not have the advantage of Craig's industry and state assistance, it received substantial inputs from ski corporations and nonresident visitors and property owners. Ski corporations played a substantial role in public services in the 1950s and 1960s, but did not attempt direct influence on social patterns in the community. Initiatives were passed to limit and control outside corporate domination of community affairs, and to balance the formal development of the community with desired informal social patterns.

Quality of Life. The need for these initiatives has shown that there is a limit to what can be done through direct local government action without extensive input from residents. During the 1970s, a broad-based concern for quality of living combined with a relatively open political process had made participation in community processes the "admission price" for full-fledged citizenship (Clifford 1980). A unique and pleasant community was thus maintained and even advanced during the rapid growth of the 1970s, and public and private services kept up with the growth.

It is probably not possible for an area to have net growth of two-thirds with rapid turnover (see Chapter 5) without experiencing some alteration in the character of the social community. Aspen has more nearly survived intact through the combination of official and citizen vigilance and responsive initiative. This combination has become a part of the community identity and spirit. Aspen gave particular attention to environmental protection, and to neighborhood and other citizen organization, in pressuring political leaders, public agencies and corporate officials to remain responsive to citizen initiatives. The community is currently rethinking the prospect of maintaining its character and unity as the population continues to grow, the gap between rich and poor widens, and "prestige" residents displace the middle class which has served as local mediators and workhorses.

Stagnant Communities

There has been less analysis of towns with little or no growth over long periods. They are often found in agricultural areas, or in other areas where resource based employment has declined. A stagnant community may be adjacent to areas experiencing growth and expansion, which suggests that stagnation may involve indigenous community organization as well as exogenous factors (Copp 1985). Community decline or stagnation is a subject worthy of much more attention (Gallaher and Padfield 1980).

Colorado. Del Norte is in southwestern Colorado (see Chapter 5). It is the county seat of Rio Grande County, a productive agricultural area at the foot of the San Juan Range. Del Norte has long been a poor county in one of the poorest and most remote areas of Colorado. Its population declined 15 percent from 1960 to 1970. During the rural migration turnaround of the 1970s, Del Norte grew modestly, from 1,569 to 1,709.

This growth of just 9 percent occurred while Colorado was experiencing a growth rate of 31 percent. The reversal of Del Norte's population decline was due mainly to high natural increase combined with a slowing of net outmigration of young adults, some return migration, and net inmigration of older adults. By 1990, the population had declined again by two percent.

Since the mid-1960s, Del Norte has undertaken several kinds of initiatives to maintain its viability, with mixed success. Seeking to capitalize on its natural setting, low-mountain climate, and relatively low cost of living, it invited new citizens who appreciated hunting and fishing, or who valued "Old West" freedoms, or who would fit in well socially.

Local issues such as school quality and costs, services for the aged, and some ethnic considerations, were addressed, and there was an attempt at "democratization" to better bridge age, ethnic, and religious differences. Traditional events and activities, some on the verge of being permanently lost, were rejuvenated and promoted, as were perceived tourist potentials. The benefits of small town neighborliness and safety were emphasized by leading citizens in the area newspapers, community service publications, and at public events. The results of these efforts were generally disappointing, although they are believed to have helped somewhat in slowing the community's long-term decline.

The initiative of leading citizens set the pace for community promotions, and local officials, most of whom were volunteers rather than professionals, responded. This put a burden on the traditional informal leadership. When they heard criticism of their motives or effectiveness, leaders professed to be "tired of it all" and withdrew without encouraging initiatives from newer potential leadership. This is reminiscent of the reaction of traditional leaders during the oil boom in Giddings.

Except for medical services, there was little need for upgrading local housing and services, because Del Norte had surplus capacity from previous periods, and nearby towns of greater size offered a full complement of commercial and professional services. Citizens sought to promote this aspect of the town, to hold more of the youth of the community, to make Del Norte more attractive, and to reinforce its sense of local pride. The Chamber of Commerce made several attempts to encourage "spend at home" programs to maintain existing and attract additional private services. Brochures were prepared and mailed to improve local employment opportunities.

Neither of these programs met with much success. Schools and medical services benefited, as did the main street and some neighborhoods. Local control probably made the difference in these areas. The fact that these efforts brought some success is also probably due to the fact that the 1970s was a period of growth and expansion for smaller towns, rural and nonmetropolitan areas nationally and regionally. In less favorable periods like the 1980s, however, it appeared that the community lacked the energy, creativity, and coordinative abilities required for sustained development.

Texas. Hearne is in Central Texas, 20 miles from Bryan. As the population of the Bryan - College Station MSA grew 143.8 percent from 1950 to 1980, Hearne grew only 11.2 percent. The last decade actually shows decline. The census count for 1990 is 286 below the 1980 population of 5,418. Hearne is not a county seat. It had been a railroad town with divisional repair facilities. It is in the Brazos Valley, a highly productive agricultural area producing cotton, sorghum, wheat and corn. Hearne has lost many low skill industrial jobs for its essentially low-skilled labor force.

Both Hearne and Del Norte have substantial minorities. In 1980 there were as many African-Americans as Anglos in Hearne. Adding the 834 persons of Hispanic origin to the 2,267 African-Americans results in a majority of the town's population (57 percent) in "minority" categories. In 1990, the proportion "minority" has risen to 65 percent. Del Norte is about one-half Hispanic. Both communities also have significant elderly. In Hearne 22 percent was 60 years of age or older, as it was in Del Norte. By 1990, the proportion of the population over 60 declined to 20 percent (Murdock and Hogue 1992).

Internal divisions characterize both communities. In Hearne, a sharp racial-ethnic segregation parallels socioeconomic divisions, although there is also a substantial low income White population. The division in Del Norte is between Hispanics and Anglos, who control most of the wealth and political influence. These divisions are the sources of occasional social tensions.

Community leaders are unable to work together in Hearne. Controllers of economic, financial, political and religious resources show little successful accomplishment or cooperation. Community efforts to bring resources together more frequently result in failure than success. The community has been plagued by embezzlement in City Hall, instability in the Police Department, rapid turnover of city managers, unfilled vacancies on the county commissioners' court, and fiscal crises.

People who have economic power and political influence also have difficulties getting elected to city council that would be uncommon in other communities. Cooperation among banks and the other controllers of wealth in civic development is notably absent (Copp 1984c). As a result, little or nothing of significance takes place in the community. The fact that the population has stabilized rather than declining is due to the fact that workers from Hearne increasingly rely on employment outside the community.

Discussion
Changes in Impacted Communities
Growth. All but one of the impacted communities grew from 50 to 80 percent during the boom period, which ranged from five to ten years. Decker was too small to capture the employment and service growth benefits of development. In effect, the development exploited Decker, as has occurred in Appalachia (Caudill 1963). Local leadership could not counter strong outside influences, while many local families were co-opted by the compensation for their coal resources.   Community disintegration resulted, with many families moving away (Jobes 1986), perhaps wealthier.

All of the communities except Decker were able to adapt. It was a struggle for some, as was the case in Giddings, where old leadership was replaced by new. Giddings and Craig had to cope with 80 percent growth. Caldwell and Aspen had fewer problems. They had an historical record of effective governance and maintenance. Aspen was most successful in managing its resource, tourism. New leadership emerged in all four of the communities, bringing experience gained outside the community to the problems of coping with the changes induced by growth.

Quality of Life. All four communities improved their quality of life. This is evident in physical infrastructure and community services. Each has better shopping and employment than prior to the development. In Decker, all indicators suggest that the quality of life declined overall (Jobes 1989). Economic organization changed with outside retailers with more resources and better skills than local merchants. With the higher level of activity, some local merchants were worse off. This paralleled national trends as smaller communities became more integrated and interdependent with the mass society, with attendant advantages and disadvantages.

Changes in Nonimpacted Communities
Communities in which there had not been new resource developments also showed changes. Even without resource impacts, both

were subject to outside economic and political control, with a reactive rather than proactive response on the part of local leaders. Both suffered from low morale and ineffective community organization, and both had been subject to embarrassing public events. Both communities had histories of weak linkages between leaders and political-economic resources. Both had substantial minority populations, and there was not a proportionate sharing of wealth among ethnic groups. Community resources and local services declined.

Variations in Findings

Some communities grew faster, depending on the resource impacts and on headquarters locations. Giddings and Decker underwent revolutionary changes in leadership while Caldwell and Aspen experienced a more gradual evolutionary change. While most communities improved as places to live, Decker did not. Population change is modest at the present time, but Decker appears to have disintegrated as a viable local community. Some towns may experience gradual growth while this is less likely in others. Aspen appears to have the most prosperous future, and Giddings and Craig have become more dominant regional trade and service centers.

Despite strong name recognition in some tourist resource communities, the permanent populations of these places if often quite modest. In Colorado, this is true of Aspen and Vail. Tourism may be a valuable resource base, but it does not have the dynamism to sustain rates of economic growth in unrelated sectors over the long run. Other kinds of developments, which may be indirectly stimulated by tourism, seem needed to bring about the kind of diversification that is analyzed by Blevins and Bradley in the next chapter.

The stagnant nonimpacted communities have little prospect of change. A lignite-fired electricity generating plant is under construction near Hearne and will provide residents with some new jobs, but Hearne will continue to function primarily as a residential suburb for people commuting to the Bryan - College Station MSA. Del Norte's outlook is more stable. It is remote and locked in by larger, more aggressive towns, such as Alamosa and Monte Vista. Unless it too should experience some new form of development, Del Norte will likely remain largely dependent on its historical agricultural base. Both communities must develop their human resource capital from low income minority groups. Both are likely to continue maintaining a passive posture toward their own futures.

Conclusion

Resource development has diverse effects on communities, with variations that depend on the nature of the resource, the pace of development, and the size of the community. In all three types of resource developments, growth patterns peaked, followed either by decline or more gradual growth. This suggests that any primary resource development will reach a growth plateau unless secondary production facilities are also attracted to the area.

The findings of this research fit well with social impact models, although these models do not predict that local merchants may be negatively impacted by the attraction of economic players from outside the community. Similarly, these models do not enable one to predict whether changes in local leadership will be revolutionary or evolutionary.

Apart from impacts during the early construction phase, there was little evidence of the boom town catastrophe model of resource development (Wilkinson et al. 1982). With the exception of Decker, most communities were able to reassert themselves as reasonably well ordered. It is possible that the highly problematic situations of some of the earlier energy boom towns provided insights which benefited subsequent local, state and federal approaches to the boom experience.

Sociological Paradigms

These findings have relatively little bearing on the relative worth of competing sociological paradigms. The structural-functional perspective makes a limited contribution to community impact analyses (Knop 1987). However, the community which results seems to be more than a moving equilibrium: in many respects, Craig, Giddings and Aspen are different and more viable than they had been before the impacts. Decker more closely approximated the catastrophe model with its virtual system breakdown.

Conflict perspectives may offer more understanding of how and why stagnant communities remain stable than do structural-functional models. The processes through which communities fail to grow and expand merit more research. Symbolic interaction and ethnomethodological perspectives contribute to understanding the community as it is experienced by its residents, most directly to the changes in quality of life dimensions.

More valuable theoretical insights for understanding and for influencing community growth and adaptation come from those theories which emphasize processes of interpersonal influence, particularly social integration and power dynamics.   The problems of structural disintegration lessen when local interaction dynamics are vigorous, balanced and effective. To the extent that interaction dynamics do not have these characteristics, the principal means for successful management of community challenges appears to be the intensity, scope and equity of interpersonal influence.   These factors are complemented by the experiences of earlier impact communities and by structural provisions such as planning and impact mitigation funding. The problems of growth and rapid assimilation are diminished and the benefits of local social and economic stimulation are distributed through the community, at least after the shocks of immediate impact (Knop 1984, 1987).

Applied Implications

Communities benefit from in-service training of new leaders in the process of adapting to crises, as the example of Caldwell illustrates. Communities must have a critical mass if they are to hope to weather the crisis; Decker was exploited, not developed. All primary resource developments involved booms of relatively short duration. Without subsequent activities, this growth and expansion plateau should be anticipated and included in response planning. While Aspen leaders have been imaginative, further growth possibilities for this community seem modest because there are many alternative locations for both tourist-oriented and derivative economic activities.   Finally, resource mobilization by local leaders was conspicuously absent in Hearne and Del Norte.

Resource development leads to migration flows, but population changes are kept within bounds because the secondary and tertiary expansion from the resource development process may take place far removed from the primary community of impact.   More distant metropolitan centers, for example, are very much a part of the system of social and economic relationships through which resource developments take place.

The greater the magnitude and pace of growth, the greater and more immediate is the adaptive challenge. The nature of this relationship is often misinterpreted. The amount and rate of growth are precipitating conditions, but other factors are more relevant for understanding and managing local adaptation. Insofar as migration (or its absence) presents local communities with adaptive challenges, it is primarily how the situation is locally perceived and responded to that determines whether the migration dynamics will be viewed as positive or negative change.

While the resources available are important components of the system of adaptive change, the mobilization of those resources is equally important. Local apathy or the inability to define and coordinate a collective response will increase the vulnerability of the affected community to exploitive rather than developmental impacts. Resistance to change may have the same effect. When adaptation is defined as necessary and at least potentially beneficial, an informed, coordinated and creative response from citizens and officials is more likely to come about. This response enters into and shapes the dynamic social processes which are at the core of the community experience. It is more likely to bring to the community a more satisfying and effective blend of structural properties and interaction processes in response to the challenges of growth and adaptation.

Chapter 8

Economic Change and Diversification in Wyoming[1]

Audie Blevins and
Edward Bradley
University of Wyoming

Introduction

There has been a long history of rural to urban migration in the United States. Except for the 1930s, urban areas consistently gained from rural migration. In the 1950s and 1960s, central cities lost population to suburban areas, while rural areas lost population both to central cities and to suburbs. As many chapters have noted, this long-term, consistent migration pattern reversed in the 1970s. Beale (1975, 1976) noted that a small but important shift in rural to urban migration had been underway as early as the 1960s. This shift had been the result of a slowing of rural outmigration and in some cases had already generated a reversal of net urban-rural migration.

While the results of the 1970 census provided little support for this shift, Beale's early findings were vindicated by the mid-1970s, when it became apparent that a migration reversal, most commonly called the nonmetropolitan migration turnaround, was underway throughout much of the United States. This new urban to rural movement was found to be significant both in magnitude and in its implications for a restructuring of the rural economy (Beale 1980; Wardwell and Gilchrist 1978).

Evidence has accumulated since the early 1980s to the effect that a reversal of patterns of geographical mobility has again taken place. Rural areas once again are losing population to urban centers, and nonmetropolitan areas have been losing migrants to metropolitan. This chapter briefly describes the nonmetropolitan turnaround of the 1970s and reviews explanations for the turnaround, as background for the two central themes of this research: the importance of economic diversification for migration growth of rural and nonmetropolitan areas; and, the effects of economic diversification on patterns of population change in Wyoming.

Wyoming is uniquely nonmetropolitan and is thus particularly well suited to study the applicability of rural turnaround explanations to the patterns of population change and migration in the Rocky Mountain region. Wyoming experienced substantial net inmigration during the 1970s. While the focus of this chapter is on the rural and nonmetropolitan growth period of the 1970s and early 1980s, it also includes a brief discussion of the end of the turnaround and concludes with a review of social policy issues related to fluctuations in rural-urban migration (Deavers and Brown 1980).

Population Change and Economic Diversification

Demographers have long been concerned with shifts in mortality and fertility rates, but to a much less extent with changes in patterns and rates of migration (Wardwell 1980). Fertility and mortality levels for urban and rural areas in the United States have steadily converged, so that migration has become the principal determinant of variations in population change patterns, both of size and composition. One of the major focuses within migration research has been on rural-to-urban migration.

Migration patterns in the United States have historically conformed to changes in the economic structure. As the economy matured and changed from primary reliance upon agriculture to manufacturing and then to service industries, the distribution of population shifted from predominantly rural to predominantly urban. This shift has been the primary focus of demographic analyses of migration since the 1940s. Rural outmigration declined in the 1970s while urban outmigration increased (Summers and Branch 1984). This population change led researchers to explore the social and economic changes that had in the past been associated with rural migration (Long and Hansen 1977).

From 1940 to 1980, the number of people working solely or primarily in agriculture dropped from 8.4 million to fewer than 2.5 million, only 2.7 percent of the labor force. There were fewer people working in agriculture in the United States in 1980 than in 1820. Nonetheless, the total rural and small town population remained stable in spite of this substantial decline in farm employment. The key to that stability has been the increase in rural nonfarm employment, particularly in manufacturing and in the trade and service sectors (Beale 1980). Since most of the rural labor force now relies upon nonfarm employment, the rural farm and rural nonfarm distinction has become extremely important to any analyses of the causes of change in migration patterns.

The economies of rural areas became more diversified during the 1970s because of the growth of rural nonfarm employment (Beale 1980). The number of manufacturing jobs in nonmetropolitan counties of the United States increased 23.9 percent in the 1970s, while in metropolitan counties this increase was only 3.9 percent (Summers and Branch 1984). This ongoing decentralization of manufacturing partially accounted for the rural migration turnaround. Nonmetropolitan population loss through migration peaked in the 1950s at three million. In the 1960s the total loss declined to 2.2 million, but in the first half of the 1970s nonmetropolitan areas gained 1.6 million people and 1.3 million in the second half of that decade.

Not all nonmetropolitan areas participated in the migration turnaround. In the 1970s, approximately 500 nonmetropolitan counties did not experience renewed population growth through migration. Similarly, not all nonmetropolitan areas had experienced the prior trend of population loss through rural to urban migration in the decade before the mid-1960s.

As Cook showed in Chapter 2 for the Pacific Northwest, nonmetropolitan areas continued to gain in the early 1980s, a net of 350,000, but by then the nonmetropolitan migration turnaround had waned and by the following year metropolitan growth rates were higher than those for nonmetropolitan areas (Engles and Forstall 1985). Census estimates for 1983 revealed that metropolitan counties grew 3.5 percent between 1980 and 1983 compared to a growth rate of 2.7 percent for nonmetropolitan counties, although 72 percent of the 877 turnaround counties continued to grow into the early 1980s (Engles and Forstall 1985). Net migration to all nonmetropolitan areas declined to only 0.2 million as the number of nonmetropolitan manufacturing jobs fell 7.5 percent (U.S. Department of Commerce 1987).

In some states, nonmetropolitan areas lost population in the early 1980s. Thus, the reversal of the nonmetropolitan migration turnaround should be located in 1982-83: the net outmigration of 22,000 for that year was the beginning of an accelerated nonmetropolitan outmigration. The U.S. Bureau of the Census (1987b) estimated that nonmetropolitan areas had lost a net of 632,000 migrants to metropolitan areas by 1986.

Explanations for the Nonmetropolitan Migration Turnaround

Prior research established that the turnaround was driven primarily by the movement of urbanites to rural nonfarm occupations, along with the decrease in rural outmigration (Beale 1975, 1976; Wardwell 1980; Wardwell and Brown 1980). Economic diversification of rural economies was an essential aspect of this movement. New opportunities in manufacturing, trade and service employment attracted urban migrants as well as providing a means by which an increasing proportion of rural workers could pursue their economic goals without moving to metropolitan centers. Changes in economic affluence, transportation, modernization of rural areas, and socio-demographic composition were also found to be important (Wardwell 1980). As Wardwell and Lyle have argued in the conclusion to Chapter 6, these organizational changes contributed to a convergence of rural and urban, nonmetropolitan and metropolitan, economies.

The reasons why people migrate are diverse, but are generally related to a perception that something can be gained by relocation. Conventional migration theory argues that the spatial distribution of economic opportunities provides the predominant force guiding migration (Blevins 1969; Murdock et al. 1978). Hathaway and Perkins (1968) noted how agricultural labor was pushed from rural origins and pulled to urban destinations during the 1960s for job-related reasons.

The turnaround was not only fueled by the growth in rural economic opportunities. It was also driven by dissatisfaction with environmental features at the points of origin for migration. In the Midwest, Lichter et al. suggested that noneconomic factors had been more important in the decision to migrate from metropolitan to nonmetropolitan areas (1985). To the extent that that was true nationally, the origin-push dimension of the turnaround was different from that of other, more traditional migration streams. It also follows that this difference has importance for the retention of nonmetropolitan migrants, an aspect of the turnaround that has been emphasized by Toney and Stinner in Chapter 3 of this book, and elsewhere in their research. It is likely, however, that this focus on noneconomic factors is conditioned by economic circumstances of relatively high levels of prosperity, as Wardwell argues in Chapters 1 and 6. Research remains inconclusive on this point.

The importance of economic diversification is thus emphasized in a number of perspectives on the causes of the migration turnaround. An alternative and partly complementary explanation focuses on urban sprawl, attributing a portion of the renewed rural growth to the spillover effects of growing metropolitan populations into adjoining nonmetropolitan counties. Individuals living in those adjacent areas might be employed in a metropolitan county while residing in a nonmetropolitan county that was extensively integrated with the proximate metropolitan area.

This explanation was not applicable to the more rapid growth of nonmetropolitan counties which were not adjacent to any metropolitan area. Wardwell (1977, 1980) recognized the importance of economic opportunities in these more remote areas, but also cited additional factors including improved transportation systems, rural modernization, and residential preferences. Improvements in transportation and communication permitted rural areas to borrow economic scale from larger metropolitan areas while structural differences between nonmetropolitan and metropolitan regions diminished through diffusion of social organization. Increasing personal affluence brought increasing residential flexibility, made metropolitan areas more accessible, and increased the ability of individuals to remain in or move to rural areas while maintaining their participation in nonfarm employment (Fliegel and Sofranko 1984). Fuguitt and Zuiches (1975), Fuguitt and Beale (1978), and Williams, Jobes and Ladzinski (1984) are among those whose research has emphasized the importance of changing residential preferences to the nonmetropolitan migration turnaround.

The Migration Turnaround in Wyoming

Wyoming provides an acid test for many of the explanations of the rural and nonmetropolitan migration turnaround. Wyoming did not have a single metropolitan county until reclassification after the 1980 census. Wyoming is also one of the states that Beale (1976) referred to as a departure from the national pattern because the turnaround appeared to have been fueled by development of abundant natural resources: coal, uranium, gas and oil. Some of these resource developments involve thousands of workers at a single construction site. Migration and population growth in the State might thus better fit the boom and bust pattern.

Beale argued that nonmetropolitan growth based on a single industry had been atypical and was found only in select areas of the Rocky Mountain region. He further argued that growth of this type was likely to be short-lived, best seen as a temporary upswing in population rather than as an example of a long-term turnaround. If Beale was correct, Wyoming would experience short-term episodes of rapid population growth in response to the development and exploitation of mineral resources, much as Copp and Knop have analyzed in Chapter 7. This suggests that growth would be unevenly and occasionally distributed within the State and would follow a boom-and-bust cycle. Some areas would be bypassed by population growth altogether, and left with chronic economic problems. Local and state institutions should then be specifically adapted to assisting communities to manage the socioeconomic disruptions associated with boom and bust cycles.

When large-scale industrial facilities were developed in Wyoming's rural areas in the 1970s, little was known about the emerging significance of residential preferences. Perhaps those responding to new job opportunities in construction and mining were those that preferred the West? Wardwell and Lyle demonstrated in Chapter 6 that the West differs from other regions of the country in terms of the importance given to quality of living motivations related to the natural environment.

Or, perhaps job-related factors determined the initial move, but residential preferences then entered into the ability of an area to retain workers? Answers to these kinds of questions are particularly important in Wyoming, where dramatic population increases have occurred in a short period of time and with little in the way of advance planning. Retention of new migrants determines the extent to which an area will experience boom and bust cycles or a cumulative population growth and economic expansion.

On the other hand, Wardwell (1977) argued that a convergence of rural and urban structural conditions had been interacting with increasing locational flexibility, personal affluence, and the borrowing of economic scale from large metropolitan areas. If this were correct, it would be reasonable to expect that nonmetropolitan areas in Wyoming and the Rocky Mountain region would continue to experience an influx of new migrants, although perhaps at a lower rate, as mineral resource developments declined. Residential preferences and flexibility would enable nonmetropolitan areas to retain at least a portion of their development-induced growth, and attract new migrants, even during periods of slow growth in employment opportunities. The next section provides a brief review of Wyoming's population growth patterns as part of the process of assessing the extent to which growth has been related to expansion of a single industry (mining), or to a diversification of its economy combined with a new importance of quality of life reasons for migration.

An Historical Overview of Population Change in Wyoming

Since 1900, Wyoming, like many other Rocky Mountain and Great Plains states, has experienced uneven population growth. The population grew fairly steadily from 1900 to 1920 from both natural increase and migration. The growth rate had been as high as 58 percent during the first decade and then declined to 33 percent in the following ten years. It was halved to 16 percent in the 1920s and declined to 11.2 percent during the decade of the Great Depression. The 1930s also witnessed a small net outmigration of less than one percent (see Table 1).

The growth rate increased slightly in the 1940s, to 15.4 percent, in spite of a continued net outmigration of 1.8 percent. Net outmigration accelerated from 1950 to 1970, reaching 6.8 percent in the 1950s and 11.9 percent in the following decade. Not until the 1970s did net outmigration reverse, and then it did so abruptly, with this decade experiencing a net inmigration of almost 30 percent. Thus the 1970s was a period of population turnaround for Wyoming, with a net increase of about 140,000, for a growth of about 42 percent, with by far the larger portion of the growth due to migration.

Despite a downturn in the economy in the first half of the 1980s, census estimates showed that nonmetropolitan areas grew 10.6 percent from 1980 to 1985, the sixth-highest nonmetropolitan growth rate in the nation. Most of the net growth of 34,800 was due to a natural increase of 27,000, while net inmigration accounted for the remaining 7,400. Eighteen of Wyoming's 21 nonmetropolitan counties continued to grow, primarily through natural increase. Interestingly, however, 13 of the 21 also experienced net inmigration in this period, although at diminished rates (U.S. Bureau of the Census 1987a). All three of the nonmetropolitan counties that lost population had experienced substantial declines in energy related developments.

With its long history of rapid growth followed by slower growth and net outmigration, the question for Wyoming remains: Is this recent growth due to temporary fluctuations, a short-lived response to higher energy prices? Or, is the growth a long-term trend resulting from shifting residential preferences, modernization of rural areas, and diversification of rural economies, which have favored Wyoming's nonmetropolitan areas? Recent census projections indicate that it will continue to grow through the 1990s from both natural increase and migration. The increases projected are substantial and would have important impacts.

Nonmetropolitan retention is of equal importance. What can nonmetropolitan communities do to provide the kinds of educational

Table 8.1. Demographic Characteristics of Wyoming, 1900 to 1986.

Characteristic	1900	1910	1920	1930	1940	1950	1960	1970	1980	1983	1986
Population (000)	93	146	194	226	250	289	330	332	471	516	507
Crude Birth Rate for census year				19.8	20.7	26.2	25.8	29.6	22.5	19.5	15.8
Crude Death Rate for census year					8.6	8.0	8.5	8.8	6.8	6.5	6.0
Percent net migration for prior decade	24.9	35.9	14.2	-0.6	-0.04	1.8	-6.8	-11.9	29.5		
Percent population change in prior period	47.9	57.7	33.2	16.0	11.2	15.4	14.1	0.7	41.3	9.6	-1.7

Sources:
1900-1970 data from U.S. Bureau of the Census 1975
1980 data from U.S. Bureau of the Census 1983
1986 population and population change from U.S. Bureau of the Census 1986
1986 birth and death rates from National Center for Health Statistics 1987

services and employment opportunities needed to retain young people? Is the quality of life afforded older people high enough to retain and attract retirees? Does net migration mask a substantial outmigration of rural residents through an even larger influx of inmigrants in a "spin-around" pattern similar to that analyzed by Jobes and Knop in Chapter 5? If this were the case, closer attention to the social disruptions attendant upon high turnover would be in order. Was the rural turnaround selective by age, gender, race and skills? Does the rate of change suggest additional adjustment problems for movers and destination communities, as Jobes and Knop have argued? The following sections address these and related topics.

Economic Structure and Employment Opportunities

Three questions stimulated by Beale's (1975, 1976) conceptual framework for explaining the turnaround orient this section. First, how closely has Wyoming's pattern of population growth followed its pattern of employment growth? Any significant divergence between the two would suggest that the framework omits one or more of the important factors affecting rural population growth.

Second, how has the lack of economic diversity in Wyoming's economy affected aggregate employment growth and stability, particularly during the cyclic downturn in mining and energy-related activity in the 1980s? To answer this question, an appropriate method of measuring economic diversity must be developed to identify how diversification has been changing over time. Finally, has Wyoming's long-term potential for further growth in aggregate employment been depressed by the fact of having mining as its principal export industry? Beale (1976) speculated that this industry would have the effect of dampening further growth.

Export base theory (North 1955) is one of the most useful methods for analyzing the prospects for growth in any state or regional economy. The theory argues that the vitality of every economy depends upon the value of the goods and services it exports. Industries which export a large proportion of their output are called "basic industries" because they bring into an economy the income used to purchase "imports" from other regions and the output of other local industries. Tourism, manufacturing, and resource processing industries such as agriculture, forestry, and mining, have traditionally comprised the basic industries of rural areas.

The phenomenon of the turnaround in the nation has been attributed in part to evolutionary change involving decentralization of

Table 8.2. Employment in Rocky Mountain Region and Wyoming, by Industry, 1970-1980.

Industry	Rocky Mountain Region					Wyoming				
	Total Employment 1970	Total Employment 1980	Percent of Total 1970	Percent of Total 1980	Rate of Growth 1970-80	Total Employment 1970	Total Employment 1980	Percent of Total 1970	Percent of Total 1980	Rate of Growth 1970-80
Agriculture:										
Farming	164,355	159,135	7.4%	4.7%	-3.2%	14,610	14,957	9.3%	5.5%	2.4%
Services	15,079	28,629	0.7%	0.8%	89.9%	1,280	2,019	0.8%	0.7%	57.7%
Mining	53,075	113,186	2.4%	3.3%	113.3%	12,454	37,916	7.9%	13.8%	204.4%
Construction	115,406	218,827	5.2%	6.4%	89.6%	9,303	25,711	5.9%	9.4%	176.4%
Manufacturing	251,936	369,139	11.4%	10.8%	46.5%	7,725	10,414	4.9%	3.8%	34.8%
Transportation	126,589	188,350	5.7%	5.5%	48.8%	11,464	19,051	7.3%	7.0%	66.2%
Wholesale	97,475	168,522	4.4%	4.9%	72.9%	4,135	10,040	2.6%	3.7%	142.8%
Retail	359,255	569,598	16.2%	16.7%	58.5%	25,620	43,814	16.3%	16.0%	71.0%
Finances	118,445	245,858	5.3%	7.2%	107.6%	5,798	12,723	3.7%	4.6%	119.4%
Services	396,130	714,247	17.9%	20.9%	80.3%	27,146	46,626	17.3%	17.0%	71.8%
Government	519,123	642,426	23.4%	18.8%	23.8%	37,431	50,600	23.8%	18.5%	35.2%
Total	2,216,868	3,417,917	100%	100%	54.2%	156,966	273,871	100%	100%	74.5%

Note: The Rocky Mountain region includes Colorado, Idaho, Montana, Utah and Wyoming.

Source: U.S. Department of Commerce 1987

manufacturing and economic diversification, including more reliance upon tourism and other export-oriented service activities. Have Wyoming and other Rocky Mountain states also been successful in expanding basic employment within their manufacturing and export service sectors? Or, did the political and business leadership within the region merely capitalize on fortuitous conditions for growth in mining?

Bureau of Economic Analysis (BEA) data on annual employment by type of industry and broad industrial sources provide the information needed to describe both growth and structural change in employment. These data for 1970 and 1980 are found in Table 2 for Wyoming and the Rocky Mountain region. The industrial sectors conform to one-digit Standard Industrial Classification (SIC) codes, but agriculture has been split in two categories, farming and agriculture service, while durable and nondurable manufacturing have been merged into a single category.

The growth rates and structural changes in Wyoming in the 1970s suggest that growth and the migration turnaround was primarily due to increasing mineral production and related construction activity. But in the Rocky Mountain region, mining is only one of nine sectors listed in Table 2 that experienced employment growth rates above the national average. Only the growth rate in agricultural employment lagged behind the nation. The portion of Wyoming's employment in mining increased from 7.9 to 13.8 percent, while the proportion in the region only increased from 2.4 to 3.3 percent. These data, particularly the rapid growth in manufacturing and service industries, suggest that economic diversification rather than mineral developments caused most of the regional growth but not the growth in Wyoming.

Following the onset of the national recession in 1981-82, growth of aggregate employment slowed in the Rocky Mountain region. As shown in Table 3, employment grew only 4.7 percent in 1980-83, while declining in Wyoming by 2.0 percent. Employment growth recovered in the region, but failed to recover in Wyoming after the end of the recession. Regionally, the rate of employment growth increased to 8.3 percent, but remained stagnant at 0.2 percent in Wyoming.

Employment growth in the region substantially led population growth in the 1970s. While the population of the region was increasing 30.9 percent, aggregate employment increased 54.2 percent, with significant growth in all industrial sectors except agriculture, as shown in Table 2. In Wyoming, both population and economic growth far exceeded that of the Rocky Mountain region, at 41.3 and 74.5 percent, respectively. Yet the relationships between population and economic growth were very

Table 8.3. Employment in Rocky Mountain Region and Wyoming, by Industry, 1980-1983.

Industry	Rocky Mountain Region					Wyoming				
	Total Employment 1980	Total Employment 1983	Percent of Total 1980	Percent of Total 1983	Rate of Growth 1980-83	Total Employment 1980	Total Employment 1983	Percent of Total 1980	Percent of Total 1983	Rate of Growth 1980-83
Agriculture:										
Farming	159,135	156,370	4.7%	4.4%	-1.7%	14,957	14,096	5.5%	5.3%	-5.8%
Services	28,629	34,363	0.8%	1.0%	20.0%	2,019	2,354	0.7%	0.9%	16.6%
Mining	113,186	103,608	3.3%	2.9%	-8.5%	37,916	30,981	13.8%	11.5%	-18.3%
Construction	218,827	221,714	6.4%	6.2%	1.3%	25,711	20,095	9.4%	7.5%	-21.8%
Manufacturing	369,139	363,512	10.8%	10.2%	-1.5%	10,414	9,203	3.8%	3.4%	-11.6%
Transportation	188,350	194,555	5.5%	5.4%	3.3%	19,051	18,304	7.0%	6.8%	-3.9%
Wholesale	168,522	167,583	4.9%	4.7%	-0.6%	10,040	9,765	3.7%	3.6%	-2.7%
Retail	569,598	599,843	16.7%	16.8%	5.3%	43,814	44,372	16.0%	16.5%	1.3%
Finances	245,858	273,800	7.2%	7.6%	11.4%	12,723	12,995	4.6%	4.8%	2.1%
Services	714,247	813,720	20.9%	22.7%	13.9%	46,626	50,374	17.0%	18.8%	8.0%
Government	642,426	650,598	18.8%	18.2%	1.3%	50,600	55,798	18.5%	20.8%	10.3%
Total	3,417,917	3,579,666	100%	100%	4.7%	273,871	268,337	100%	100%	-2.0%

Note: The Rocky Mountain region includes Colorado, Idaho, Montana, Utah and Wyoming.

Source: U.S. Department of Commerce 1987

Table 8.4. Employment in Rocky Mountain Region and Wyoming, by Industry, 1983-86.

Industry	Rocky Mountain Region Total Employment 1983	1986	Percent of Total 1983	1983	Rate of Growth 1983-86	Wyoming Total Employment 1983	1986	Percent of Total 1983	1983	Rate of Growth 1983-86
Agriculture:										
Farming	156,370	152,020	4.4%	3.9%	-2.8%	14,096	13,290	5.3%	4.9%	-5.7%
Services	34,363	39,780	1.0%	1.0%	15.8%	2,354	2,612	0.9%	1.0%	11.0%
Mining	103,608	80,487	2.9%	2.1%	-22.3%	30,981	22,393	11.5%	8.3%	-27.7%
Construction	221,714	234,163	6.2%	6.0%	5.6%	20,095	23,012	7.5%	8.6%	14.5%
Manufacturing	363,512	378,214	10.2%	9.8%	4.0%	9,203	9,259	3.4%	3.4%	0.6%
Transportation	194,555	203,350	5.4%	5.2%	4.5%	18,304	17,256	6.8%	6.4%	-5.7%
Wholesale	167,583	167,076	4.7%	4.3%	-0.3%	9,765	8,951	3.6%	3.3%	-8.3%
Retail	599,843	644,581	16.8%	16.6%	7.5%	44,372	43,957	16.5%	16.3%	-0.9%
Finances	273,800	326,154	7.6%	8.4%	19.1%	12,995	13,972	4.8%	5.2%	7.5%
Services	813,720	963,713	22.7%	24.9%	18.4%	50,374	56,324	18.8%	20.9%	11.8%
Government	650,598	686,596	18.2%	17.7%	5.5%	55,798	57,888	20.8%	21.5%	3.7%
Total	3,579,666	3,876,134	100%	100%	8.3%	268,337	268,914	100%	100%	0.2%

Note: The Rocky Mountain region includes Colorado, Idaho, Montana, Utah and Wyoming.

Source: U.S. Department of Commerce 1987

similar in the state and region: Wyoming's population increased 55 percent as much as did employment; for the region this ratio was 57 percent.

The relationship between population and economic growth weakened after 1980. From 1980 to 1986, population increased 7.6 percent while aggregate employment declined 1.8 percent. The divergence between these rates was particularly large in the early years of the decade. From 1980 to 1983, population grew 9.6 percent as employment declined 2.0 percent. Thus, Wyoming's growth has been less stable and more cyclic than that of the region. In metropolitan areas, differences in industrial diversification have been found to explain much of the variation in economic stability over time (Brewer 1985; Conroy 1974; Kort 1981). Increased diversification is nearly synonymous with increased economic stability.

Theoretically, diversification is a less important factor in explaining cyclical instability in nonmetropolitan regions. According to Thompson (1965), nonmetropolitan areas tend to be much more specialized; thus, those regions that specialized in relatively unstable industries would exhibit more instability than those specialized in more stable industries. Nonmetropolitan regions with diversified economies usually are more unstable than those specialized in stable industries, but more stable than those specialized in the most unstable industries (Bender et al. 1985; Killian and Hady 1988).   Development policies often presume that increased diversification will reduce instability, but this is incorrect if rural and nonmetropolitan regions have specialized in relatively stable industries.

In order to examine how economic diversification has been changing in the Rocky Mountain region and in Wyoming, a traditional measure called the "national average index" was used to compute values for 1970 to 1986. The national average index of diversification (Smith and Weber 1984) calculates the variance from national patterns of an economy's distribution of employment among sectors. National average employment in each sector is used as a norm from which deviations in diversification are measured. The index values in Table 5 were computed from annual employment data for the 11 aggregated sectors presented in Tables 2-4. The formula used is:

$$\text{National Average Index} = \sum_{i=1}^{11} \frac{\left[\dfrac{q_{is}}{q_s} - \dfrac{q_{in}}{q_n}\right]^2}{\dfrac{q_{in}}{q_n}}$$

where:

$q_i(s, n)$ = total employment in sector i of state or region (s) or nation (n),

q_s = total employment in the state or region (s), and,

q_n = total employment in the nation.

If the regional or state distribution of employment were exactly the same as the national, the value of the index would be zero because the numerator would be zero for all sectors. This would be a diversified economy with ideal balance in sectoral composition. Thus the size of the national average index values indicate the extent to which an economy lacks diversification.

Although both the Rocky Mountain region and Wyoming had high rates of population and employment growth in the 1970s, the industrial composition of their economies became more dissimilar. Table 5 shows that Wyoming's rapid growth in aggregate employment occurred as its economy became more specialized with the boom in mining and related construction. In the region, growth was more uniformly distributed across industrial sectors. Strong growth in manufacturing and service employment enabled the region to remain well diversified despite substantial growth in mining and construction activities.

Since 1980, neither the relatively well diversified economy of the region nor the relatively specialized economy of Wyoming has performed well in creating additional employment. Both economies have become more diversified, but this has been due to employment losses in mining combined with some employment gains in service sectors. The more diversified regional economy has shown more growth and stability than the economy of Wyoming. Total employment in the region increased 13.4 percent from 1980 to 1986, while employment in Wyoming decreased 1.8 percent.

Most of the population growth in Wyoming in the 1970s may be explained by the increases in employment brought about by energy and mineral developments. That close relationship ceased in the 1980s.

Table 8.5.   Industrial Diversification of Employment in Wyoming and the Rocky Mountain Region, 1970-1986.

National Average Index of Industrial Diversification

Year	Wyoming	Change	Region	Change
1970	0.885		0.121	
1971	0.770		0.103	
1972	0.831	0.061	0.096	-0.007
1973	0.874	0.043	0.095	-0.001
1974	1.016	0.142	0.092	-0.003
1975	1.118	0.102	0.084	-0.008
1976	1.209	0.091	0.084	0.000
1977	1.472	0.263	0.088	0.004
1978	1.608	0.136	0.089	0.001
1979	1.669	0.061	0.089	0.000
1980	1.722	0.053	0.092	0.003
1981	1.636	-0.086	0.095	0.003
1982	1.360	-0.276	0.081	-0.014
1983	1.212	-0.148	0.068	-0.013
1984	1.175	-0.037	0.064	-0.004
1985	1.019	-0.156	0.054	-0.010
1986	0.823	-0.196	0.050	-0.004

Note: The Rocky Mountain region includes Colorado, Idaho, Montana, Utah and Wyoming.

Employment in mining and construction declined 40.9 and 10.5 percent, respectively, from 1980 to 1986, while population increased 7.6 percent.

The employment data in Table 2 were analyzed using the shift-share technique developed by Kalbacker (1979) in order to better explain the pronounced differences in employment growth between Wyoming and the region.   The technique is useful for analyzing state and regional employment growth (Hastings and White 1984).   This analysis of Wyoming's growth shows how regional influences (Standard Growth), initial employment structure (Industrial Mix) and local advantages and disadvantages (Competitive Share) have affected growth. According to this method,

Actual Growth = Standard Growth + Industrial Mix + Competitive Share

or, $[(R_i/R)\, r_i] = [(S_i/S)\, s_i] + [(R_i/R - S_i/S)\, s_i] + [(R_i/R)\, (r_i - s_i)]$

where R = base year total employment in state,
R_i = base year employment in sector i in state,
S = base year total employment in base region,
r_i = rate of employment growth in sector i in state, and
s_i = rate of employment growth in sector i in base region.

The three components of employment change for each sector necessarily total to the actual employment change during the period. This analysis provides a means of estimating how Wyoming's employment grew by sector compared to the standard rate for the Rocky Mountain region. Differences between the state and regional trends are then explained by industrial mix and competitive share components. Employment change related to the industrial mix of economic activities indicates whether the economic structure in 1970 consisted predominantly of sectors which subsequently grew slowly or rapidly. Employment change due to competitive share measures the comparative strength of Wyoming in getting more or less of its fair share of employment growth in the various sectors. Wyoming's competitive share effects should reflect specific local attributes which promote or restrain growth. These include the availability and quality of human and natural resources, the quality of public and private services, the availability of amenities, tax levies for state and local governments, and the effectiveness of state and local economic development programs.

Data in Table 6 indicate that Wyoming's employment grew differently from that of the region in the 1970s. Most of the difference is due to the rapid growth in the State's mining and construction employment. These activities contributed 26.7 percent to the overall growth rate, while they contributed only 7.3 percent to the employment growth in the region. Some of this difference is due to the fact that these activities, which also grew rapidly in the region, initially provided a disproportionate share of employment in Wyoming. Nevertheless, most of the employment increase contributed by mining and construction occurred because of Wyoming's local comparative advantages, such as its abundance of mineral resources, as indicated by the 7.23 local share value for mining. The shift-share results also show that growth in manufacturing and service industries did not occur in Wyoming to the extent that it did elsewhere in the region. It is possible that the boom in mining and construction activity raised wage rates to levels that inhibited employment growth in manufacturing and service sectors during the 1970s.

The results of the shift-share analysis of Wyoming employment relative to the Rocky Mountain region from 1980 to 1983 is presented in Table 7, and the corresponding data for 1983-86 will be found in Table 8. The data reveal that aggregate employment declined 2.0 percent in the first period, with six of eleven sectors experiencing losses. Job losses were so severe in mining, construction and manufacturing that modest

Table 8.6   Shift-Share Analysis of Wyoming Relative to the Rocky Mountain Region, 1970-1980.

Industry	Actual Growth	Standard Growth	Net Relative Change	Industrial Mix	Competitive Share
Agriculture:					
Farming	0.22	-0.24	0.46	-0.06	0.52
Services	0.47	0.61	-0.14	0.12	-0.26
Mining	16.22	2.71	13.51	6.28	7.23
Construction	10.45	4.67	5.78	0.64	5.14
Manufacturing	1.72	5.29	-3.57	-3.00	-0.57
Transportation	4.84	2.79	2.05	0.78	1.27
Wholesale	3.76	3.20	0.56	-1.28	1.84
Retail	11.59	9.49	2.10	0.07	2.03
Finances	4.41	5.75	-1.34	-1.77	0.43
Services	12.41	14.35	-1.94	-0.46	-1.48
Government	8.39	5.56	2.83	0.10	2.73
Total	74.48	54.18	20.30	1.42	18.88

Note: The Rocky Mountain region includes Colorado, Idaho, Montana, Utah and Wyoming.

employment gains in retail trade, financial services, other services and government sectors could not fully offset the loss of 13,762 jobs. These losses accounted for about 70 percent of the difference between the employment growth rates in the State and region from 1980 to 1983. While experiencing a decline in aggregate employment, the economy of Wyoming did begin to become somewhat more diversified.

From 1983 to 1986, job losses in the mining sector in Wyoming were even greater than during the first three years of the decade. Aggregate employment grew 0.2 percent, because growth in construction and service employment was able to fully compensate for the continuing loss in mining employment. The highly specialized Wyoming economy thus performed far less well in generating employment growth than did the well-diversified economy of the Rocky Mountain region, where employment increased 8.3 percent.

Discussion: Policy Implications and Future Research

During the 1970s, population in the Rocky Mountain region increased 30.9 percent while total full and part-time employment increased 54.2 percent. Significant employment growth occurred in all major industrial sectors except agriculture (Table 2). The economic changes characteristic of the rural renaissance and associated with the migration turnaround were occurring in the region. The economy was more diversified as employment grew rapidly in all service-producing sectors, and decentralization of manufacturing contributed to employment growth of 46.5 percent in that sector. Employment in mining and construction nearly doubled during the decade, but these highly cyclic industries accounted for slightly less than ten percent of the region's total employment in 1980.

In contrast, population and employment growth rates for Wyoming in the 1970s far exceeded those for the region, at 41.3 and 74.5 percent, respectively. Beale's characterization of Wyoming's migration turnaround as an aberration from general national patterns is supported by the results of this study. The aberration did not stem from Wyoming's unusually high rate of growth in total employment, but rather from the extent to which it was concentrated in particular industries.

Growth in manufacturing contributed 5.3 percent to total employment of the region, but only 1.7 percent to Wyoming (see Table 6). Growth in the service-producing sectors, however, increased total employment at about the same rates in the region and State. Growth in mining and construction increased total employment just 7.4 percent in the Rocky

Table 8.7 Shift-Share Analysis of Wyoming Relative to the Rocky Mountain Region, 1980-83.

Industry	Actual Growth	Standard Growth	Net Relative Change	Industrial Mix	Competitive Share
Agriculture:					
Farming	-0.32	-0.08	-0.24	-0.01	-0.23
Services	0.12	0.17	-0.05	-0.02	-0.03
Mining	-2.53	-0.28	-2.25	-0.89	-1.36
Construction	-2.05	0.08	-2.13	0.04	-2.17
Manufacturing	-0.44	-0.16	-0.28	0.11	-0.39
Transportation	-0.27	0.18	-0.45	0.04	-0.49
Wholesale	-0.10	-0.03	-0.07	0.01	-0.08
Retail	0.20	0.88	-0.68	-0.04	-0.64
Finances	0.10	0.82	-0.72	-0.29	-0.43
Services	1.37	2.91	-1.54	-0.54	-1.00
Government	1.90	0.24	1.66	-0.01	1.67
Total	-2.02	4.73	-6.75	-1.60	-5.15

Note: The Rocky Mountain region includes Colorado, Idaho, Montana, Utah and Wyoming.

Table 8.8 Shift-Share Analysis of Wyoming Relative to the Rocky Mountain Region, 1983-86.

Industry	Actual Growth	Standard Growth	Net Relative Change	Industrial Mix	Competitive Share
Agriculture:					
Farming	-0.30	-0.12	-0.18	-0.02	-0.16
Services	0.10	0.15	-0.05	-0.01	-0.04
Mining	-3.20	-0.65	-2.55	-1.93	-0.62
Construction	1.09	0.35	0.74	0.07	0.67
Manufacturing	0.02	0.41	-0.39	-0.27	-0.12
Transportation	-0.39	0.25	-0.64	0.06	-0.70
Wholesale	-0.30	-0.01	-0.29	0.00	-0.29
Retail	-0.16	1.25	-1.41	-0.02	-1.39
Finances	0.36	1.46	-1.10	-0.54	-0.56
Services	2.22	4.19	-1.97	-0.73	-1.24
Government	0.78	1.00	-0.22	0.14	-0.36
Total	0.22	8.28	-8.06	-3.25	-4.81

Note: The Rocky Mountain region includes Colorado, Idaho, Montana, Utah and Wyoming.

Mountain region, but 26.7 percent in Wyoming.

As a consequence of this disproportionate growth, 23.2 percent of Wyoming's total employment in 1980 was in the mining and construction sectors. This type of growth confirms Beale's explanation of and concern over rural and nonmetropolitan growth in single or closely related industries that are characterized by a high cyclic instability.

In the early 1970s, social scientists and government officials discovered that the local units of government that were serving rapidly growing communities could neither accommodate nor control inmigration without additional financial assistance or regulatory authority from higher levels of government (Denver Research Institute 1976; Gilmore and Duff 1975). The review of the State's tax and revenue system by Thompson and Schutz (1978) revealed why.

Property taxes were the principal source of revenue for local government. The revenues Wyoming received from state and federal mineral royalties were the principal source of revenue for state revenue sharing programs. But since property taxes and mineral royalties each fail to generate additional revenue during the construction period for a new project, the revenue they do provide comes after the time in which it is most needed.

In addition, Wyoming law tightly restricted the taxing and bonding authority of local governments. The intent of the law was to equalize local tax levies throughout a state with ample but unevenly distributed mineral resources. Nevertheless, it made local governments less able to accommodate rapid growth. Further, state law earmarked a significant portion of its mineral severance tax revenues to finance a permanent mineral trust fund. Interest from this account flows into the state's general fund account, as a means of stabilizing state revenues.

Later in the decade, politicians enacted legislation that enabled local and state government units to respond to rapid population shifts. They were driven by the knowledge of boom town crises and the prospects for continued growth but also the possibility of imminent rapid decline. New state grant and loan programs were authorized to support needed public facilities and services in impacted municipalities and school districts during the construction phase of large-scale developments. County governments were given authority to engage in land use planning and to implement land use controls. An industrial siting act was passed, requiring developers of large-scale projects to prepare plans for alleviating the environmental and socioeconomic impacts of their projects on local communities.

Much of this flurry of activity helped to reduce the social and economic disruptions in those communities which experienced growth after the mid-1970s. But it failed to rectify existing problems in areas where the major migration impacts had occurred earlier. Another problem still remaining for the State and for local communities was the inability to reliably predict future movements of people into and out of Wyoming.

Wyoming experienced an economic downturn in 1980-83, particularly in mining, construction and manufacturing, with a net loss of 13,762 jobs in these industries. The losses were partially offset by gains in retail trade, finance, service and government employment, resulting in a net decrease of 5,534. But while employment was declining 2.0 percent, population grew 9.6 percent, or about 45,000. Population growth continued in 18 of the 21 nonmetropolitan counties. From 1983 to 1986, aggregate employment and population remained stable. Thus, the rapid economic and population growth of the 1970s was not followed by a rapid decline in the 1980s.

In recent years, both the State and local communities have been increasing their efforts to diversify local economies through recruitment of existing firms and encouragement of people to start new businesses. Government officials and community leaders must carefully evaluate local economic opportunities and study economic development strategies, to make sure these economic development programs are fundamentally sound.

Without grounding predictive models in migration data, it is difficult to formulate regional social policies to effectively adapt to variations in growth. The boom-and-bust cycle of migration that responds to massive developments of energy sources usually produces a brush-fire approach in which social policy is geared to the short-term solution of large-scale disruptions, such as the need for temporary housing, school facilities, and social services. Migration that is responsive to both economic factors and quality of life motivations suggests the need for social policies with a longer-term focus, such as the bond financing of infrastructure improvements, permanent schools, recreation complexes, and mental health centers.

Lloyd and Wilkinson (1985) found that community activeness and solidarity were important in attracting rural manufacturing development in nonmetropolitan communities of Pennsylvania. In the preceding chapter, Copp and Knop have similarly argued that these traits were instrumental in adapting to energy-related rapid growth in Colorado,

Montana and Texas. Enhancement of community activeness and solidarity could be particularly important for achieving economic diversification and population retention in areas of Wyoming that are heavily dependent upon single industries.

Further research should focus not only on the economic factors which promote employment growth, but also on residential preferences which promote population retention, when economic conditions permit. Migration must be seen both as an independent and as a dependent variable. Explanations of why individuals move into nonmetropolitan areas are as important as models of their community impacts.

Two models have been proposed and reviewed in this chapter. One suggests that employment fluctuation predicts migration, while the other suggests that when economic conditions are equal, residential preferences influence movement patterns. The data for Wyoming from the 1970s and early 1980s support both models. In the 1970s, the State experienced substantial increases in employment, and also substantial increases in population growth. Both employment and population growth significantly exceeded regional and national rates for the period.

In the 1980s, Wyoming experienced continuing population growth at slower rates, and continuing net inmigration, combined with a sharp cyclic downturn in employment beginning in 1981. Thus employment could not have been the primary determinant of population growth in this period. Wyoming was apparently able to attract migrants through factors other than employment opportunities, particularly to nonmetropolitan areas.

The widespread rural migration turnaround began to diminish in Wyoming after 1983, as substantial losses in mining employment continued. The volatile nature of rural population growth and the factors affecting rural net migration patterns remain key issues in understanding the socio-economic trends and problems of nonmetropolitan America.

Note

1. This research was supported through the University of Wyoming Agricultural Experiment Station under Regional Project W-118. An earlier version of this chapter was published in the Journal of the Community Development Society, Spring, 1988.

Chapter 9

Economic Recession and Nonmetropolitan Migration in the 1980s[1]

John M. Wardwell
Washington State University

Corinne M. Lyle
University of Idaho

Introduction

The nonmetropolitan migration turnaround began in the late 1960s in the northeastern U.S. and continued through the late 1970s (Richter 1985). This was a time of rapid growth in real and particularly in nominal income. This favored residential relocation to nonmetropolitan places (Hoch 1981). With more disposable income, individuals and households could engage in consumption patterns not possible at lower income levels or lower rates of growth. Those patterns involved increased expenditures for outdoor recreation, extended travel, and greater residential space favoring rural areas.

The economic context of migration changed radically in the early 1980s. The nation sustained the worst recession since the Great Depression of the 1930s. From 1978 to 1983, median household income declined in constant 1985 dollars from $24,839 to $22,694 (U.S. Bureau of the Census 1986b, T. 723, p. 431). Median income of families declined from $27,421 in 1975 to $26,116 in 1982 (T. 731, p. 436). Even in families in which the wife was in the paid labor force, constant dollar income declined from $33,266 in 1975 to 32,651 in 1982 (T. 737, p. 439). The impact was more severe in nonmetropolitan areas than metropolitan in both employment declines and real incomes (Beale and Fuguitt 1986; Fuguitt 1985).

The attribution of the diminishing of nonmetropolitan growth to the recession has been based on the documentary data available on net migration and population growth, employment and income trends in this decade (Beale and Fuguitt 1986; Bluestone and Hession 1986; Brown 1987). There have been too few studies of residential preferences conducted among nonmetropolitan migrants since the onset of the economic recession to infer that declining growth could be due to changing values or residential preferences, or to suggest that these preferences have changed once again, in favor of metropolitan locations. Rather, the data suggest that diminished income and diminished rural and nonmetropolitan employment opportunities are primarily responsible.

Noneconomic factors were most frequently cited to explain the appearance of the nonmetropolitan migration turnaround (Dillman 1979; Morrison and Wheeler 1976). Three basic motivations have traditionally been emphasized. These are economic maximization, community/kinship ties, and residential and lifestyle preferences. Prior to the turnaround, most studies concluded that the dominant factor influencing long-distance migration was economic maximization. In economic terms, persons in the labor force moved to locations where the real value of the expected net benefit from migration was greatest (Greenwood 1975; Ritchey 1976; Shaw 1975). Studies conducted since 1975 suggested that economic factors had become less important predictors of migration. Migrants seemed more willing to trade income gains for other quality of life considerations (Dailey and Campbell 1980; Williams and Sofranko 1979).

The turnaround from population loss to population gain through net migration in rural areas occurred in nearly all subregions of the country and at all levels of sizes of counties, and for most categories of migrants (Beale 1975; Wardwell and Brown 1980). The pervasiveness of this change across types of places and migrants suggested that structural convergence between urban and rural areas had gone far enough to sustain an equilibrium in movement patterns (Long 1981; Wardwell 1977). Opportunities for employment and economic advancement were becoming more similar. As a result, movement from one type of place to the other was being roughly balanced by an equal movement in the opposite direction. This situation would persist until further change upset the balance of economic opportunities (Williams 1981). The economic recession played just that role in the migration patterns of the 1980s.

In an economic equilibrium, movement from one type of place to another would have to be explainable with noneconomic causes. If places had converged on economic determinants, other factors related to quality of life and residential preferences would become more important in influencing the decision to move and choice of location (Zuiches 1980). Consequently, explanations of the new patterns of the 1970s broadened beyond economic to include social and environmental considerations (Zelinsky 1977).

Community and kinship ties were important migration motivations prior to the turnaround. Numerous studies had shown that migrants frequently followed other family members in well-beaten paths (Morrison 1973; Ritchey 1976). Relatives or friends encouraged and directed migration by providing information before the move and adjustment assistance afterwards (Lansing and Mueller 1967). Evidence from a number of studies indicated that a prior residence or the location of family and/or friends in an area accounted for a higher percentage of migration to nonmetropolitan areas than that previously found for metropolitan-directed migration (Sofranko and Williams 1980; Voss and Fuguitt 1979).

Residential or lifestyle preferences are another set of noneconomic motivations for migration (Dillman 1979; Zelinsky 1971; Zuiches 1980). This component includes accessibility of parks and recreational facilities, convenience to work, less crime, higher air and water quality, child-raising considerations, and lower cost of living (DeJong and Sell 1977). These were associated with community size in the minds of potential migrants and expressed in the form of preferences for communities under 50,000 in size (Dillman and Dobash 1972; Fuguitt and Zuiches 1975).

A related set of factors associated with large urban living operated as push forces, through dissatisfaction with residence. Smaller places in recreation areas with quality of life attributes in addition to employment attracted new inmigrants (Christenson et al. 1983; Dailey and Campbell 1980; DeJong and Fawcett 1981). Studies of migration conducted since the turnaround began generally found that quality of life reasons for moving had surpassed jobs and other economic considerations, once the decision to move was reached (Long and DeAre 1980).

Thus, by far most of the effort devoted to explaining the nonmetropolitan migration turnaround had concentrated either on the role of changing residential preferences, or on the role of changes in the social infrastructure of smaller communities and unincorporated areas. Both approaches also noted the importance of growth in employment opportunities and the removal of other economic constraints upon migration to smaller-sized destinations, and some noted as well the effects of income growth on migrants' hierarchies of values (Brown and

Wardwell 1980; Hawley and Mazie 1981; Williams 1982). But these factors were understandably not emphasized in the explanation of a phenomenon that appeared to be primarily noneconomic in nature.

As a consequence, Williams (1982) was one of the few who identified the economic conditions under which the nonmetropolitan migration turnaround could continue through the 1980s. None of the surveys of reasons for moving had identified fewer than one-third of the nonmetropolitan migrants giving economic factors as their primary reason for moving. The continuing importance of economic motivation was recognized by all. Most of the attention was simply devoted to documenting and understanding the remaining two-thirds, to those who had given noneconomic factors as the most important reason for the move they had made.

There were thus no deductions drawn as to what the impact of a deep economic recession which was felt more severely in nonmetropolitan areas would be on the direction and volume of net migration flows between metropolitan and nonmetropolitan areas. For example, if the preferences disclosed by surveys conducted in the 1970s had been applied to 1975-80 gross migration streams under varying economic assumptions, the deductions drawn would have been of value for anticipating and understanding the turnaround of the turnaround in the 1980s.

An example will illustrate this point. Until Adamchak's (1987) study of low-amenities counties in Kansas appeared, no survey of reasons for moving found fewer than one-third giving primarily economic reasons for a move to a nonmetropolitan destination; most studies indicated this proportion varied between two-fifths and three-fifths, depending in part upon the type of origin. If one were to assume that a severe economic recession would cause one-half of the one-third of metropolitan-to-nonmetropolitan migrants that been primarily economically motivated to move instead to another metropolitan destination [or, to not move], and the same reasoning applied to nonmetropolitan outmigration, the resulting decline in net nonmetropolitan migration might be enough to account for most or all of the changes observed since 1980.

In fact, when this reasoning was applied to the 1975-80 gross migration stream from metropolitan to nonmetropolitan areas, this factor alone would have been more than sufficient to account for the observed return of net nonmetropolitan loss. That is, if the 7,337,000 migrants from metropolitan areas from 1975-80 were decreased by one-sixth solely as a result of diminishing nonmetropolitan economic opportunities, and the 5,993,000 migrants from nonmetropolitan areas increased by one-fourth (because all surveys indicated that a higher proportion of nonmet-to-nonmet migrants were economically motivated), the net nonmetropolitan migration experience would have been changed from the observed gain of 1,344,000 during this period to a net loss of 1,328,000. That latter figure is close to the rate of nonmetropolitan loss which occurred from 1980 to 1985.

This example uses the classification of counties prior to the results of the 1980 census and the changed definition of metropolitan statistical areas. Since the larger and more rapidly growing nonmetropolitan counties in the 1970s were among those most likely to have been reclassified following the 1980 census, it is likely that their economic experience in the 1980s has not been as severe as that of the counties not reclassified. If this were the case, it would further support the hypothesis that the nonmetropolitan migration losses of the 1980s were primarily, if not entirely, attributable to economic changes (Fuguitt, Brown, and Beale 1989).

Nonmetropolitan growth had diminished considerably by 1981-82, but it remained far above the levels of the 1950s and 1960s. While metropolitan counties were once again growing more rapidly than nonmetropolitan (Engels 1986), the difference was slight and indicated a shifting equilibrium between the two categories as much as a return of traditional metropolitan dominance (Johnson 1989). The change however, was steady throughout the 1980s (Frey and Speare 1992). Did the economic recession influence migration independently of residential preferences, or had preferences begun to shift prior to the onset of the recession?

The primary objectives of this chapter are to explore the relationships between (1) negative economic outcomes associated with metropolitan-to-nonmetropolitan moves, including those induced by the economic recession, (2) reasons for moving, and (3) satisfaction with the move and future mobility intentions. The analysis will shed some light on the extent to which the recession may have affected the nonmetropolitan migration turnaround, and provide some basis for evaluating what future migration experiences of nonmetropolitan areas may be as the economic recession is followed by renewed and strengthened economic growth.

Research Design

In the West, the annualized nonmetropolitan growth rate declined 25 percent from 1970-80 to 1980-83. In the 1980-83 period, nonmetropolitan and metropolitan growth rates were essentially the same

(20.2 and 19.1 per 1000, respectively). In contrast, from 1970 to 1980, nonmetropolitan growth rates had been 30 percent higher than metropolitan. Nonetheless, nonmetropolitan growth rates in the West remained much higher than in any other region into the early 1980s; in fact, Western nonmetropolitan growth at that time was more rapid than was that of any other region in the 1970s (Beale and Fuguitt 1986:50).

However, in 1983-85, nonmet counties that were just beginning to lose population through migration appeared throughout the West, and Current Population Survey data indicate that the West was losing population through migration between it and the other regions of the country (U.S. Bureau of the Census 1986a). This research was conducted in an eight-county, largely nonmetropolitan, area in northeastern Washington and northern Idaho which made up the fastest growing subregion of the commercial and agricultural trading area centered on Spokane. The four counties of Washington are Ferry, Pend Oreille, Stevens, and the non-city portion of Spokane. The four counties in Idaho are Benewah, Bonner, Boundary and Kootenai (see Figure 1 of Chapter 6).

Changes in Growth Patterns

Between 1960 and 1970, the study area experienced net outmigration, as did most rural and nonmetropolitan counties of the nation. The area grew by 13.2 percent, but after accounting for natural increase, only one county had more people moving in than out: the other nonmetropolitan counties of the region had net outmigration rates ranging from about five percent (Benewah, Boundary and Stevens) to nearly twenty percent (Pend Oreille).

In the next decade, population growth and migration changed dramatically. The population increased 51.7 percent. All of the counties experienced substantial net inmigration, ranging from 20 percent for the two most slowly-growing counties to nearly 60 percent in the two most rapidly-growing. Six of the eight counties experienced a reversal from net outmigration to net inmigration, the primary criterion for definition as turnaround counties (data in Table 1 of Chapter 6).

The recession was more severe in the study area than in most nonmetropolitan counties. Unemployment rates approaching and even exceeding 25 percent occurred in these counties, as they did in other resource-based nonmetropolitan counties of the Inland Northwest and throughout the western region. The unemployment rate at the time of our research ranged from 10.5 to 27.4 percent, and remained well above the national average of 9.4 percent. Much of the net outmigration in these counties in the 1980s may be attributed to the severity and duration of the recession.

The combination of sparse population density, distance from and dependence upon a single small metropolitan center, diminishing employment in resource-based industries, and outdoor activities provided an ideal setting in which to examine the relationships between reasons for moving, the economic recession, and residential preferences. The Inland Northwest region is more comparable to the high amenities counties studied by Sofranko and Williams (1980) or by Voss and Fuguitt (1979) than to the low amenities counties studied by Adamchak (1987).

Research Hypotheses

Prior research had established that by far the majority of recent nonmetropolitan migrants remain active in the labor force, with employment participation rates and incomes increasingly convergent with metropolitan levels (Bowles 1978). For those migrants of labor force ages who are active in the labor force, the necessity of working to maintain an acceptable material standard of living in order to continue residence at the nonmetropolitan destination is self-evident. However, the definition of "an acceptable standard of living" might vary considerably with migrants' stated reasons for moving. Migrants moving for social or environmental reasons, for example, might well anticipate a decline in their former, urban standard of living, experience such a decline, and remain quite satisfied with the outcomes of their decision to move (Zelinsky 1977). Those motivated primarily by economic considerations might express more dissatisfaction with adverse economic outcomes.

We included four measures of economic outcomes, three personal and one structural. The structural item relates directly to the economic depression. We asked respondents whether local economic conditions had made it harder or easier to remain in their new locations, or had had no effects. Our primary personal measure was derived from coding the choices migrants made when asked to identify the primary gains and losses that they associated with the move. The other two measures were based on their reports of whether incomes immediately following the move and in 1981 were lower or higher than they had been prior to the move.

Interrelationships of Measures of Economic Loss

Three hypotheses guided our work. The first was that all four measures of economic outcomes would be directly associated with five specific measures of gain or loss related to employment, income and living costs. We expected to find that the greater the economic distress by any measure, the smaller the proportion of migrants reporting that they had gained with respect to these dimensions and the greater the proportion reporting that they had lost. We expected a high interrelationship between these measures of economic outcomes. We would be surprised if respondents who indicated that the local recession had made it harder for them to remain, or that their most significant loss was economic, or that either the postmove or 1981 incomes were lower than prior to the move, did not also report that they'd lost ground economically as a result of their move.

Reasons for Moving, Economic Outcomes and Satisfaction

Our second hypothesis was that respondents who moved primarily for economic reasons would be more likely to associate negative economic outcomes with dissatisfaction in noneconomic areas than would respondents who moved primarily for noneconomic reasons. We also expected that the structural economic outcome (i.e., effects of the recession) would be more strongly associated with noneconomic measures of satisfaction than would any of the three personal measures.

We thought that reasons given for moving mediate the relationships between economic outcomes and noneconomic satisfaction. Dissatisfaction effects of negative economic outcomes were expected to be greater for those who gave economic reasons for their move than for those who gave noneconomic reasons. Migrants who reported that they moved to the Inland Northwest for noneconomic reasons would be better able to rationalize a personal economic loss by reporting greater gains on noneconomic dimensions. Finally, an economic loss that has been structurally induced is more difficult to reconcile than one that was expected as a result of the move.

Economic Outcomes, Dissatisfaction, and Future Mobility

Our final hypothesis dealt with the relationships between post-move economic experiences, subsequent dissatisfaction, and mobility intentions. We asked the respondents if they had any regrets over their decision to move, if they viewed the move as temporary or permanent, and if they could imagine conditions under which they would move back to their place of origin. We hypothesized that these indicators would respond to negative economic outcomes: those indicating negative economic outcomes would be more likely to express regrets, view the move as temporary, and anticipate the possibility of returning to their origin. However, we expected these effects to be greatest with the structural cause of economic distress, and for those who indicated that they moved primarily for economic reasons.

Data Collection

Complete details of research methods are in Rowe and Wardwell (1987) and are summarized in Chapter 6. The survey was conducted in the spring of 1982, at the depth of the recession. It was not known at that time that net outmigration had already become characteristic of many of the counties that had recently been experiencing exceptionally high annual growth rates. We did not know, for example, that our study counties would show the extreme change from high net inmigration in 1970s to low rates of net outmigration. It was known, however, that the regional and national economy had taken a radical turn for the worse since the migrants had made their decision to move to the Inland Northwest. We wanted to know to what extent and in what ways the recession was affecting their retrospective evaluation of the decision to move to the area, whether it was making it more difficult for them to remain in their chosen locations, and whether it affected their future migration plans.

Slightly over one-half (53.4 percent) of the migrants came to the area from a metropolitan location, and the rest from some other nonmetropolitan area. The samples of migrants and residents are equally divided between the two states.

Qualification

Our sample was necessarily restricted to migrants who had resided in their destination choice from the time of their move until we conducted our survey in the spring of 1982. Consequently, our analysis cannot include individuals who moved out the study area because of economic (or any other) outcomes associated with their move prior to that time. Thus, two of our measures understate economic-dissatisfaction relationships: definition by the respondent of the move as temporary rather than permanent and identification of conditions under which the respondent would move back to the place of origin.

Findings

We first explore the frequency of negative economic outcomes in income changes, gains and losses associated with the move, and the respondents' association of economic outcomes with the recession. We then look for covariation in these frequencies with reasons for moving to the Inland Northwest. Finally, we examine the effects of these outcomes on whether the migrants regretted having made the move, on the degree of satisfaction expressed with noneconomic aspects, and on future mobility intentions.

The first hypothesis was very strongly supported by the data in Table 1. This table presents 20 two-by-two tables cross-tabulating economic outcomes (column variables) with reported gains and losses associated with the move (row variables). For example, in the first cell of Table 1, 42 percent of those who indicated that the recession had made it harder for them to remain also indicated that they had lost income as a result of the move, compared to 17 percent of those who said that the recession had not made it harder for them to remain.

However, there was an evident difference between objective measures of post-move income (self-reported) and perceptions of gain and loss. For example, in Columns 3 and 4 of the first row, only 43 percent of those who said that their income was higher in the year immediately following their move also indicated that they gained with respect to their own income (and only 31 percent say they gained with respect to their spouse's income). Similarly, just 50 percent of those who indicated that their own income was lower following the move also indicated that they had lost income. Migrants were clearly including factors other than nominal income change in their calculations of gains and losses. These factors may include perceived changes in the cost of living, in the spouse's ability to find employment, or changes in the mix of household expenditures from origin to destination.

All but 4 of these 20 cells were significant (the four including three of the cost of living measures in the bottom row of the table, and the cell in row four, column four, 1981 income and job advancement for spouse). By any of the four measures of economic outcome, economic distress was associated with a loss in employment of self and spouse, and with a loss of income of self and spouse. While only one of the cost of living relationships was significant, this does not necessarily contradict the hypothesis: it is possible for migrants to have simultaneously experienced negative economic outcomes as measured by the column variables and still report that they had gained through their move with respect to the cost of living comparison between their new location and their place of origin.

Table 9.1 Effects of Measures of Economic Outcomes Associated with Move on Migrants' Reported Gains or Losses in Income, Employment and Living Costs (figures in percents).

	Effect of Economic Conditions on Residence		Area of Most Significant Loss		Income in Year after Move		Income in 1981	
	Harder to Stay	Easier to Stay	Economic	Not Economic	Less	More	Less	More
Higher pay, self:								
gain	20 ns	38	20	41	16	43	18	37
loss	42	17	48	17	50	10	44	20
Higher pay, spouse:								
gain	20 *	26	17	24	13	31	17 *	27
loss	28	13	32	14	42	4	28	16
Job advancement, self:								
gain	32	44	29	46	27	48	28	43
loss	30	13	38	10	38	7	42	14
Job advancement, spouse:								
gain	20	34	22	33	20	36	25 ns	33
loss	23	12	27	10	34	5	25	13
Living costs:								
gain	36 ns	40	41 ns	38	48 *	33	42 ns	38
loss	21	15	23	17	15	19	17	17

Notes: All relationships significant at $p < .001$ unless noted: * $= .005 < p < .05$; ns $= .05 < p$

Individual cell sizes not shown to reduce detail; all component cells were based on the reduced sample size of 385 (not including those reporting no changes in economic conditions).

These findings show covariation of several indicators of the same global concept (i.e., economic outcomes associated either with the move itself or with the economic recession). The results establish systematic regularities in the data that permit us to examine other findings with confidence. The four measures of economic outcomes that form the column variables in Table 1 are themselves highly interrelated (data not shown). Individuals who reported that the local economic conditions had made it harder for them to remain were also much more likely to report that their most significant loss associated with the move was in employment or income, that their post-move income was lower than prior to the move, and that their income in 1981 was lower than prior to the move. The strong relationship between income just after the move and income in 1981 is particularly important, because it casts doubt on the hypothesis in the literature that migrants accept a temporary economic loss because they expect to make up that loss in ensuing years. These data suggest that loss at time of move is a predictor of continuing loss years later.

Reasons for Moving, Economic Outcomes and Satisfaction

We did not expect economic outcomes to directly affect satisfaction, either in general terms or with regard to noneconomic aspects of the move. We did explore this possibility in the data, by examining the effect of each of the four measures of economic outcomes on 20 indicators of noneconomic satisfaction (i.e., percents reporting gains and losses in such areas as "time with family," "social position," "safety from crime," "residential space," "leisure opportunities," etc). While these data are not shown in the tables, the results are of interest.

Nearly three-quarters of the 80 possible relationships were not significant, and when significant were more likely to be in the opposite direction. That is, migrants who reported economic distress by one measure or another were more likely to report gains in noneconomic areas than were those who did not report negative economic outcomes. For example, 79 percent of those saying that the recession had made it more difficult to remain in their locations reported that they had gained from the move with respect to access to the physical environment, compared to 66 percent of those saying that the recession had not made it harder for them to remain. In another example, 80 percent of those who reported that their income was lower following the move said that they had gained in terms of air and water quality; the corresponding percent for those who reported a higher income following the move was 63.

Nine of 22 significant relationships were in this direction: respondents reporting negative economic outcomes were more likely to report gains in noneconomic areas than were those reporting positive economic outcomes. These 9 items cluster in the areas of social aspects of the community (size, less crime, housing space) and aspects of the physical environment (attractions, access, air and water quality).

We did expect that reasons for moving would interact with economic outcomes to affect satisfaction. Individuals who moved to the area for noneconomic reasons may well have expected to incur economic costs in doing so, and subsequently report satisfaction with noneconomic consequences of their move. It is evident that in these cases, they were even more likely to report such satisfaction.

Introducing a control over reasons for moving enabled us to evaluate this. We compared the proportions reporting gains in each of the 20 noneconomic dimensions for groups formed by looking simultaneously at economic outcomes and reasons for moving. We examined the data in columns arranged in order of ascending proportions reporting gains, as expected from the hypothesis: people moving for economic reasons who had been negatively affected by the recession were expected to be least satisfied with their move; people moving for economic reasons and not negatively affected by the recession were expected to be most satisfied; those moving for noneconomic reasons were expected to be intermediate between these extremes. The data were examined only for those who gave economic reasons or noneconomic reasons for both the decision to leave the place of origin and the decision to choose the destination location. This reduced the sample for this table from the 385 used in Table 1 to 260, a reduction of approximately one-third in sample size (data in Table 2).

Fourteen of the 20 comparisons of economically-motivated migrants who had or had not suffered economically as a result of the recession were in the expected direction, although the differences were not significant in three of these cases; in the five cases where the differences were not in the expected direction, only two were significant. Support for the hypothesis was found in items dealing with social aspects of community living and with items relating to costs of living. However, the expected monotonic relationship across all four categories was found only with one item (church spirit). A weaker monotonic relationship across three of the four categories appeared more frequently, in seven items dealing with ownership of a business, similarity of people, leisure, lifestyle and access to the environment.

Table 9.2   Effects of Economic Recession and Primary Reason for Moving on Migrants' Report Gains in Noneconomic Domains (figures in percent).

Items	Effect of Economic Conditions				Recession Effects Controlling Reasons		Reasons Effects Controlling Recession	
	Harder to Stay Reason for Move		Not Harder to Stay Reason for Move		$=(4)-(1)$	$=(3)-(2)$	$=(2)-(1)$	$=(3)-(4)$
	Economic	Noneconomic	Economic	Noneconomic				
	(1)	(2)	(3)	(4)	(5)	(6)	(7)	(8)
Distance to work	40	29	26	40	0	-3	-11	-14
Time with family	44	43	49	29	-15	6	-1	20
Own prop/bsns	50	63	73	59	9	10	13	14
Social position	31	40	28	33	2	-12	9	-5
Housing costs	50	63	52	68	18	-11	13	-16
Residential space	25	82	70	38	13	-12	57	32
Community size	50	85	81	55	5	-4	35	26
Safety	25	70	63	33	8	-7	45	30
Similar people	25	45	47	30	5	2	20	17
Raising children	38	69	66	60	22	-3	31	6
Leisure time	69	83	85	53	-16	2	14	32
Community services	25	6	11	33	8	5	-19	-22
Community facilities	38	7	20	45	7	13	-31	-25
Church spirit	13	18	21	31	18	3	5	-10
Personal lifestyle	56	72	83	52	-4	11	16	31
Weather/climate	44	59	60	45	1	1	15	15
Attractive env	69	85	85	59	-10	0	16	26
Air/water quality	38	92	78	48	10	-14	54	30
Access to env	69	86	79	57	-12	-7	17	22
New/fun experiences	38	58	66	44	6	8	20	22

We also examined the hypothesis by comparing the differences between the effect of the recession on the noneconomic gains of those moving for economic reasons with the effect on those moving for noneconomic reasons. A positive difference was in the expected direction: greater gains were associated with no negative effects of the recession. A greater difference between those moving for economic reasons than for those moving for noneconomic reasons supports the hypothesis. Fourteen of the differences were in the expected direction for the economically motivated; nine were as expected for migrants motivated by noneconomic reasons. The difference between the differences was in the expected direction for 10 of the 14, and was strongest in the areas of time with family, social position, housing, raising children and church spirit. Once again, social aspects of community living showed the greatest noneconomic effects of the recession on satisfaction with move, and the effects were greater for those motivated primarily for economic reasons.

Perceptions of gains in the physical environment were most impervious to the recession. Items that directly contradicted the hypothesis by showing a greater difference in the expected direction for those motivated by noneconomic reasons for moving were few and concentrated in the personal realm. These data provided some support for the hypothesis, but the support was often weak and occasionally equivocal. It appeared that there were factors operating in the relationships between reasons for moving, economic experience in the recession, and perceptions of gains and losses that were not captured in our hypotheses.

Accordingly, we compared the effects of reasons for moving on gains and losses, controlling for economic experience, with the effects of economic experience controlling for reasons. That is, we compared the differences between those moving for economic and noneconomic reasons and experiencing negative outcomes of the recession with the differences between those who had not had any negative economic experiences as a result of the recession [data also in Table 2]. We wished to compare both the signs and size of differences to evaluate the relative strengths of the effects of reasons for moving and impacts of the recession.

The results were surprising and unexpected. Thirty-five of the differences were statistically significant, compared to only 14 of the differences without controls. Of these 35 differences, all but 7 were in the expected direction; only 5 of the 14 statistically significant differences without controls were in the expected direction. Of the differences that were both significant and in the expected direction with controls, in all cases they were greater than the corresponding differences without controls. Of the seven statistically significant differences with controls that were not in the expected direction, all dealt with four items: distance to work, housing costs, community services and facilities. These items have to do with conditions of employment, economic factors or structural aspects of the community. We have noted already how closely the structural items were related to economic growth orientations.

To clarify these relationships and simplify detail, we constructed satisfaction scales for the several dimensions on which migrants might report gains and losses, similar to reasons for moving. The scales were constructed through factor score procedures (Rowe 1984). Table 3 reports relationships between economic outcomes, reasons for moving, and scales measuring gains and losses in four areas: employment-economic, social infrastructure, social relationships and recreation-environment. As in the analyses of individual items reported above, main reasons for moving have been coded only as economic or noneconomic. Our primary interest is to compare the relative impacts of the recession on satisfaction with the move, controlling for reasons for moving, with the impacts of reasons controlling for satisfaction.

The results are again surprising and significant. Economically and non-economically motivated migrants who had negative experiences with the recession (Columns 1 and 2) differed in perceptions of gain and loss on all five measures. Both groups reported higher gains in social relationships and the natural environment than in the economic-infrastructure areas, with the noneconomically motivated scores consistently higher than the economic.

Among migrants who had not had negative experiences associated with the recession (Columns 3 and 4), the economically motivated had significantly higher gains in the economic-infrastructure areas, while the non-economically motivated reported higher gains in social relationships and in recreation-environment. However, if we compare the weighted averages of the gain scores for the economically motivated in both economic experience categories with the corresponding gain scores for the noneconomically motivated, we consistently find that the differences in gain-loss perception by type of reason for move (Columns 7 and 8) are greater than the differences by recession experience (Columns 5 and 6).

One example will serve to illustrate: the recession had no effect at all on satisfaction with gains in social relationships when reasons for moving

Table 9.3   Effects of Economic Recession and Primary Reason for Moving on Migrants' Report Gains in Noneconomic Domains (scale scores).

| | Effect of Economic Conditions | | | | Recession Effects | | Reasons Effects | |
| | Harder to Stay Reason for Move | | Not Harder to Stay Reason for Move | | Controlling Reasons $=(4)-(1)$ | $=(3)-(2)$ | Controlling Recession $=(2)-(1)$ | $=(3)-(4)$ |
Scales	Economic (1)	Noneconomic (2)	Economic (3)	Noneconomic (4)	(5)	(6)	(7)	(8)
Total gain-loss scale	3.6	3.8	4.0	3.7	3.7	3.9	3.6	3.9
F significance level			0.011			0.011		0.046
Job-related scale	3.8	2.9	3.5	4.1	3.1	3.7	4.0	3.2
F significance level			0.000			0.000		0.000
Facilities/services	3.2	2.8	3.2	3.5	2.9	3.3	3.4	3.0
F significance level			0.000			0.001		0.001
Social scale	3.5	4.3	4.2	3.7	4.1	4.1	3.6	4.2
F significance level			0.000			n.s.		0.000
Environmental scale	4.0	4.4	4.5	3.9	4.4	4.3	3.9	4.4
F significance level			0.000			n.s.		0.000

N = 253

are not controlled -- the mean satisfaction score for both groups is 4.1. However, the mean gain score for economically motivated migrants is just 3.6, while for the noneconomically motivated it was 4.2. Similarly, the difference of 4.4 and 4.3 as the effect of the recession upon recreation-environment gains expands to the difference between 4.5 for the noneconomically motivated and 3.9 for the economically motivated migrants.

These results strongly support the argument that reasons for moving are closely related to perception of gains and losses in noneconomic dimensions, regardless of economic experience during the recession. The only exceptions were found in items that are much more closely related to economic dimensions. We will return to this finding in our concluding discussion.

Data similar to those discussed have been examined to study the effect of reason for moving on the relationships between the other three measures of negative economic outcomes and noneconomic gains and losses. As expected, reasons for moving had much less of an effect with the personal indicators than on the relationships between perceptions of gain/loss and the structural economic indicator. Migrants were less likely to associate noneconomic losses with personal negative economic outcomes than with recession-induced hardships, regardless of reasons for moving.

Economic Outcomes, Satisfaction with Move, and Future Mobility

Table 4 presents the relationships between the four measures of economic outcomes and three indicators of the respondents' evaluation of their move. As expected, all four outcomes measures were closely associated with whether the respondents express regrets at having made the move. Nearly 30 percent of those who felt the recession had made it harder for them to remain expressed regrets at having moved, compared to only nine percent of those who felt the recession had not made it more difficult. This difference was greater than for any of the other three measures of negative economic outcomes, all of which had a relationship in the expected direction. By any of the four measures, about one-fourth of those experiencing negative economic outcomes expressed regrets, compared to about one-tenth of those not experiencing negative outcomes.

Only the recession measure was associated with future mobility: 35 percent of those who said the recession had made it harder for them to stay said that their move may have been temporary, and 43 percent

Table 9.4 Economic Outcomes, Satisfaction with Move, and Future Mobility Expectations (figures in percents).

A. Negative Economic Outcomes and Post-Move Satisfaction

	Effect of Economic Conditions on Residence		Area of Most Significant Loss		Income in Year after Move		Income in 1981	
	Harder to Stay	Easier to Stay	Economic	Not Economic	Less	More	Less	More
Regrets at having made this move?								
Yes	30	9	22 ns	14	24	11	31	13
No	70	91	78	86	76	89	69	87
Was present move:								
temporary?	35	21	24 ns	27	25 ns	25	30 ns	25
permanent?	65	79	76	73	75	75	70	75
Would you move back?								
Yes	43	31	34 ns	35	36 ns	33	35 ns	35
No	57	69	66	65	64	63	65	65

B. Post-Move Satisfaction and Future Mobility

	Regrets at having made this move?		Was move:	
	Yes	No	Temp	Perm
Was present move:				
temporary?	63	19		
permanent?	37	81		
Would you move back?				
Yes	67	29	58	27
No	33	71	42	73

All relationships significant unless indicated "ns"

indicated they may move back to their origin, compared to 21 and 31 percent, respectively, of those who indicated that the recession had not made it harder (Panel A). The three personal measures of economic outcomes had no relationships with either measure of future mobility. In Panel B, the effect of dissatisfaction on future mobility was evident: 63 percent of those expressing regrets viewed the move as temporary, and 67 percent indicated they may move back to their origin, compared to 19 and 29 percent, respectively, of those not expressing regrets.

Thus, negative economic outcomes did affect migrants' satisfaction, and did have a greater effect upon those who moved primarily for economic reasons. Satisfaction was directly related to future mobility intentions.   However, only economic outcomes associated with the recession showed any relationship to future mobility intentions.

Summary: Economic Recession and Migrant Satisfaction

These findings support the argument that the decline in rates of population growth since 1980 may be attributed to the effects of the recession on migrants who moved to the area primarily for economic reasons.   Accordingly, the effects on satisfaction are particularly important.

- The relationships between reasons for move, economic outcomes of the move, and satisfaction with the move were strong and direct.
- People who moved primarily for employment or income reasons had more positive economic outcomes as a result of the move. But if they had experienced negative economic outcomes through the recession, they were much more likely to be dissatisfied. About one-fourth of those who experienced negative outcomes expressed overall regret at having made the move, compared to about one-tenth of those who had not experienced any adverse economic consequences as a result of the move.
- Individuals who had moved for noneconomic reasons were more likely to express general satisfaction with the move if they had experienced negative economic outcomes than if they had not experienced such negative economic consequences.
- Satisfaction was directly related to future mobility plans. Nearly one-half of those adversely affected by the recession indicated they would move back to a former residence.

Conclusion: The Evidence for Equilibrium

The premise on which this study is based is that changes have occurred in the social and economic structure of the nation in its transition from an agricultural to an industrial and then post-industrial economy and society. These changes set the stage for the migration turnaround and now contain the new and expanded bases on which migrants make their decisions to move. The overriding hypothesis has been that structural convergence, or the growing similarities between urban and rural places in the conditions of working and living, was at least as important for the recent growth of nonmetropolitan areas as were the continuing differences between them. Surveys of where people wanted to live indicated that far more people would like to live in smaller-sized places than were moving to those places. We believe that those desires could not be implemented until rural and nonmetropolitan areas could offer people opportunities and conveniences for working and living similar to those found in large urban areas.

These findings provide support for this equilibrium, or convergence, hypothesis. We expect that future movement between metro and nonmetro places will roughly reflect the balance of economic opportunities. Continued change in rural areas offers people the chance to live in a place of their size-preference without foregoing the conveniences of modern living. People must have adequate income and employment in order to move to or remain in any place. Whenever these economic necessities are equally available in large and small areas, people have the freedom to choose one over the other according to other values. We find no evidence in these data that values or preferences for nonmetropolitan living changed as a result of the recession. Rather, these data suggest that if economic conditions were to change again so as to facilitate living and working in rural areas, a return to the migration trends of the 1970s would be likely. Whether such a change will occur is outside the scope of sociological theories of migration. What sociologists must do, however, is better understand the economic conditions under which migrants' noneconomic motivations may influence their decisions.

Note

1. The research reported in this chapter was supported by Project 0354, Washington State University College of Agriculture and Home Economics, Agricultural Research Center, and by Project R-871, University of Idaho College of Agriculture, Agricultural Experiment Station, contributing projects to Western Regional Project W-118. We wish particularly to thank J. Patrick Smith for his helpful comments on an earlier draft.

Chapter 10

Metropolitan-Nonmetropolitan Differences in Public Policy Orientations in Utah[1]

William F. Stinner and
Luis Paita
Utah State University

Introduction

Many have observed that inmigrants might be harbingers of political change (Lyons and Durant 1980; Clarke 1981). They may arrive with new attitudes and aspirations. This is by no means unequivocal. The dispersal of inmigrants from other locations into metropolitan and nonmetropolitan destinations adds an additional and perhaps critical dimension. Aggregate opinion distributions in each area on various state policy issues may or may not be affected. Effects will vary with the extent to which inmigrant attitudes are congruent with those of prior residents. This process of assimilation or conflict has implications for overall differences in sociopolitical attitudes in metropolitan and nonmetropolitan areas.

Our specific objectives in this chapter are to determine the degree to which the policy orientations of nonmetropolitan residents in Utah differ from those of metropolitan residents, and to assess the extent to which native and inmigrant attitudes have contributed to the differences between areas. Our research is guided by three perspectives: the "urban way of life," "convergence," and "institutionalist" perspectives.

The analyses examine attitudes regarding four recent public policy issues in Utah. The first has to do with siting a community/neighborhood group home for recovering alcoholics and drug abusers. The second involves copayment of nursing home costs by children of elderly parents on Medicaid. The third deals with installation of air bags in new cars.

The final policy issue addresses environmental impacts associated with location of a nuclear waste repository in southern Utah.

Data were gathered through telephone interviews with a random sample of 992 Utah adults in November and December of 1984 by the Survey Research Center of the University of Utah. The response rate was 75 percent. Inmigrants are classified as returnees or in one of three groups based on their duration of residence in Utah at the time of the survey. The scope of the analyses is limited in that the mechanisms of underlying differences are not identified. This limitation is inherent in the size and nature of the data file.

Theoretical Perspectives
The Urban Way of Life Hypothesis

One point of view holds that nonmetropolitan people are more conservative, or traditional (see Willits et al. 1982 for a review of this perspective). The small size, low density and relative isolation of nonmetropolitan areas generate and sustain traditional conservative views. The large size, high density and diversity of metropolitan areas stimulate an "urban way of life" characterized by continuous ideational reinvigoration which leads to more moderate and liberal attitudes.

Migration outcomes are associated with this thesis. Metropolitan areas receive migrants attracted by greater freedom and the more diverse environment. The dispositions of these migrants reinforce the dominant urban mentality. Nonmetropolitan areas, on the other hand, are said to be characterized by the outmigration of people with more liberal views. This reinforces their sociocultural conservatism. Returning migrants do not disturb the dominant traditionalism; many are seeking to recapture their former way of life. In Petersen's (1975) terminology, their attempt to recapture and preserve the old reinforces nonmetropolitan conservatism. The combined patterns of selective in- and outmigration leave the "cake of custom" intact.

According to the urban way of life hypothesis, attitudes of inmigrants from out of state who settle in nonmetropolitan areas would be expected to more closely resemble the conservative sociopolitical orientations of nonmetropolitan natives. Similarly, inmigrants from out of state who go to metropolitan areas should hold orientations more similar to the moderate and liberal views of prior metropolitan residents. Inmigrants are attracted in part on the basis of which of the two milieus they perceive to be most compatible with their own predispositions. Migration thus reinforces the prevailing patterns and metropolitan-nonmetropolitan differentials persist through migration experiences.

The Convergence Hypothesis

The convergence hypothesis stresses the increasing socioeconomic integration of nonmetropolitan areas into the national mainstream, as a consequence of social, economic and technological change (Wardwell 1980). It may be that these developments also impact nonmetropolitan residents so as to generate some convergence in attitudes, although this is not a part of the convergence hypothesis. The convergence orientation is a structural theory dealing with migration behaviors rather than a social psychological theory of attitudes and migration motivations.

The 1970s witnessed a major turnaround in nonmetropolitan population growth through migration. Decreased nonmetropolitan outmigration coincided with increased inmigration (Fuguitt 1985). Various surveys showed that new nonmetropolitan migrants held attitudes which diverged from those of prior residents and more closely resembled those of prior residents of metropolitan areas (Ploch 1980; Stinner and Toney 1980).

According to this extension of the convergence hypothesis, the impacts of change on nonmetropolitan areas may have attracted new inmigrants in increasing numbers with moderate and liberal sociopolitical attitudes. If this has taken place, metropolitan-nonmetropolitan differences would be expected to diminish. Nonmetropolitan residents may be becoming no more conservative in their policy orientations than metropolitan residents.

The Institutionalist Perspective

A third perspective may be drawn from the distinctive Utah setting. With its Mormon domination, Utah has historically been noted as being a politically conservative state (O'Dea 1957; Leone 1979; May 1980; Barrus 1984; Hrebenar 1981; Stinner et al. 1988). In fact, one recent study ranked Utah's degree of political conservatism the highest in the nation (Wright et al. 1985).

A strong version of this thesis would suggest that the institutional commitment to a conservative perspective would cause metropolitan-nonmetropolitan attitudinal differences on specific policy issues to vary in ways unrelated to either the urban way of life or convergence hypotheses. That is, according to the institutionalist perspective, metropolitan and nonmetropolitan orientations would be expected to be similar and both to be strongly conservative.

The sociopolitical attitudes of inmigrants might either mirror the dominant institutional perspective or indicate some potential for change. Inmigrants might be attracted to Utah by the conservatism of the state. This suggests a conservative orientation among both prior residents and new inmigrants in both metropolitan and nonmetropolitan settings. With pervasive normative support for sociocultural conservatism, any "deviants" among the new migrants could be rapidly assimilated in either type of destination area.

A weaker version of this hypothesis suggests outcomes more closely approximating either the urban way of life or convergence models. That is, increasing socioeconomic integration of Utah into the national mainstream may have brought about a weakening of the dominant conservative orientation, so that the institutionalist force may operate less strongly in metropolitan than in nonmetropolitan areas. The close-knit social networks of nonmetropolitan places may more effectively support the dominant traditional outlooks (Stinner and Toney 1980).

If this were the case, metropolitan-nonmetropolitan attitudinal differences would conform to the urban way of life hypothesis. On the other hand, recent inmigrants might have generated an approximation of the convergence model. These inmigrants to both metropolitan and nonmetropolitan destinations may be less conservative than prior residents, thus contributing to lower levels of conservatism in both areas.

In our research, a conservative stance implies: (1) a strong endorsement of *laissez-faire*; (2) advocacy of fiscal austerity; (3) pro-family sentiments with emphasis on familial responsibility in providing for the needs of individuals; and, (4) lower levels of concern for environmental quality. A liberal perspective would be expected to include a view of governmental intervention as appropriate to meeting the welfare needs of the citizens and a greater concern for environmental quality. (See Conover and Feldman 1981; Buttel and Flinn 1978; Van Liere and Dunlap 1980; Dunlap and Van Liere 1984).

In terms of the specific policy issues examined in this research, the conservative orientation toward *laissez-faire* policies coupled with strong proscriptive norms toward intemperance implies less tolerance toward or support for governmental siting of group homes for recovering alcoholics and drug abusers. The strong pro-family orientation emphasizing familial responsibility over governmental intervention in the welfare of family members implies greater support for children's copayments for indigent parents' nursing home costs. *Laissez-faire* sentiments also imply relatively greater opposition to legislation require air bag installation in new cars. Finally, a conservative orientation would be more likely to favor growth that would result from siting of a nuclear waste repository with a corresponding deemphasis of potential for environmental harm.

However, some degree of cognitive dissonance is also possible from the conservative orientation. Hostility toward the federal government and an ideological commitment to the "preservation of Zion" are also both conservative perspectives and these orientations may generate concern over the possible adverse environmental impacts of the nuclear waste repository. With regard to this issue, the outcome may be greater similarity with the liberal concerns regarding environmental quality.

The liberal perspective, on the other hand, is expected to be associated with support for governmental attempts to meet the welfare needs of recovering alcoholics and drug abusers, support for governmental intervention in the promotion of automotive safety, and with perceived harm from the proposed siting of a nuclear waste repository.

The results of the analyses confirm these interpretations of traditional conservative and moderate-liberal orientations in the context of these policy issues (see Table 1). The data indicate that persons who identify themselves as politically conservative are significantly less likely to approve group homes for recovering alcoholics and drug abusers at both the community and neighborhood levels. They are also less likely to approve air bag installation in new automobiles. They are less likely to perceive environmental harm from the siting of nuclear waste dumps; and, they are more likely to approve children's copayments for the nursing home costs of parents on Medicaid than are those who identify themselves as politically moderate or liberal.

Procedures

The migrant status variable is based on an abbreviated migration history. Persons who were born in Utah and have not been out of the state for longer than a two-year period are classified as natives. Returnees are persons born in Utah but who left the state at some point for two or more years and since returned. Those born outside the state and resident in Utah at the time of the survey were asked the year in which they moved to Utah to stay. These were classified as follows: (1) long-term inmigrants had 15 or more years of residence in the state; (2) middle-term inmigrants had 5 to 14 years' residence; and, (3) recent inmigrants had arrived within the last five years. Natives constituted 42 percent of the sample, and 19 percent were returnees. Migrants were roughly evenly

Table 10.1. Orientations on Selected Policy Issues by Political Self-Identification (percent approving; percent perceiving environmental harm)

Political Self-Identification	Group Homes for Recovering Alcoholics or Drug Abusers In:		Children's Copayments Nursing Home Costs Parents on Medicaid	New Car Air Bags	Environmental Harm from Nuclear Waste Repository	(N)
	Community	Neighborhood				
Total	47.4	32.7	59.2	65.3	54.9	992
Conservative	43.2	28.7	63.6	59.4	51.3	505
Moderate	48.2	33.1	53.6	69.4	57.9	278
Liberal	56.5	41.6	56.0	74.2	59.8	209
X2	10.58	11.24	8.49	17.08	5.72	
p	<.01	<.01	<.02	<.001	<.06	
Eta	0.103	0.106	0.092	0.131	0.076	

divided between the three categories, with 16 percent long-term, 12 percent middle-term and 11 percent recent. Note that interstate migration only is of interest to this research; no questions on migration within Utah were asked of the respondents.

Attitudes toward group home siting for recovering alcoholics and drug abusers are analyzed at both the community and neighborhood levels. The question was worded:

> How would you feel about small neighborhood residences for eight or fewer people who are recovering alcohol and drug abusers in your town or city? ... in your neighborhood?

Response options ranged from strongly in favor (1) to strongly opposed (5).

The analysis of attitudes regarding children's copayment of nursing home costs for Medicaid recipients is based on responses to the following question:

> The government's Medicaid program currently pays for the nursing home care of elderly people who cannot afford it. A number of states may start requiring the adult children of Medicaid recipients to pay a portion of their parents' nursing home costs. The exact amount that adult children would have to contribute would depend on their income. How would feel about such a law?

Again, response options arranged from strongly in favor (1) to strongly against (5).

Responses to the next question were analyzed regarding orientations toward installation of air bags:

> If a law were proposed in Utah requiring all new cars to come equipped with air bags or other automotive restraining devices, how would you feel about such a law?

Strongly in favor responses were coded "1," with other responses ranging to the code of "5" for strongly against such a law.

Finally, orientations toward nuclear waste repository siting were measured with responses to the following question:

> To what extent do you think the environmental quality will change in Southeastern Utah if a nuclear waste site is located at Gibson Dome?

Response options for this question ranged from no deterioration (1) to serious deterioration (5).

Results are first presented for the percentages of respondents in the two extreme response categories regarding the four policy issues. The aim herè is to describe the basic differences across and within metropolitan and nonmetropolitan areas and among natives and the three categories of inmigrants.

The analyses then employs multivariate logit techniques for each of the four policy issues. This examines the degree to which all subgroups differ from nonmetropolitan natives, presumed to be the most conservative. Logit analysis is used in part because the various dependent variables are dichotomous with categorical explanatory variables (Feinberg 1980).

The group home siting issue can be used as an example to demonstrate the logit model. With "favoring group homes" as the dependent variable, the logit model without interactions is as follows:

$$L_n \frac{P(F)}{1-P(F)} = a + b_{ij} \tag{1}$$

where L_n refers to the natural logarithmic function, $P(F)$ is the probability that the respondent favored group homes, and "a" and b_{ij} are the logit coefficients. Equation (1) expresses the logarithm of the odds of favoring group homes as a linear function of characteristics "j."

Since the interest at this stage of the analysis is in the joint effect of residence and migrant status, a composite derived from the two measurements is used as the independent variable. Equation (1) is thus reduced to a linear logit model with one predictor:

$$L_n \frac{P(F)}{1-P(F)} = a + b_i \tag{2}$$

The quantity "a" indicates the mean or overall effect of the independent variable on policy attitudes, and is similar to the intercept term in an ordinary regression equation. A significant positive b_i (Beta) coefficient indicates that being in category "i" of the independent variable increases the probability that a respondent favored group homes. In all cases, the interpretation is relative to the suppressed reference category, nonmetropolitan natives.

Except for the implication of being positive or negative, the values of b_i do not provide information that is directly useful, unlike the ordinary regression coefficient whose interpretation is straightforward. For this reason we include the Tau coefficient, the antilog of the Beta coefficient. This translates the additive model in equation (2) into a multiplicative model in equation (3) which contains odds rather than log odds:

$$\frac{P(F)}{1 - P(F)} = t \times {}^{t_i} \tag{3}$$

where "t" and t_i are the antilogs of "a" and b_i respectively. Again using the group home siting example, an antilog of 2.00 for short-term migrants in nonmetropolitan areas would indicate that they are twice as likely to approve the issue than the reference group of nonmetropolitan natives.

Findings
In the first section, we report the results of the descriptive analyses for each policy issue. Following this presentation, we turn to the findings from the multivariate log analyses.

Descriptive Analyses
Table 2 contains the descriptive data for the policy issues. Percentages favoring group homes, children's copayments, air bag installation, and perceiving environmental harm are cross-classified by metropolitan-nonmetropolitan residence and by migrant status.

Metropolitan-nonmetropolitan differences are not large, with no consistent tendency toward either conservative or liberal responses across all issues. The largest differences (nine percent) are found for approval of the group home issue (50 vs 41 percent) and new car air bag approval (68 vs 59 percent). On all other issues, the differences are only three to four percent. When the group home issue is focused on the neighborhood, for example, 34 percent of metropolitan and 31 percent of nonmetropolitan residents approve. Both categories of residents give a conservative response on the copayments issue, with metropolitan residents slightly more likely to so respond (60 vs 56 percent). A slight majority of both residence categories perceive environmental harm from siting a nuclear waste repository (56 and 53 percent).

In sum, nonmetropolitan residents do not differ significantly from metropolitan, nor is there any set pattern to the responses. Both categories give more conservative responses regarding group home siting and copayments for nursing home costs. Each category tends toward less

Table 10.2. Orientations on Selected Policy Issues by Residence and Migrant Status.
(percent approving; percent perceiving environmental harm)

Residence, Migrant Status	Group Homes for Recovering Alcoholics or Drug Abusers in: Community Met	Non	Neighborhood Met	Non	Children's Nursing Home Copayments Met	Non	New Car Air Bags Met	Non	Environmental Harm from Nucl Waste Met	Non	(Number) Met	Non
Total	50	41	34	31	60	56	68	59	56	53	732	260
Natives	50	38	36	31	57	53	69	56	63	55	286	127
Migrants	49	45	33	32	63	60	67	62	51	51	446	133
Return	40	43	29	28	62	55	63	62	55	55	139	47
Non-Return	53	45	35	34	63	62	68	62	49	49	307	86
Long-Term	49	40	33	23	52	50	63	53	52	60	138	30
Middle-Term	52	41	30	28	71	69	74	56	45	41	87	32
Short-Term	61	58	44	54	72	68	71	83	48	46	82	24

Difference = Metropolitan minus Nonmetropolitan

Residence, Migrant Status	Community	Neighborhood	Nursing Home	Air Bags	Nucl Waste
Total	9	3	4	9	3
Natives	12	5	4	13	8
Migrants	4	1	3	5	0
Return	-3	1	7	1	0
Non-Return	8	1	1	6	0
Long-Term	9	10	2	10	-8
Middle-Term	11	2	2	18	4
Short-Term	3	-10	4	-12	2

conservative responses to car air bag installation and nuclear waste siting, although only a bare majority exhibit this response on the latter issue.

When natives only are considered, differences between residence categories increase on issues other than the nursing home copayments. Among inmigrants, differences contract. Inmigration appears to be contributing to a diminishing of metropolitan-nonmetropolitan differences.

However, while nonmetropolitan inmigrants are more approving of community group home siting than natives, less than a majority approve in either category (45 and 38 percent). When the focus shifts to the neighborhood, inmigrant approval levels drop substantially and no longer differ from those of prior residents. Inmigrants to either destination category are more likely to give approval to nursing home copayments than natives in either area. Inmigrants are less likely to perceive environmental harm than natives, with 51 percent of inmigrants to either area type identifying potential environmental harm from nuclear waste siting.

No model receives consistent support from these findings, but the institutionalist perspective may be somewhat more strongly supported. The nursing home copayments results conform to the expectations of this model. Metropolitan-nonmetropolitan differences are small. Inmigrants reinforce the dominant conservative orientation in both settings. When the focus of group home siting is on the community, the data support the convergence model. But when the focus shifts to the neighborhood, the institutionalist model clearly prevails.

The data on the new car air bag installation issue support the convergence model. This is the only issue on which outcomes are consistent. A relatively less conservative orientation (i.e., higher approval levels) among nonmetropolitan inmigrants compared to their native counterparts contributes to a contraction in the metropolitan-nonmetropolitan differential, but it is smaller than that which would be expected from the differences between natives.

Finally, on the nuclear waste siting issue, inmigrants contribute to a more conservative orientation in nonmetropolitan and particularly in metropolitan areas. Inmigrants to both areas appear more conservative (relatively lower likelihood of perceived harm) than natives. Differences are again smaller than expected on the basis of patterns among natives, but the shift is clearly in the conservative direction. This pattern would thus appear to also support the institutionalist model.

Differences between migrant categories appear first in the comparison of returning and nonreturning migrants. Variations by destination area are not large nor consistent. Nonreturning migrants to metropolitan areas are more approving of group homes (53 and 45 percent) and new car air bags (68 and 62 percent) than are migrants to nonmetropolitan areas.

Differences between returning migrants are negligible for the group home siting at either neighborhood or community levels. There are also no differences in perception of environmental harm. With respect to nursing home copayments, however, differences between returning migrants are greater than between nonreturnees (62 and 55 percent, compared to 63 and 62 percent).

Within metropolitan and nonmetropolitan areas, returning and nonreturning migrants to nonmetropolitan destinations differ little if at all on community siting of group homes and new car air bag installation. Both migrant categories are equally conservative on group homes and equally liberal on car air bags, and both groups are more approving than are the nonmetropolitan natives. A slightly larger difference is found at the neighborhood group home siting level, with nonreturning inmigrants indicating greater approval than returnees (34 and 28 percent), and slightly higher approval than among natives.

Nonetheless, the approval level remains quite low. Nonreturning migrants are somewhat more approving of nursing home copayments than are returning migrants (62 and 55%). Returnees are just barely above natives in approval level, while nonreturning migrants are about nine percent higher. Returnees are more likely to perceive environmental harm than nonreturnees (55 and 49%), although their level of support is no higher than that among nonmetropolitan natives.

The slight increase in overall conservative orientation in nonmetropolitan areas with regard to this issue (i.e., higher approval level) is due primarily to the impact of nonreturning migrants. This group is more conservative than are returning migrants. The results for both groups conform to the expectations of the institutionalist model.

Regarding the group home siting issue, both nonreturning and returning migrants are less conservative than natives when the focus is at the community level, but when the focus shifts to the neighborhood, natives fall between the two migrant groups. Returnees are somewhat more conservative than natives, and nonreturning migrants slightly less conservative. The patterning in both groups supports the institutionalist model.

Both inmigrant categories are supportive of new car air bag installation, the liberal orientation. They thus lend support to the convergence model. Through migration impacts, nonmetropolitan respondents more closely approach the liberal orientation of metropolitan residents on this issue. Regarding environmental attitudes, nonreturning migrants are more conservative than returning in either destination category. The shift toward a more conservative orientation in both areas is due to the relatively more conservative attitudes of nonreturning migrants.

Differences by duration of residence among migrants on the group home siting issue and the installation of air bags on new cars are smaller, the shorter the duration of residence. Recent inmigrants to nonmetropolitan areas have minimally lower approval levels of group home siting in the community than recent migrants to metropolitan areas (58 and 61 percent). The differential is greater between the other two categories, approaching that found between natives of the two residence areas. At the neighborhood level, recent nonmetropolitan migrants have higher approval levels than their metropolitan counterparts, while among the longer-term migrants the differential is about the same as that found at the community level. Recent nonmetropolitan migrants are also more likely to approve car bag installation than are recent migrants to metropolitan areas, reversing the pattern found among longer- and middle-term inmigrants.

No significant variations across duration of residence appears with the nursing home copayments issue. Differences do appear in the perception of environmental harm, but in the direction opposite to the above and still quite minimal, particularly among recently arriving migrants.

Recent nonmetropolitan arrivals are considerably more approving of group homes in both community and neighborhood, of nursing home copayments, and of new car air bag installation, than are longer-term migrants and natives. The long-term migrants resemble the natives, while short-term migrants are less likely to perceive environmental harm than either long-term migrants or natives. Long-term migrants are slightly more likely to perceive harm than natives. These patterns also generally characterize the corresponding metropolitan groups.

Only among recent nonmetropolitan arrivals is there majority support for group home siting in community and neighborhood. In metropolitan areas, majority support is evident among both recent and middle-term migrants at the community level but evaporates at the neighborhood level.

Consequently any shift away from the institutionalist model would have to be due to recent arrivals. Their small numbers can have only slight effects on the prevailing conservative orientation.

Patterns among both recent and middle-term returning migrants support the institutionalist model with nursing home copayments. Their relatively more conservative orientation on this issue contributes to an increase of approval levels in both metropolitan and nonmetropolitan areas. Recently arriving nonreturning migrants contribute to a more liberal orientation on the air bag issue, but again, their small numbers in nonmetropolitan areas can effect only a small impact.

Finally, recently arriving nonreturning inmigrants in both metropolitan and nonmetropolitan areas shift attitudes on the environmental issue in a more conservative direction. Among both middle- and short-term migrants in both areas, less than a majority perceive potential harm from the location of a nuclear waste repository. Both groups thus contribute support to the institutionalist model.

Multivariate Analyses

The main purpose of the multivariate analyses is to compare effects across subgroups for the various policy issues with nonmetropolitan natives. The results are in Table 3. Within nonmetropolitan areas, we observe generally similar profiles with the exception of the most recent nonreturning migrants. Even with this group, significant differences are not consistent across all issues.

Significant differences appear in the issue of group home siting in either community or neighborhood and in approval of air bag installation on new cars. Recent nonreturning migrants in nonmetropolitan areas are more than five times more likely to approve group homes in their community, and eight times more likely to approve the homes in their neighborhoods, than are natives. They are 13 times more likely to approve air bag installation. But with the other two issues, copayments and environmental concern, none of the migrant subgroups significantly differ from nonmetropolitan natives.

When the metropolitan migrant and resident subgroups are examined, greater differences are observed. Metropolitan natives and all subgroups of nonreturning migrants to metropolitan areas are significantly more likely to approve group homes in their communities than are nonmetro-politan natives. The differences range from 6.5 times more likely among recent metropolitan migrants to 2.7 and 2.8 times more likely among longer-term nonreturning migrants and metropolitan natives, respectively.

Table 10.3. Logit Analysis for Selected Policy Issues by Residence and Migrant Status.

| Residence, Migrant Status | Group Homes for Recovering Alcoholics or Drug Abusers in: | | | | Children's Copayments Nursing Home | | New Car Air Bags | | Environmental Harm from Nuclear Waste | |
| | Community | | Neighborhood | | | | | | | |
	Beta	Tau	Beta	Tau	Beta	Tau	Beta	Tau	Beta	Tau
Constant	-0.22	0.80	-1.45***	0.24	0.88***	2.41	1.27	3.55	0.16	1.17
Nonmetropolitan										
Natives										
Return Migrants	0.40	1.49	-0.33	0.72	0.20	1.22	0.46	1.59	0.01	1.01
Non-Return										
Long-Term	0.20	1.23	-0.52	0.59	-0.22	0.80	-0.21	0.81	0.38	1.46
Middle-Term	0.25	1.29	-0.05	0.95	1.31	3.69	0.02	1.02	-1.14	0.32
Short-Term	1.63*	5.12	2.08**	8.02	1.11	3.03	2.56**	12.96	-0.73	0.48
Metropolitan										
Natives	1.02**	2.76	1.59	1.80	0.31	1.37	1.11***	3.04	0.68	1.97
Return Migrants	0.15	1.16	-0.11	0.90	0.74	2.10	0.61	1.84	-0.04	0.96
Non-Return										
Long-Term	0.99**	2.69	0.26	1.29	-0.46	0.63	0.59	1.80	-0.23	0.79
Middle-Term	1.12**	3.08	-0.03	0.97	1.57***	4.83	1.55***	4.70	-0.82	0.44
Short-Term	1.87***	6.49	1.28**	3.60	1.64***	5.14	1.27**	3.56	-0.60	0.55

*   p < .10
**   p < .05
*** p < .01

This pattern shifts markedly when the focus is on locating a group home in the neighborhood. Only recent nonreturning inmigrants differ significantly from nonmetropolitan natives, 3.6 times more likely to approve. This could reflect differences in the geographic scope of metropolitan and nonmetropolitan communities. Location of a group home may be defined as more acceptable if thought to be located somewhere else in a large city than in one's own neighborhood. In smaller nonmetropolitan communities it may be that an adverse impact would be anticipated regardless of the location, if all locations were perceived to be in close proximity.

Regarding copayments, only middle- and short-term metropolitan nonreturning migrants differ significantly from nonmetropolitan natives. Both groups are about five times more likely to approve copayments than are nonmetropolitan natives. They thus exhibit a more conservative orientation than do the natives. Conversely, these two migrant subgroups are 4.7 and 3.6 times more likely to approve air bag installation than are natives. On this issue, metropolitan natives also are three times more likely to approve than are their nonmetropolitan counterparts. The two metropolitan migrant groups and metropolitan natives are less conservative than nonmetropolitan on this issue.

None of the migrant subgroups are more likely to see environmental harm from nuclear waste siting. Most recent arrivals in nonmetropolitan Utah resemble prior residents on some issues, prior metropolitan residents on others. They are less conservative on the group home and new car air bag installation issues, as are metropolitan residents. On the other hand, they are as conservative on the nursing home copayment and environmental issues. With copayments they differ from nonreturning migrants to metropolitan areas.

Conclusion

No one conceptual model can account for all of the patterns found in the data; however, the institutionalist model received stronger overall support than did either of the other two. Metropolitan residents are less conservative than nonmetropolitan residents on group home siting in the community and on automotive safety legislation. These findings support the urban way of life hypothesis. However, when the group home focus is shifted to the neighborhood, metropolitan residents are as decidedly conservative as are nonmetropolitan residents. This supports the institutionalist perspective. Metropolitan and nonmetropolitan residents are slightly less conservative on the environmental issue, supporting the convergence hypothesis, but more conservative on the nursing home copayments issue, supporting the institutionalist model.

Differences between metropolitan and nonmetropolitan natives expanded, but only by a few percentage points. Once again, the results are equivocal in distinguishing between competing hypotheses. Nonmetropolitan natives are more conservative regarding the siting of group homes in the community, installation of air bags in new cars, and nuclear waste siting, than are metropolitan natives. These results support the urban way of life explanation. If changes are underway in differences between areas on these kinds of issues, they are not readily apparent among natives at the time of our survey.

On the other hand, the results regarding neighborhood siting of group homes and nursing home copayments lend support to the institutionalist interpretation. Metropolitan and nonmetropolitan natives are equally conservative on these issues. The multivariate analyses showed no significant differences on these issues, reinforcing the institutionalist hypothesis. But the lack of significant differences between natives on the environmental issue suggests convergence. Migrants appear to be producing some diminishing of metropolitan-nonmetropolitan variations in some public policy issues in Utah. The contractions are not all that great, however, and the differences among natives were small to begin with.

Moreover, on some issues, inmigrants are contributing slightly to more liberal perspectives, whereas on others they are reinforcing conservative attitudes. Recent nonreturning migrations are primarily responsible in both instances. This subgroup is considerably more liberal in their orientations toward group home siting, regardless of whether the focus of the question is on the community or neighborhood. They are also more liberal with regard to automotive safety legislation, but more conservative on the nursing home copayment and environmental issues than are the nonmetropolitan natives.

More generally, migrant patterns support the convergence model on group home siting and automotive safety legislation issues. But they lend support to an institutionalist model regarding the nursing home copayments and environmental issues. Their contribution to convergence, moreover, is slight because of their comparatively small numbers.

The more liberal orientations of recent migrants in nonmetropolitan areas are insufficient to offset the high degree of conservatism among their native counterparts regarding the siting of group homes at either the community or neighborhood levels. There is minor convergence toward the somewhat less conservative posture of metropolitan residents concerning community group homes and automotive safety legislation. On the other hand, the orientations of both nonmetropolitan and metropolitan residents toward group homes in their own neighborhoods are quite conservative.

The significant increments in approval among recent migrants to metropolitan areas are insufficient to produce a more liberal orientation. Less than a majority of these migrants support the idea of neighborhood group homes. Nonmetropolitan migrants reinforce conservative orientations on the nursing home copayment and environmental issues, although the size of the difference is again small.

In general, the neighborhood group home issue supports the institutionalist model. The automotive safety legislation issue supports the convergence interpretation, with convergence being produced by migrants. Among natives, the pattern conforms more to that expected under the urban way of life hypothesis.

The issues examined in this research are selective. Different results might be obtained with more social issues, such as pornography, liquor laws and women's rights. These are issues on which institutional positions have been clearly articulated. In the case of the specific issues included in this research, much may depend upon the future migration of recent migrants to Utah.

Public policy orientations are a particularly important matter in the Utah context. The desirability of "cultural pluralism" increasingly surfaces in discussions that are focused on economic growth, as the state develops job creation strategies to accommodate the large numbers of children now approaching labor force entry ages. A greater volume of inmigration implies more competition in the labor market as well as pressures for the elimination of any discriminatory tendencies in job placement. More research of a longitudinal nature is needed to untangle these complex but important relationships.

Note

1. This research was supported by Utah State University Agricultural Experiment Station Projects 836 and 837, and Western Regional Project W-118. We acknowledge the assistance of Dr. Ken Smith, Director, Survey Research Center, University of Utah, in providing us a copy of the data tape for analysis.

Appendix — Participants in W118: 1982-1992

Ahearn, Mary C.	See Stevens, Joe B.
Bacigalupi, Tad	See Knop, Edward
Backmann, Kenneth F.	See Copp, James H.
Blevins, Audie L.	Department of Sociology
	University of Wyoming, Laramie, Wyoming 82071
Bradley, E. B.	Department of Agricultural Economics
	University of Wyoming, Laramie, Wyoming 82071
Bouvier, Leon F.	See Martin, Philip L.
Bohren, Lenora	See Knop, Edward
Byun, Yongchan	See Stinner, William F.
Calvert, Jerry W.	See Jobes, Patrick C.
Carpenter, Edwin H.	Department of Agricultural Economics
	University of Arizona, Tucson, AZ 87521
Cook, Annabel K.	Department of Rural Sociology
	Washington State University, Pullman, WA 99164
Copp, James H.	Department of Rural Sociology
	Texas A & M, College Station, TX 77843
Eastman, Clyde	Department of Agricultural Economics
	New Mexico State University,
	Las Cruces, NM 88003
Eckert, J.	See Knop, Edward
Gilchrist, C. Jack	Department of Sociology
	Montana State University, Bozeman, Montana 59717
Golesorkhi, Banu	See Toney, Michael B.
Jensen, Katherine	See Blevins, Audie
Jobes, Patrick C.	Department of Sociology
	Montana State University, Bozeman, Montana 59717
Kan, Stephen J.	See Stinner, William F.
Keywon, Cheong	See Stinner, William F.
Kershaw, Terry	See Wardwell, John M.
Knop, Edward	Department of Sociology
	Colorado State University, Ft. Collins, CO 80523
Larson, Don C.	See Toney, Michael B.

Martin, Philip L.   Department of Agricultural Economics
                           University of California, Davis, CA 95616
Mines, Richard   See Martin, Philip L.
Pitcher, Brian L.   See Stinner, William F.
Rowe, Corinne M.   Corinne M. Lyle
                           Department of Agricultural Economics
                           University of Idaho, Moscow, Idaho 83843
Seyfrit, Carole L.   See Toney, Michael B.
Shearman, Gayle A.   See Wardwell, John M.
Stevens, Joe B.   Department of Agricultural and Resource Economics
                           Oregon State University, Corvallis, OR 97331
Stewart, Christopher   See Wardwell, John M.
Stinner, William F.   Department of Sociology
                           Utah State University, Logan, Utah 84321
Swanson, Linda L.   USDA/ARED, Room 340,
                           1301 New York Avenue NW
                           Washington, D. C. 20005
Tinnakul, Nithet   See Stinner, William F.
Toney, Michael B.   Department of Sociology
                           Utah State University, Logan, Utah 84321
Van Loon, Mollie   See Stinner, William F.
Wardwell, John M.   Department of Rural Sociology
                           Washington State University, Pullman, WA 99164
Wheat, Leonard F.   See Wardwell, John M.
Williams, Anne S.   See Jobes, Patrick C.
Williams, James D.   See Eastman, Clyde
Wilson-Figueroa   See Toney, Michael B.

Bibliography

Adamchak, Donald J.
  1987 Further Evidence on Economic and Noneconomic Reasons for
        Turnaround Migration. Rural Sociology, 52: 109-118.

Albrecht, Stan L.
  1990 Great Basin Kingdom--Socio-Cultural Case Study. Presented at the
        1990 Lowry Nelson Symposium, Rural Villages in the Twenty-First
        Century, Logan, Utah.

Arrington, Leonard J. and David Bitton
  1978 The Mormon Experience: A History of Latter-Day Saints. New York:
        Alfred S. Knopf.

Ballard, Chester C. and James H. Copp
  1982 Coping with Change in an Oil Boom Town. Small Town, :4-8.

Ballard, Chester C., Myrna S. Hoskins and James H. Copp
  1981 Local Leadership Control of Small Community Growth. College
        Station: Texas Agricultural Experiment Station Department of Rural
        Sociology Technical Report No. 81-3.

Barsby, Steve L. and Dennis R. Cox
  1975 Interstate Migration of the Elderly: An Economic Analysis. Lexington,
        MA: Lexington Books.

Beale, Calvin L.
  1975 The Revival of Population Growth in Nonmetropolitan America.
        Washington, D.C. U.S. Department of Agriculture Economic Research
        Service, No. ERS 605.

  1976 A Further Look at Nonmetropolitan Population Growth Since 1970.
        American Journal of Agricultural Economics, 58: 953-58.

1980   The Changing Nature of Rural Employment. Pp. 37-49 in David L. Brown and John M. Wardwell (editors), New Directions in Urban-Rural Migration. New York: Academic Press.

Beale, Calvin L. and Glenn V. Fuguitt
   1985   Metropolitan and Nonmetropolitan Growth Differentials in the United States since 1980. Madison: University of Wisconsin Center for Demography and Ecology Paper No. 85-6.

   1986   Metropolitan and nonmetropolitan growth in the United States since 1980. Pp. 46-62 in Joint Economic Committee, Congress of the United States, New Dimensions in Rural Policy. Washington, D.C.: U.S. Government Printing Office.

Bellah, Robert N., Richard Madsen, William M. Sullivan, Ann Swindler and Steven M. Tipton
   1985   Habits of the Heart. Berkeley: University of California Press.

Bender, Lloyd D., Bernal L. Green, Thomas L. Hady, John A. Kuehn, Marlys K. Nelson, Leon B. Perkins and Peggy R. Ross
   1985   The Diverse Social and Economic Structure of Nonmetropolitan America. Washington, D.C.: U.S. Department of Agriculture Economic Research Service, Rural Development Research Report No. 49.

Bernstein, Susan C.
   1982   Unusual Utah. American Demographics 4: 20-23, 41.

Blackwood, Larry G. and Edwin H. Carpenter
   1978   The Importance of Anti-Urbanism in Determining Residential Preferences and Migration Patterns. Rural Sociology, 43: 31-47.

Blevins, Audie L.
   1969   Migration in Southern Cities: A Push-Pull Analysis. Social Science Quarterly, 50: 337-353.

Bluestone, Herman
   1979   Income Growth in Nonmetro America: 1968-75. Washington, D.C.: U.S. Department of Agriculture Economic Development Division Rural Development Research Report No. 14.

Bluestone, Herman and John Hession
   1986   Patterns of Change in the Nonmetro and Metro Labor Force Since 1979. Pp. 121-133 in Joint Economic Committee, Congress of the United States, New Dimensions in Rural Policy.

Bogue, Donald J. and Calvin L. Beale
1961   Economic Areas of the United States.   New York: Free Press of
       Glencoe.

Bouvier, Leon and Philip Martin
1985   Population Change and California's Future.   Washington, D.C.:
       Population Reference Bureau.

Bowles, Gladys K.
1978   Contributions of Recent Metro-Nonmetro Migrants to the Nonmetro
       Population and Labor Force. Agricultural Economics Research, 30:15-
       22.

Brewer, H. L.
1985   Measures of Diversification: Predictors or Regional Economic
       Instability. Journal of Regional Science, 25: 463-69.

Briggs, Vernon
1984   Immigration Policy and the American Labor Force. Baltimore: The
       Johns Hopkins University Press.

Brooks, Richard O.
1974   New Towns and Communal Values. New York: Praeger.

Brown, David L. (ed)
1987   Rural Economic Development in the 1980s. Washington, D.C.: U.S.
       Department of Agriculture Economic Research Service, ERS Staff
       Report No. AGES870724

Brown, David L. and John M. Wardwell (eds.)
1980   New Directions in Urban-Rural Migration. New York: Academic.

Carpenter, Edwin H.
1977   The Potential for Population Dispersal: A Closer Look at Residential
       Locational Preferences. Rural Sociology 42: 352-370.

Campbell, Ken
1986   Relative Priorities in Residential Location Choice: The Case of a Fast-
       Growing Nonmetropolitan County.   Irvine, CA: University of
       California Department of Social Sciences Ph. D. Dissertation.

Caudill, Harry M.
   1963   Night Comes to the Cumberlands: A Biography of a Depressed Area. Boston: Little, Brown.

Center for Population Research and Census
   1982   Intercensal Estimates of Oregon by County: 1970-1980. Portland: Portland State University.

   1986   Population Estimates of Oregon Counties and Incorporated Cities. Portland: Portland State University.

Chiswick, Barry
   1980   An Analysis of the Economic Progress and Impact of Immigrants. Washington, D.C.: U.S. Department of Labor.

Christenson, James A., Lorraine E. Garkovich and Gregory S. Taylor
   1983   Proruralism Values and Migration Behavior. Population and Environment 6: 166-78.

Clifford, Peggy
   1980   To Aspen and Back. New York: St. Martin's Press.

Congressional Research Service
   1987   U.S. Immigration Law and Policy: 1952-1986. Published by the Senate Committee on the Judiciary, Senate Print 100-100.

Conroy, Michael E.
   1974   Alternative Strategies for Regional Industrial Diversification. Journal of Regional Science, 14: 31-46.

Cook, Annabel
   1986   Factors Relating to Nonmetropolitan County Change in the Pacific Northwest, 1980-84. Presented at the Rural Sociological Society annual meetings, Blacksburg, VA, August.

   1987   Nonmetropolitan Migration. Rural Sociology 52: 409-18.

   1990   Retirement Migration as a Community Development Option. Journal of the Community Development Society 21: 83-101.

Copp, James H.
   1984a   After the Boom: A Follow-up Study of an Oil Boom Town. Presented at Southern Association of Agricultural Scientists, Nashville.

1984b Social Impacts of Oil and Gas Development on a Small Rural Community. College Station: Texas A&M University Center for Energy and Mineral Resources, CEMR-MS-8.

1984c The Stagnating Community. Presented at the Southwestern Sociological Association, Fort Worth (March).

1985 Leadership and Linkages in Rural Community Growth: A Resource Mobilization Interpretation. Presented at the Southern Association of Agricultural Scientists, Biloxi (February).

1987 Community Effects of Retrenchment in the Oil and Gas Industry. Presented at the Southern Rural Sociological Association, Nashville.

Corbett, Michael
1981 A Better Place to Live. Emmaus, PA: Rodale Press.

Crapo, Richley H.
1987 Grass-Roots Deviance from Official Doctrine: A Study of Latter-Day Saints (Mormon) Folk Beliefs. Journal for the Scientific Study of Religion 26: 465-485.

Dailey, George H., Jr. and Rex R. Campbell
1980 The Ozark-Ouachita Uplands: Growth and Consequences. Pp. 233-65 in David L. Brown and John M. Wardwell (editors), New Directions in Urban-Rural Migration. New York: Academic Press.

Deavers, Kenneth L. and David L. Brown
1980 The Rural Population Turnaround: Research and National Public Policy. Pp. 51-66 in David L. Brown and John M. Wardwell (eds.), New Directions in Urban-Rural Migration. New York: Academic.

DeJong, Gordon F. and J. T. Fawcett
1981 Motivations for Migration: An Assessment and a Value-Expectancy Research Model. Pp. 13-58 in Gordon DeJong and R. Gardner (eds.), Migration Decision-Making. New York: Pergamon Press.

DeJong, Gordon F. and R. Gardner (eds.)
1981 Migration Decision-Making. New York: Pergamon Press.

DeJong, Gordon F. and Ralph J. Sell
1977 Population Redistribution, Migration and Residential Preferences. Annals of the American Academy of Political and Social Science, 429: 130-42.

Denver Research Institute
   1976   Socioeconomic Impact of Western Energy Resource Development.
          Washington, D.C.: Council on Environmental Quality.

Deseret News
   1991   Church Almanac. Salt Lake City: Deseret News.

Dillman, Don A.
   1978   Mail and Telephone Surveys: The Total Design Method. New York:
          John Wiley and Sons.

   1979   Residential Preferences, Quality of Life, and the Population
          Turnaround. American Journal of Agricultural Economics, 61: 960-66.

   1985   The Social Impacts of Information Technologies in Rural North
          America. Rural Sociology, 50: 1-26.

Dillman, Don A. and Russell Dobash
   1972   Preferences for Community Living and Their Implications for
          Population Redistribution. Pullman, WA: Washington Agricultural
          Experiment Station Bulletin No. 764.

Engels, Richard A.
   1986   The Metropolitan/Nonmetropolitan Population at Mid-Decade.
          Presented at the Population Association of America annual meetings,
          San Francisco, April.

Engles, Richard A. and Richard L. Forstall
   1985   Metropolitan Areas Dominate Growth Again. American Demographics,
          7: 23-35, 45.

Engles, Richard and Mary Kay Healy
   1979   Rural Renaissance Reconsidered. American Demographics 1: 16-18.

Fisher, James S. and Ronald L. Mitchelson
   1981   Forces of Change in the American Settlement Pattern. Geographical
          Review 71: 298-310.

Fliegel, Frederick and Andrew J. Sofranko
   1984   Nonmetropolitan Population Increase, the Attractiveness of Rural
          Living, and Race. Rural Sociology, 49: 298-308.

Francaviglia, Richard V.
  1970   The Mormon Landscape: Definition of an Image in the American West. Proceedings of the Association of American Geographers.

Freudenburg, William
  1982   The Effects of Population Growth on the Social and Personal Well-Being of Boom Town Residents. Pullman: Washington State University Agricultural Research Center.

Frey, William H.
  1988   Migration and Metropolitan Decline in Developed Countries. Population and Development Review, 14:595-628.

Frey, William H. and Alden Speare, Jr.
  1992   The Revival of Metropolitan Population Growth in the United States: An Assessment of Findings from the 1990 Census. Population and Development Review, 18: 129-146.

Fuguitt, Glenn V.
  1985   The Nonmetropolitan Population Turnaround. Annual Review of Sociology, 11: 259-280.

Fuguitt, Glenn V. and Calvin L. Beale
  1978   Population Trends of Nonmetropolitan Cities and Villages in Subregions of the United States. Demography, 15: 605-20.

Fuguitt, Glenn V., David L. Brown and Calvin L. Beale
  1989   The Population of Rural and Small Town America. New York: Russell Sage

Fuguitt, Glenn V. and James J. Zuiches
  1975   Residential Preferences and Population Distribution. Demography, 12: 491-505.

Gallaher, Art, Jr. and Harland Padfield (editors)
  1980   The Dying Community. Albuquerque: University of New Mexico Press.

Gershuny, J.
  1978   After Industrial Society: The Emerging Self Service Economy. London: MacMillan.

Gilmore, John S. and Mary K. Duff
   1975   Boom Town Growth Management: A Case Study of Rock Springs - Green River, Wyoming. Boulder, CO: Westview Press.

Glasgow, Nina and Calvin L. Beale
   1985   Rural Elderly in Demographic Perspective.   Rural Development Perspectives 3: 22-26.

Greenwood, Michael J.
   1975   Research on Internal Migration. Journal of Economic Literature, 13: 397-433.

Grubel, H.G. and M.A. Walker
   1989   Service Industry Growth: Causes and Effects.   Vancouver, B.C., Canada: The Fraser Institute.

Guile, Bruce R.
   1988   Introduction to Service Industries: Policy Issues. Pp. 1-14 in Bruce R. Guile and James Brian Quinn (editors), Technology in Services. Washington, D.C.: National Academy Press.

Hathaway, Dale E. and Brian E. Perkins
   1968   Occupational Mobility and Migration from Agriculture. Pp. 185-237 in Report of the National Commission on Rural Poverty. Washington, D.C.: U.S. Government Printing Office.

Hastings, Steve E. and Jeffrey D. White
   1984   Employment Growth in the Northeast: 1970-79. Dover: University of Delaware Agricultural Experiment Station Bulletin No. 455.

Hawley, Amos H.
   1971   Urban Society: An Ecological Approach. New York: Ronald Press.

Hawley, Amos H. and Sara Mills Mazie
   1981   Nonmetropolitan America in Transition. Chapel Hill, NC: University of North Carolina Press.

Heaton, Tim B.
   1986   The Demography of Utah Mormons. In T.K. Martin, T.B. Heaton and S.J. Bahr (editors), Utah in Demographic Perspective. Salt Lake City: Signature Books.

Heaton, Tim B., William B. Clifford and Glenn V. Fuguitt
   1981   Temporal Shifts in the Determinants of Young and Elderly Migration
          in Nonmetropolitan Areas. Social Forces 60: 41-60.

Hirschl, Thomas A. and Gene F. Summers
   1982   Cash Transfers and the Export Base of Small Communities. Rural
          Sociology 47: 295-316.

Hoch, Irving
   1981   Energy and location. Pp. 285-356 in Amos H. Hawley and Sara Mills
          Mazie (eds.), Nonmetropolitan America in Transition. Chapel Hill, NC:
          UNC Press.

Ilvento, Thomas W. and Alan E. Luloff
   1982   Anti-Urbanism and Nonmetropolitan Growth: A Re-evaluation. Rural
          Sociology 47: 220-33.

Jackson, Richard H.
   1978   Mormon Perception and Settlement. Annals of the Association of
          American Geographers 68: 317-334.

Jacobson, Cardell K.
   1991   Black Mormons in the 1980s: Pioneers in a White Church. Review of
          Religious Research 33: 146-152.

Jobes, Patrick C.
   1980   Changing Country, Changing Town: A Research Report. Bozeman:
          Montana Agricultural Experiment Station.

   1984   Migration Into the Gallatin Valley: Preliminary Findings. Presented at
          the Rural Sociological Society, College Station, Texas, August.

   1986   A Small Rural Community Responds to Coal Development. Sociology
          and Social Research, 70: 174-177.

   1987   Nominalism, Realism and Planning in a Changing Community.
          International Journal of Environmental Studies

   1989   Disintegration of Ranching Communities in Southeastern Montana.
          Environmental Impact Assessment Review, 9: 149-156.

Johnson, Kenneth M.
   1989   Recent Population Redistribution Trends in Nonmetropolitan America.
          Rural Sociology, 54: 301-326.

Johnson, Kenneth M. and Ross L. Purdy
  1980   Recent Nonmetropolitan Population Change in Fifty Year Perspective.
         Demography 17: 57-70.

Kalbacker, Judith Z.
  1979   Shift-Share Analysis. Agricultural Economics Research, 31: 12-25.

Kephart, William M.
  1982   Extraordinary Groups: The Sociology of Unconventional Life Styles.
         New York: Saint Martin's Press.

Kershaw, Terry
  1985   Attitudes Toward Economic Growth, Personal Economic Experience
         and Reasons for Moving. Pullman, WA: Washington State University
         Department of Sociology Ph.D. Dissertation.

Killian, Molly S. and Thomas Hady
  1988   What is the Payoff for Diversifying Rural Economics?   Rural
         Development Perspectives, 5: 2-7.

Knop, Edward
  1982   Craig, Colorado, Pre- and Post-Impact: Citizens' Assessments.
         Presented at the Western Social Science Association, Denver (April).

  1984   Community Conceptions and Development Approaches in Sociology.
         High Plains Applied Anthropologist, 5: 12-14.

  1987   Alternative Perspectives on Community Impacting: Toward
         Complementary Theory and Application. Sociological Inquiry, 57:
         272-91.

Knop, Edward and Ted Bacigalupi
  1984   Migration Patterns and Management Challenges in Three
         Nonmetropolitan Communities, 1970-1980. Ft Collins: Colorado State
         University Agricultural Experiment Station Technical Report 84-17.

Kort, John R.
  1981   Regional Economic Instability and Industrial Diversification in the U.S.
         Land Economics, 57: 596-608.

Krout, John A.
  1982   The Changing Impact of Sustenance Organization Activities on
         Nonmetropolitan Net Migration. Sociological Focus 15: 1-13.

Lansing, John B. and Eva Mueller
  1967   The Geographic Mobility of Labor. Ann Arbor, MI: University of
         Michigan SRC.

Larson, Don C.
  1988   Mormon Return Migration: A Return to Zion. Logan: Utah State
         University Ph.D. Dissertation.

Leon, Arthur William
  1984   Place Image Choice. Seattle: University of Washington Department of
         Geography Ph.D. Dissertation.

Lichter, Daniel, Glenn V. Fuguitt and Tim B. Heaton
  1985   Components of Nonmetropolitan Population Change: The Contribution
         of Rural Areas. Rural Sociology, 50: 12-25.

Lloyd, Robert C. and Kenneth P. Wilkinson
  1985   Community Factors in Rural Manufacturing Development. Rural
         Sociology, 50: 27-37.

Long, John F.
  1981   Population Deconcentration in the U.S. Washington, D.C.: U.S. Bureau
         of the Census Special Demographic Analysis, CDS

Long, Larry H. and Diana DeAre
  1980   Migration to Nonmetropolitan Areas: Appraising the Trends and
         Reasons for Moving. Washington, D.C.: U.S. Bureau of the Census
         Special Demographic Analysis, CDS 80-2.

Long, Larry H. and Kristen Hansen
  1977   Reasons for Interstate Migration. Washington, D.C.: U.S. Bureau of the
         Census Current Population Reports Series P-23, No. 81.

Louv, Richard
  1985   America II. New York: Penguin Books.

Marans, Robert W., Don A. Dillman and Janet Keller
  1980   Perceptions of Quality of Life in Rural America. Ann Arbor, MI:
         University of Michigan Survey Research Center.

Martin, Philip
  1981   Germany's Guestworkers. Challenge (July-August): 34-42.

1986   Illegal Immigration and the Colonization of the American Labor Market. Washington, D.C. Center for Immigration Studies.

1992   Testimony Before the California Assembly's Select Committee on California-Mexico Affairs, Sacramento, July 28.

Martin, Philip and Marion Houstoun

1982   European and American Immigration Policies. Law and Contemporary Problems 45: 29-54.

Martin, Philip and Ellen Sehgal
1980   Illegal Immigration: The Guestworker Option. Public Policy 28: 207-30.

Martin, Thomas K., Tim B. Heaton and Stephen J. Bahr (editors)
1986   Utah in Demographic Perspective. Salt Lake City: Signature Books.

Massey, Douglas S.
1986   The Settlement Process Among Mexican Migrants to the United States. American Sociological Review 51: 670-684.

Meinig, Donald M.
1965   The Mormon Culture Region: Strategies and Patterns of the Geography of the American West. Annals of the Association of American Geographers, 55: 191-220.

Miller, James P. and Herman Bluestone
1987   Prospects for Service Sector Employment Growth in Nonmetro America. Pp. 6-1 to 6-21 in Economic Research Service (editor), Rural Economic Development in the 1980s: Preparing for the Future. Washington, D.C.: U.S. Department of Agriculture.

Mines, Richard and Carole Nuckton
1982   The Evolution of Mexican Migration to the U.S.: A Case Study. Berkeley, CA: Giannini Foundation Report No. 82-1.

Morrison, Peter A.
1973   A Demographic Assessment of New Cities and Growth Centers as Population Redistribution Struggles. Public Policy, 21: 367-82.

Morrison, Peter A. and Judith Wheeler
1976   Rural Renaissance in America?   Washington, D.C.: Population Reference Bureau No. 31.

Mulder, William
1954   Mormonism's "Gathering:" An American Doctrine with a Difference. Church History 23: 248-264.

Muller, Thomas and Thomas Espenshade
1985   The Fourth Wave: California's Newest Immigrants. Washington, D.C.: The Urban Institute

Murdock, Steve H. and Md. Nazrul Hogue
1992   Demographic and Socioeconomic Change in the Texas Population 1980 to 1990.   College Station: Texas Agricultural Experiment Station Department of Rural Sociology Technical Report 92-4.

Murdock, Steve H. and F. Larry Leistritz
1979   Energy Development in the Western United States: Impact on Rural Areas. New York: Praeger Publishers.

Murdock, Steve H., John D. Montel, F. Larry Leistritz, Pamela Hopkins, and Rita Hamm
1981   An Analysis of the Construction Impacts of Coal Development in Rural Texas: The Case of Fayette County.   College Station: Texas Agricultural Experiment Station Technical Report 81-2.

Murdock, Steve H., James S. Wieland and F. Larry Leistritz
1978   An Assessment of the Validity of the Gravity Model for Predicting Community Settlement Patterns in Rural Energy-Impacted Areas in the West. Land Economics, 54: 461-71.

National Center for Health Statistics
1987   Annual Summary of Births, Marriages, Divorces, and Deaths, United States, 1986. Hyattsville, MD: Public Health Service Monthly Vital Statistics Report Vol. 35, No. 13, DHHS Pub. No. (PHS) 87-1120.

Nelson, Lowry
1952   The Mormon Village. Salt Lake City: University of Utah Press.

Newman, William M. and Peter L. Halvorson
1984   Religion and Regional Culture: Patterns of Concentration and Change Among American Religious Denominations, 1952-1980. Journal for the Scientific Study of Religion, 23: 304-315.

North, Douglass C.
   1955   Location Theory and Regional Economic Growth. Journal of Political
          Economy, 63: 243-58.

Noyelle, Thierry J. and Thomas M. Stanback
   1984   The Economic Transformation of American Cities.   Totowa, NJ:
          Rowman and Allanheld.

O'Dea, Thomas F.
   1957   The Mormons. Chicago: University of Chicago Press.

Office of Financial Management
   1979   Population Trends for Washington State.   Olympia: State of
          Washington.

   1986   Population Trends for Washington State.   Olympia: State of
          Washington.

Olien, Roger M. and Diana Davids Olien
   1982   Oil Booms: Social Change in Five Texas Towns. Lincoln: University
          of Nebraska Press.

Oregon State
   1980   Resident Labor Force Employment and Unemployment.   Salem:
          Employment Division.

   1983   Resident Labor Force Employment and Unemployment.   Salem:
          Employment Division.

   1986   Resident Labor Force Employment and Unemployment.   Salem:
          Employment Division.

   1990   Resident Labor Force Employment and Unemployment.   Salem:
          Employment Division.

Pacific Northwest Executive
   1990   Economic Developments in the Pacific Northwest. Pacific Northwest
          Executive 6: 3,8-10.

Personick, Valerie A.
   1987   Industry Output and Employment through the End of the Century.
          Monthly Labor Review 110: 9, 30-45.

Petrulis, M.F.
   1979   Regional Manufacturing Employment Growth Patterns. Washington,
          D.C.: U.S. Department of Agriculture Economic Development
          Division, Rural Development Research Report No. 13.

Ploch, Louis A.
   1978   The Reversal in Migration Patterns. Rural Sociology 43: 292-303.

Population Reference Bureau
   1992   The United States Population Data Sheet.   Washington, D.C.:
          Population Reference Bureau, Inc.

Poston, Dudley L., Jr.
   1984   Regional Ecology: A Macroscopic Analysis of Sustenance
          Organization. In M. Micklin and H.M. Choldin (editors), Sociological
          Human Ecology. Boulder: Westview Press.

Price, Daniel O. and Melanie M. Sikes.
   1975   Rural-Urban Migration in the U.S.   Washington, D.C.: U.S.
          Government Printing Office.

Quinn, Bernard, Herman Anderson, Martin Bradley, Paul Goetting and
          Peggy Shriver
   1982   Churches and Church Membership in the United States, 1980: An
          Enumeration by Region, State and County Based on Data Reported by
          111 Church Bodies. Atlanta: Glenmary Research Center.

Renshaw, Vernon, Howard Friedenberg and Bruce Twine
   1978   Workforce Migration Patterns, 1970-76. Survey of Current Business
          58: 17-20.

Richter, Kerry
   1985   Nonmetropolitan Growth in the Late 1970s: The End of the
          Turnaround? Demography 22: 245-263.

Riddle, Dorothy I.
   1987   The Role of the Service Sector in Economic Development: Similarities
          and Differences by Development Category. Pp. 83-104 in Orio Giarini
          (editor), The Emerging Service Economy. New York: Pergamon Press.

Ritchey, P. Neal
   1976   Explanations of Migration. Annual Review of Sociology 2: 363-404.

Rowe, Corinne M. (Lyle)
    1984   Migration Turnaround: Analysis of the Relative Values of Motivators Resulting in Migration to Nonmetropolitan Areas. Pullman: Washington State University Department of Sociology Dissertation.

Rowe, Corinne M. (Lyle) and John M. Wardwell
    1987   Population Growth and Migration in the Inland Northwest. Pullman: Washington State University College of Agriculture and Home Economics, Agricultural Research Center Bulletin 0994.

Schwarzweller, Harry K.
    1979   Migration and the Changing Rural Scene. Rural Sociology 44: 7-23.

Shaw, R. Paul
    1975   Migration Theory and Fact: A Review and Bibliography of Current Literature. Philadelphia: Regional Science Research Institute.

Shearman, Gayle A.
    1983   The Salience of Structural Change as a Factor in the Migration Turnaround. Pullman: Washington State University Department of Sociology M.A. Thesis.

Singelmann, Joachim
    1978   From Agriculture to Services: The Transformation of Industrial Employment. Beverly Hills: Sage Publications.

Smith, Gary
    1986   Transfer Payments and Investment Incomes: Sources of Growth and Cyclical Stability for Nonmetro Counties of Oregon and Washington. Pullman: Washington State University College of Agriculture and Home Economic Agricultural Research Center Bulletin No. 0981.

Smith, Gary W. and Bruce A. Weber
    1984   Growth, Diversification, and Cyclical Instability in the Oregon Economy, 1960-1979. Corvallis: Oregon State University Agricultural Experiment Station Bulletin No. 712.

Sofranko, Andrew J. and James D. Williams (eds.)
    1980   Rebirth of Rural America. Ames, IA: North Central Regional Center Rural Development. U.S. Bureau of the Census

    1986a   Current Population Reports, Series P-20, No. 407, Geographical Mobility: March 1983 to March 1984. Washington, D.C. U.S. Government Printing Office. U.S. Bureau of the Census

1986b Statistical Abstract of the United States, 1987. Washington, D.C. U.S. Government Printing Office.

SPSS
1988 SPSS-X Users Guide, Third Edition. Chicago: SPSS Inc.

Stark, Rodney
1984 The Rise of a New World Faith. Review of Religious Research 26: 18-27.

Stinner, William F. and Stephan H. Kan
1983 Patterns of Population Growth and Distribution in Utah: 1950-1980. Utah Agricultural Experiment Station Research Report No. 91. Logan, Utah: Utah Agricultural Experiment Station.

Stinner, William F. and Michael B. Toney
1980 Migrant-Native Differences in Social Background and Community Satisfaction in Nonmetropolitan Utah Communities. Pp. 313-31 in David L. Brown and John M. Wardwell (editors), New Directions in Urban-Rural Migration. New York: Academic Press.

1981 Energy Resource Development and Migrant-Native Differences in Composition, Community Attachment and Satisfaction, and Migration Intentions. Logan, Utah: Utah State University Agricultural Experiment Station Research Report No. 52.

Summers, Gene F.
1977 Industrial Development in Rural America. Journal of the Community Development Society 8: 6-18.

Summers, Gene F. and Kristi Branch
1984 Economic Development and Community Social Change. Annual Review of Sociology, 10: 141-66.

Swanson, Linda L.
1984 Changing Patterns of Migration to Growing Nonmetro Areas of the Western U.S., 1955-80. Presented at the Population Association of America annual meetings, Minneapolis, May.

1986 What Attracts New Residents to Nonmetro Areas? Washington D.C.: U.S. Department of Agriculture Economic Research Service Rural Development Research Report No. 56.

Tellez, Luis
    1991   Cited in New York Times, November 27, p. A1.

Thompson, Layton S. and Willard D. Schutz
    1978   Taxation and Revenue Systems in Wyoming. Laramie: University of
            Wyoming Agricultural Experiment Station Research Journal No. 137.

Thompson, Wilbur R.
    1965   A Preface to Urban Economics. Baltimore: Johns Hopkins Press.

Thornton, Arlon
    1979   Religion and Fertility: The Case of Mormonism. Journal of Marriage
            and the Family, 41: 131-142.

Toney, Michael B., Banu Golesorkhi and William F. Stinner
    1985   Residence Exposure and Fertility Expectations of Young Mormon and
            Non-Mormon Women in Utah. Journal of Marriage and the Family, 47:
            459-465.

Toney, Michael B., Brian L. Pitcher and William F. Stinner
    1985   Geographical Mobility and Locus of Control. Journal of Psychology
            119: 361-68.

Trepanier, Cecyle
    1991   The Cajunization of French Louisiana: Forging a Regional Identity. The
            Geographical Journal, 157: 161-171.

Uhlenberg, Peter
    1973   Noneconomic Determinants of Migration. Rural Sociology 38: 296-
            311.

U.S. Bureau of the Census
    1972   Geographic Profile of Employment and Unemployment, 1983. Bulletin
            2216. Washington, D.C. U.S. Government Printing Office.

    1975   Historical Statistics of the United States, Colonial Times to 1970.
            Washington, D.C.: U.S. Government Printing Office.

    1981   Characteristics of the Population, 1970 Census of Population: Oregon,
            Washington. Washington, D.C. U.S. Government Printing Office.

    1983a   General Social and Economic Characteristics, 1980 Census of
            Population, Oregon, Washington. Washington, D.C. U.S. Government
            Printing Office.

1983b   County and City Data Book. Washington, D.C.: U.S. Government Printing Office.

1984   Gross Migration for Counties: 1975-1980. 1980 Census of Population Supplementary Report. Washington, D.C. U.S. Government Printing Office.

1986a   Patterns of Metropolitan Area and County Population Growth 1980 to 1984. Washington, D.C.: Current Population Reports Series P-25, No. 976.

1986b   Statistical Abstract of the United States. Washington, D.C. U.S. Government Printing Office.

1986c   West: 1984 Population and 1983 Per Capita Income Estimates for Counties and Incorporated Places. Current Population Reports Series P-26, No. 84-W-SC.

1987a   Estimates of the Population of Wyoming Counties and Metropolitan Areas: July 1, 1981 to 1985. Washington, D.C.: Current Population Reports Series P-26, No. 85-WY-C.

1987b   Geographical Mobility. Washington, D.C.: Current Population Reports Series P-20, No. 407.

1988   Current Population Reports, Series P-20, Geographical Mobility, March 1985 to March 1986. Washington, D.C.: U.S. Government Printing Office.

1990   West: 1988 Population and 1987 Per Capita Income Estimates for Counties and Incorporated Places. Current Population Reports Series P-26, No. 88-W-SC.

1991   1990 Census of Population and Housing Public Law 94-171 Data (CD-ROM). Washington, D.C.: Data User Services Division.

U.S. Department of Commerce
1987   Total Full-Time and Part-Time Employment Estimates. Washington, D.C.: Bureau of Economic Analysis Regional Economic Information System Data File.

U.S. Department of Labor
1983   Workers Without Jobs. Washington, D.C.: Government Printing Office.

1984   Geographical Profile of Employment and Unemployment, 1983: Washington D.C.: U.S. Government Printing Office Bulletin No. 2216.

1989   The Effects of Immigration on the U.S. Economy and Labor Market. Washington, D.C.: U.S. Government Printing Office.

U.S. Immigration and Naturalization Service
  Annual Statistical Yearbooks. Washington, D.C.: U.S. Government Printing Office.

U.S. Select Commission on Immigration and Refugee Policy (SCIRP).
  1981   Immigration and the National Interest. Washington, D.C.: U.S. Government Printing Office.

Voss, Paul R.
  1980   A Test of the "Gangplank Syndrome" Among Recent Migrations to the Upper Great Lakes Region. Journal of the Community Development Society, 11: 95-111.

Voss, Paul R. and Glenn V. Fuguitt
  1979   Turnaround Migration in the Upper Great Lakes Region. Madison, WI: Applied Population Laboratory Series 70-12.

Wardwell, John M.
  1977   Equilibrium and Change in Nonmetropolitan Growth. Rural Sociology 42: 156-79.

  1980   Toward a Theory of Urban-Rural Migration in the Developed World. Pp. 71-114 in David L. Brown and John M. Wardwell (editors), New Directions in Urban-Rural Migration. New York: Academic Press.

  1982   Revitalization of Rural America. Pp. 49-79 in Donald Hicks and Norman J. Glickman (editors), Transition to the 21st Century. Greenwich, CT: JAI Press.

Wardwell, John M. and David L. Brown
  1980   Population Redistribution in the United States During the 1970s. Pp. 5-35 in David L. Brown and John M. Wardwell (eds.), New Directions in Urban-Rural Migration. New York: Academic.

Wardwell, John M. and Annabel K. Cook
  1982   The Demographic Context of Western Growth. Pp. 1-23 in Bruce A. Weber and Robert E. Howell (eds.), Coping with Rapid Growth in Rural Communities. Boulder, CO: Westview Press.

Wardwell, John M. and C. Jack Gilchrist
  1978 External Validation of Migration Findings from the Continuous Work
        History Sample. Pp. 333-43 in Policy Analysis with the Social Security
        Data Files. Washington, D.C.: U.S. Government Printing Office.

  1980 Employment Deconcentration in the Nonmetropolitan Migration
        Turnaround. Demography 17: 145-158.

Washington State
  1980 Annual Averages Washington State Resident Labor Force and
        Employment by Labor Area.   Olympia: Employment Security
        Department.

  1983 Annual Averages Washington State Resident Labor Force and
        Employment by Labor Area.   Olympia: Employment Security
        Department.

  1986 Annual Averages Washington State Resident Labor Force and
        Employment by Labor Area.   Olympia: Employment Security
        Department.

  1990 Annual Averages Washington State Resident Labor Force and
        Employment by Labor Area.   Olympia: Employment Security
        Department.

Wilkinson, Kenneth P., James G. Thompson, Robert E. Reynolds, Jr.,
        and Lawrence M. Ostresh
  1982 Local Social Disruption and Western Energy Development: A Critical
        Review. Pacific Sociological Review, 25: 275-96.

Williams, Anne S. and Patrick C. Jobes
  1990 Economic and Quality of Life Considerations in Urban-Rural
        Migration. Journal of Rural Studies, 6: 187-194.

Williams, Anne S., Patrick C. Jobes and C. Jack Gilchrist
  1986 Gender Roles, Marital Status and Urban-Rural Migration. Sex Roles 15:
        627-43.

Williams, Anne S., Patrick C. Jobes and Richard Ladzinski
  1984 Migration into the Gallatin Valley: Preliminary Findings. Bozeman:
        Montana State University Department of Sociology.

Williams, James D.
   1981   The Nonchanging Determinants of Nonmetropolitan Migration. Rural
          Sociology 46: 183-202.

   1982   Turnaround Migrants: Grubby Economics or Delightful Indulgence in
          Ruralism? The Rural Sociologist, 2: 104-108.

Williams, James D. and David B. McMillen
   1980   Migration Decision-Making Among Nonmetropolitan-Bound Migrants.
          Pp. 189-211 in David L. Brown and John M. Wardwell (eds.), New
          Directions in Urban-Rural Migration. New York: Academic Press.

Williams, James D. and Andrew Sofranko
   1979   Motivations for the Inmigration Component of Population Turnaround
          in Nonmetropolitan Areas. Demography 16: 239-255.

Yepsen, Roger
   1987   Back to the Country: Is the Rural Life for You? Practical Homeowner
          II: 48-52.

Zelinsky, Wilbur
   1961   An Approach to the Religious Geography of the United States: Patterns
          of Church Membership in 1952.   Annals of the Association of
          American Geographers, 51: 139-193.

   1971   The Hypothesis of the Mobility Transition. Geographical Review, 61:
          219-249

   1974   Selfward Bound: Personal Preferences Patterns and the Changing Map
          of American Society. Economic Geography 50: 144-179.

   1977   Coping with Migration Turnaround: The Theoretical Challenge.
          International Regional Science Review 2: 175-78.

Zuiches, James J.
   1982   Residential Preferences. Pp. 247-255 in Don A. Dillman and Daryl J.
          Hobbs (editors), Rural Society in the U.S.: Issues for the 1980s.
          Boulder, CO: Westview Press.

   1980   Residential Preferences in Migration Theory. Pp. 163-188 in David L.
          Brown and John M. Wardwell (eds.), New Directions in Urban-Rural
          Migration. New York: Academic Press.

1981   Residential Preferences in the U.S. Pp. 72-115 in Amos H. Hawley and Sara Mills Mazie (eds.), Nonmetropolitan America in Transition. Chapel Hill, NC: University of North Carolina Press.

Zuiches, James J. and Michael L. Price
1980   Industrial Dispersion and Labor-Force Migration: Employment Dimensions of the Population Turnaround in Michigan. Pp. 333-359 in David L. Brown and John M. Wardwell (eds.), New Directions in Urban-Rural Migration. New York: Academic Press.

Zuiches, James J. and Jon H. Rieger
1978   Size of Place Preferences and Life Cycle Migration: A Cohort Comparison. Rural Sociology, 43: 618-633.

Index

Editors' Biographical Sketches

John M. Wardwell earned the Ph.D. in sociology from the University of North Carolina at Chapel Hill. He is a demographer with the Departments of Sociology and Rural Sociology at Washington State University. He has participated in editing three books on migration in the United States. Most recently his research has focused on migration impacts on local school districts in sending and receiving communities. Wardwell has also advised local school district superintendents and administrators in several states on patterns of growth anticipated. He has been active in developing demographic curricula for use in the interactive telecommunications systems of extended degree programs for place-bound rural and urban students. In the future, he intends to actively pursue the adaptation of traditional college teaching formats to the use of telecommunications capabilities in education.

James H. Copp is a rural sociologist at Texas A&M University where he teaches courses on rural sociology, social change, minority groups, and Russia and the former USSR. He held a joint appointment in the Department of Rural Sociology, where he conducted research on oil booms and busts.

Copp earned his Ph.D. at the University of Wisconsin. He has held appointments with Kansas State University, The Pennsylvania State University, and the Economic Research Service of the U. S . Department of Agriculture. He is a past president of the Rural Sociological Society and edited the journal, Rural Sociology. He is currently working with Jon Rieger of the University of Louisville on an introductory rural sociology textbook.

About the Contributors

Audie L. Blevins received his Ph.D. from the University of Texas at Austin. He is Professor of Sociology at the University of Wyoming. His research is focused on rural migration. He is interested in community transformations as a result of local option gambling. He also works in historical demography, and his current project concerns the history of birth control in England during the 19th Century.

Edward B. Bradley is an Agricultural Economist at the University of Wyoming. He received his Ph.D. from the Pennsylvania State University and a B.A. degree from the University of Wisconsin. He teaches methodology courses and has been heavily involved in an exchange program with universities in France, Russia and Taiwan.

Annabel Kirschner Cook is an Extension and Research Sociologist in the Department of Rural Sociology at Washington State University in Pullman. She completed the Ph.D. at Washington State University. The interaction between local sociodemographic trends and community change and development is her principal focus. She has analyzed changes in timber dependent areas, retirement migration, and the growth of single-parent families in rural areas. She is the creator and author of Washington Counts! which tracks major social trends at state and county levels.

James H. Copp is a rural sociologist at Texas A&M University where he teaches courses on rural sociology, social change, minority groups, and Russia and the former USSR. He earned his Ph.D. at the University of Wisconsin. He has conducted research on oil booms and busts. He is currently working on an introductory rural sociology textbook.

Patrick C. Jobes has conducted research on rural communities and migration since the early 1970s. His Ph.D. was granted by the University of Washington in 1970. He has taught at the University of Colorado and at Montana State University and has been a member of the Western regional migration project since 1979. He now is lecturer of sociology at the University of New England in New South Wales, Australia.

Edward Knop was educated in sociology and anthropology at the University of Minnesota, where he earned the Ph.D., at the University of Arizona for the M.A., and at Wartburg College (B.A.). He now inhabits the Sociology Department of Colorado State University in Ft. Collins. His research and applied work emphasizes dynamics between sustainability and development in community, population and natural resource interrelations.

Corinne M. Lyle holds a Ph.D. in sociology from Washington State University and is Associate Director of the Cooperative Extension System of the University of Idaho. She is an Extension Rural Sociologist in the Department of Agricultural Economics and Rural Sociology. She is currently working on programming issues for cooperative extension, with emphasis on the assessments of needs, issues and concerns of rural communities and residents, and evaluation of commuity impacts of educational programs.

Philip L. Martin studied labor economics and agricultural economics at the University of Wisconsin in Madison, where he earned his Ph.D. He is Professor of Agricultural Economics at the University of California at Davis, and is Chair of the University of California's Comparative Immigration and Integration Program. He has published extensively on farm labor, labor migration, economic development and immigration issues.

Luis Paita is a Ph.D. candidate in the Department of Sociology of Utah State University. He holds a Master's Degree in Applied Statistics and specializes in methods of research and quantitative analysis. He works as a Health Services Research Consultant at the Utah Department of Health.

William F. Stinner received his doctoral degree in sociology from The Pennsylvania State University. He is Professor of Sociology and Faculty Research Associate with the Population Research Laboratory, Department of Sociology, Social Work and Anthropology at Utah State University. His research interests include migration and community change, and the social demography of health and the life course.

Michael B. Toney is a demographer who received his Ph.D. in sociology from Brown University. He has specialized in migration studies and the demography of the West. He is the Director of the Population Research Laboratory at Utah State University.

John M. Wardwell earned the Ph.D. in sociology from the University of North Carolina at Chapel Hill. He is a demographer with the Departments of Sociology and Rural Sociology at Washington State University. He has written on migration theory, urban and rural social change, and migration. He teaches courses in population, resources and the future, and demography.

James J. Zuiches is Dean of the College of Agriculture and Home Economics, and Director of the Agricultural Research Center at Washington State University. He earned the Ph.D. in sociology from the University of Wisconsin at Madison and his B.A. from the University of Portland, Oregon. Zuiches served as Program Director for Food Systems and Rural Development for the W. K. Kellogg Foundation and was Sociology Program Research Director for the National Science Foundation. He has also worked as Associate Director for the Agricultural Experiment Station for New York State, located at Cornell University, and as a faculty member at Michigan State University. He was elected President of the Rural Sociological Society and serves as a member of the National Research Council.